9/09

3000 800064 28874
St. Louis Community College

D0076105

Meramec Library
St. Louis Community College
11333 Big Bend Blvd.
Kirkwood, MO 63122-5799
314-984-7797

Culture and Customs
of Serbia and Montenegro

Serbia and Montenegro. Cartography by Bookcomp, Inc.

Culture and Customs of Serbia and Montenegro

CHRISTOPHER DELISO

Culture and Customs of Europe

GREENWOOD PRESS
Westport, Connecticut • London

Library of Congress Cataloging-in-Publication Data

Deliso, Christopher M., 1974–
  Culture and customs of Serbia and Montenegro / Christopher Deliso.
    p. cm. — (Culture and customs of Europe)
  Includes bibliographical references and index.
  ISBN 978–0–313–34436–7 (alk. paper)
  1. Serbia—Civilization.   2. Montenegro—Civilization.   3. Serbia—Social life and customs.
4. Montenegro—Social life and customs.   I. Title.
  DR1952.D45   2009
  949.7103—dc22   2008032966

British Library Cataloguing in Publication Data is available.

Copyright © 2009 by Christopher Deliso

All rights reserved. No portion of this book may be
reproduced, by any process or technique, without the
express written consent of the publisher.

Library of Congress Catalog Card Number: 2008032966
ISBN: 978–0–313–34436–7

First published in 2009

Greenwood Press, 88 Post Road West, Westport, CT 06881
An imprint of Greenwood Publishing Group, Inc.
www.greenwood.com

Printed in the United States of America

The paper used in this book complies with the
Permanent Paper Standard issued by the National
Information Standards Organization (Z39.48–1984).

10 9 8 7 6 5 4 3 2 1

Contents

Series Foreword		vii
Preface		ix
Chronology		xiii
1	Land, People, and History	1
2	Religion and Thought	29
3	Marriage, Gender, Family, and Education	45
4	Holidays, Customs, and Leisure Activities	61
5	Cuisine and Fashion	83
6	Literature	101
7	Media and Cinema	115
8	Performing Arts	135

9   Art and Architecture   151

Selected Bibliography   171

Index   175

Series Foreword

THE OLD WORLD and the New World have maintained a fluid exchange of people, ideas, innovations, and styles. Even though the United States became the de facto world leader and economic superpower in the wake of a devastated Europe in World War II, Europe has remained for many the standard bearer of Western culture.

Millions of Americans can trace their ancestors to Europe. The United States as we know it was built on waves of European immigration, starting with the English who braved the seas to found the Jamestown Colony in 1607. Bosnian and Albanian immigrants are some of the latest new Americans.

In the Gilded Age of one of our great expatriates, the novelist Henry James, the Grand Tour of Europe was de rigueur for young American men of means, to prepare them for a life of refinement and taste. In a more recent democratic age, scores of American college students have Eurailed their way across Great Britain and the Continent, sampling the fabled capitals and bergs in a mad, great adventure, or have benefited from a semester abroad. For other American vacationers and culture vultures, Europe is the prime destination.

What is the New Europe post–Cold War, post Berlin Wall in a new millennium? Even with the different languages, rhythms, and rituals, Europeans have much in common: they are largely well educated, prosperous, and worldly. They also have similar goals and face common threats and form alliances. With the advent of the European Union, the open borders, and the Euro and considering globalization and the prospect of a homogenized Europe, an updated survey of the region is warranted.

Culture and Customs of Europe features individual volumes on the countries most studied and for which fresh information is in demand from students and other readers. The Series casts a wide net, inclusive of not only the expected countries, such as Spain, France, England, and Germany, but also countries such as Poland and Greece that lie outside Western Europe proper. Each volume is written by a country specialist, with intimate knowledge of the contemporary dynamics of a people and culture. Sustained narrative chapters cover the land, people, and brief history; religion; social customs; gender roles, family, and marriage; literature and media; performing arts and cinema; and art and architecture. The national character and ongoing popular traditions of each country are framed in an historical context and celebrated along with the latest trends and major cultural figures. A country map, chronology, glossary, and evocative photos enhance the text.

The historied and enlightened Europeans will continue to fascinate Americans. Our futures are strongly linked politically, economically, and culturally.

Preface

THERE IS NO country in Europe today that has been more misunderstood and misrepresented than Serbia. This is largely the result of how international media and certain governments, including that of the United States, have tended to depict the country since the violent disintegration of the federation of Yugoslavia in the early 1990s, a process that spawned three wars and culminated with a NATO bombing campaign against Serbia for control of its southwestern province, Kosovo, in 1999. According to all too many news reports, government communiqués, and sensationalizing exposés to have come out in recent years, the Serbs are to blame for all of those events: they are at best irrational nationalists and genocidal monsters at worst. By 2008, this line of thinking has become such an ingrained part of Western conventional wisdom that journalists and public officials rarely have to support any comment denouncing Serbia and its people with facts.

The truth, of course, is less black and white. Owing to limitations of space, however, this book cannot possibly get into all the details of Serbia's recent (and less recent) history, the dissolution of Yugoslavia, and Western diplomatic and military interventions in the region. In any case, some books taking a more critical view of these complex events have started to appear.[1] Nevertheless, few Americans are aware of the interesting facts that indicate the historical affinity between their country and Serbia, such as that the largest airlift of downed American pilots in history occurred when Serbian rebels and civilians, at great danger to themselves, sheltered and helped evacuate some 500 American airmen shot down over Nazi-occupied Serbia during World War II.[2]

The scope and size of this book, however, preclude any sustained discussion of complex historical episodes. Instead, it seeks simply to give some introduction to the unique aspects of daily life, history, art, and culture that make Serbia one of Europe's most distinctive and significant places. Serbs are warmhearted, hospitable people who keep their traditions close to their hearts and delight in festivals, celebrations, and generally doing things "big." Most foreign tourists who visit leave quite pleasantly surprised with their experience.

The same goes for Montenegro, which has been spared many of Serbia's recent troubles, using historically tried and tested diplomatic skills and a unique geographical positioning to its advantage. Although Serbia's smaller neighbor has throughout history always been living in Serbia's shadow—literally, under some of Europe's most sweeping mountain peaks—Montenegro is now coming into its own. Even before it and Serbia decided to peacefully part ways in May 2006, tourism had started to take off. In the past few years, foreign investors have been snapping up property on Montenegro's gorgeous Adriatic coast, and the new influx of tourists is only increasing. Outsiders are always eager to discover Europe's "next big thing," and Montenegro, with its beaches, medieval castles, and mountain sports, is right up there. And Serbia too is receiving more and more visitors, with the capital, Belgrade, now recognized as one of Europe's most dynamic and fun cities, and music gatherings like the Guča Trumpet Festival and EXIT Festival in Novi Sad attracting massive audiences and increasing their international presence.

Of course, Serbia and Montenegro both have their flaws and problems, just like anywhere in the world. However, day to day, outsiders will find that they are among the safest places in Europe to travel. All things considered, now seems to be the perfect time for the outside world to embrace these countries, which, despite their very close historical and cultural ties, offer much variety and much to see and do. Hopefully, in some small way this book offers an introduction to some of the facets of life, culture, and history that will inspire readers to visit or at least learn more about two of the most unique and unknown countries in Europe.

NOTES

1. A few examples of such works include veteran journalist Peter Brock's *Media Cleansing, Dirty Reporting: Journalism and Tragedy in Yugoslavia* (Los Angeles: GM Books, 2005), an expert analysis of biased and fraudulent media coverage of the recent wars in Yugoslavia; Canadian war reporter Scott Taylor's on-the-ground testimony from Serbia during the Kosovo bombardment, *Inat: Images of Serbia and the Kosovo Conflict* (Ottawa: Esprit de Corps Books, 2000), British author John

Laughland's *Travesty: The Trial of Slobodan Milošević and the Corruption of International Justice* (London: Pluto Press, 2007), on the politically motivated indiscretions of The Hague tribunal for war crimes; former National Security Agency Balkans analyst John Schindler's *Unholy Terror: Bosnia, Al-Qa'ida, and the Rise of Global Jihad* (St. Paul, MN: Zenith Press, 2007), on the close connections of the Bosnian Muslim wartime government and Islamic terrorism; and Noam Chomsky's *The New Military Humanism* (London: Pluto Press, 1999).

2. Veteran American airmen thus saved went to their graves in recent years still pleading with the U.S. government to recognize and commemorate the bravery of these Serbs. For political reasons, they were unsuccessful. For the whole story, see *The Forgotten 500: The Untold Story of the Men Who Risked All for the Greatest Rescue Mission of World War II* (New York: NAL/Penguin Group, 2007).

Chronology

6th–1st centuries B.C.	Turks, then Celts, and finally Romans settle today's Serbia; Illyrian tribes rule coastal Montenegro.
A.D. 6th–7th centuries	Serb tribes are among the Slavic Great Migration to the Balkans.
825–1120	Vlastimirović and Vojislavljievié dynasties create first Serb states of Raška and Zeta/Duklja in present-day Montenegro
9th century	Serbs converted to Orthodox Christianity following mission of Byzantine monks Cyril and Methodius to Morava in 863.
1166	Stefan Nemanja founds Nemanjić dynasty and endows churches.
1219	Serbian Orthodox Church becomes autocephalous from Byzantium; Nemanja's son, the monk Sava, becomes patriarch.
1331–1355	Reign of Stefan Dušan, creator of advanced legal code and endower of churches; Serbia becomes an empire, controlling much of the western Balkans.
1371	Prince Vukašin Mrnjavčević's forces defeated by Turks at Battle of Maritsa in Bulgaria; Ottomans expand in Balkans.
1389	Battle of Kosovo between Serbs and Turks. Heavy casualties on both sides; Prince Lazar and Sultan Murad I die in battle,

and most Serbian nobles killed. Ottoman conquest accelerates.

1429	The despot Đurađ Branković moves Serbian capital north to the fortified city of Smederevo.
1459	Ottomans capture Smederevo and conquer all of Serbia soon after.
1517	*Vladika* system (rule of bishop-prince) begins in semi-independent Montenegro.
1679	Beginning of Montenegrin Petrović Njegos dynasty; will rule until 1918.
1690	Mass migration northward of the Serbs during the Austro-Turkish war; Turks spread Islam in Kosovo and Raška/Sandžak.
1699	Treaty of Karlovci between Christian powers and Turkey ends long war; Vojvodina incorporated into Austria; Sremski Karlovci becomes revived Serbian center under Austrian rule.
1737–1739	Ottomans raze Belgrade after third Austro-Turkish war; second Great Migration of Serbs into Austrian territories.
1766	Under Greek influence, Ottoman sultan abolishes Serbian patriarchate; Serbian church subjugated to Constantinople.
1804	The first Serbian uprising, led by Karađorđe Petrović, breaks out after Turkish atrocities against Serbs.
1815	The second Serbian uprising, led by Miloš Obrenović, drives out Turkish forces; Serbia becomes autonomous principality.
1847	*The Mountain Wreath*, Montenegro's greatest epic poem, written by enlightened *Vladika* Petar II Petrović Njegos.
1852	*Vladika* system abolished in Montenegro in favor of secular principality.
1868	Serbian government finalizes adoption of linguist Vuk Stefanović Karadžić's innovative language reforms.
1877–1878	Russo-Turkish War liberates Bulgaria; independent principality of Serbia formed with Treaty of Berlin.
1882	Kingdom of Serbia declared by Miloš Obrenović.
1885	After a border provocation, Bulgaria defeats Serbia in short war; Great Powers forced to accept unification of Bulgaria.

1903	Serbian King Petar Karađorđević takes power in a coup d'état.
1908	Austro-Hungarian Empire formerly annexes Bosnia-Herzegovina, while Young Turk revolution forces Ottoman Sultan Abdulhamid to reinstate Constitution of 1876; Europe-wide diplomatic crisis.
1910	Montenegrin Prince Nikola I proclaims himself king.
1912	First Balkan war. Serbia, Montenegro, Greece, and Bulgaria ally against Turkey; Serbia sweeps south to occupy half of Macedonia.
1913	Second Balkan war; Bulgaria attacks Greece and Serbia, but loses much of its recent gains.
1914	Austro-Hungarian successor to the throne, Archduke Franz Ferdinand, assassinated by Bosnian Serb Gavrilo Princip in Sarajevo on June 28.
	Austro-Hungary declares war on Serbia on July 28, setting off a chain reaction of war declarations; Serbia defeats first two Austrian invasions.
1914–1915	Third Austro-Hungarian invasion overwhelms Serbia. Led by the king, Serbian army marches through Albanian mountains, in winter, to the sea, and rehabilitates on the Greek island of Corfu.
1918	Allied breakthrough on Macedonian front in September; Serbian and French armies sweep northward, liberating Serbia.
	Kingdom of Serbs, Croats, and Slovenians proclaimed in Belgrade on December 1.
1928–1929	Montenegrin member of Parliament assassinates Croat politician Stjepan Radić; King Aleksandar I bans ethnic parties, renaming the country Yugoslavia.
1934	King Aleksandar I assassinated in Marseilles by a Bulgarian-Macedonian revolutionary group.
1941	Bombing of Belgrade by the Nazis on April 6 causes widespread damage and kills up to seventeen thousand people; Yugoslavia capitulates eleven days later; resistance groups emerge.
1945	Yugoslavia fully liberated by Tito's Partisan fighters; Communist Yugoslavia replaces royalist predecessor.

1948	Tito breaks with Stalin, navigating a diplomatic course between Communism and the West.
1961	Tito hosts the first summit of Non-Aligned Countries in Belgrade; gains prominence as international statesman.
1974	New constitution allows more decentralization of powers; ethnic separatism slowly begins.
1980	Josip Broz Tito dies on May 4; Communist system continues.
1991–1995	Slovenia, Croatia, Macedonia, and Bosnia and Herzegovina claim independence; savage fighting in Croatia and Bosnia.
1995	Dayton Agreement signed on December 14 by international leaders and Yugoslav President Slobodan Milošević, Croatian President Franjo Tuđman, and Bosnian president Alija Izetbegović, formally ending Bosnian War.
1999	Albanian separatist fighting in Kosovo leads NATO to begin seventy-eight-day air campaign on March 24; many civilian killed and refugee crisis develops.
	Yugoslav troops evacuate Kosovo after NATO bombing; Albanian ethnic cleansing of two hundred thousand Kosovo Serbs begins.
2000	Yugoslav President Slobodan Milošević toppled after mass street demonstrations on October 5.
2003	Prime Minister Zoran Đinđić assassinated by Belgrade gangsters on March 12.
2004	Anti-Serb pogrom by 50,000 Kosovo Albanians destroys churches and homes, displacing 3,500 Kosovo Serbs.
2006	Slobodan Milošević dies during proceedings at The Hague Tribunal on March 11.
	Montenegro holds successful independence referendum on June 6, becoming an independent state.
2008	Kosovo Albanians declare independence from Serbia on February 17.
	Serbia signs Stabilization and Association Agreement with European Union on April 29, an important step towards E.U. membership.

1

Land, People, and History

THERE IS NO race which has shown a more heroic desire for freedom than the Serbs or achieved it with less aid from others or at more sacrifice to itself.
—Lord Temperley, British historian

SERBS AND MONTENEGRINS

THROUGHOUT HISTORY, THE Serbs and Montenegrins, neighbors, allies, and close ethnic kin, have undergone cyclical processes of self-estrangement and unity. With the 2006 referendum by which Montenegro's people voted to dissolve the short-lived Serbia and Montenegro state union—itself the last iteration of the former Yugoslavia—Montenegrins recovered the independent statelet they had last enjoyed almost a century before. However, the tightness of the result (just more than 55 percent voted in favor, and claims of fraud and illegal voting dogged the proceedings), and the fact that many Montenegrins consider themselves Serbs, indicates that there is no great cultural schism in the offing. A large majority in both countries consists of Orthodox Christians, and they speak essentially the same language. And here, as elsewhere in Europe, religion and language are crucial in determining national identity.

Serbs and Montenegrins are closely related Balkan peoples, ultimately descendents of Slavic, Celtic, and other tribes who settled the region starting in the sixth century. Their heritage, national narrative, customs, and social rituals derive largely from the heritage of the Serbian kingdoms of the twelfth to fourteenth centuries, which expanded not only territory but also Slavic literacy and learning, as well as art and architecture, in the cultural milieu of Byzantium. From that empire, based in Constantinople (modern-day Istanbul, Turkey) the Serbs in the late ninth century also began to adopt the Orthodox Christian religion, a decision that would have momentous consequences for the future of the nation.

In the Serbian popular imagination, cultural production, and prevailing national narrative, the story of the Serbian nation is that of a bitter, four-hundred-year struggle to preserve Serbian Christian (and so Western) culture against the attacks and abuses of the Muslim Ottoman Empire. While there are no doubt many Serbs and Montenegrins who do not view their history in such simplistic terms, it is certainly true that this national narrative has had, and continues to have, a significant influence on everything from political life to popular culture. For Westerners, the long and often bitter memories of Serbs and Montenegrins may indeed seem baffling. However, appreciating the past and present of these nations is enhanced by also considering their historical legacy.

LANGUAGE

Although regional politics have made linguistic designations controversial, it is safe to say that Serbs and Montenegrins speak essentially the same language with regional variations. In Yugoslav times, the national language was known as Serbo-Croatian, but with Croatia's independence in the early 1990s, a process of linguistic revision occurred by which Zagreb created or changed numerous words to form a tongue of its own. The same process was repeated, to a lesser extent, in Bosnia, though both Croatian and Bosnian remain very similar to Serbian. Now that Montenegrin is an independent state, there are attempts being made to create a national language (e.g., the constitution states that Montenegrin is the official language of the land). However, standard Serbian, Serbian regional dialects, and the language of the Montenegrins all remain variations on the same theme.

All of these languages (along with Slovenian, Macedonian, and Bulgarian) belong to the South Slavic linguistic group. A major difference occurs with orthography: Croatia, Slovenia, and Bosnia (i.e., Bosnian Muslims) use the Latin script exclusively, whereas the other nations all use Cyrillic as well.

Matters are still more complicated, however: not only are slight differences between the Cyrillic alphabet used in each country, even in Latin transliteration, but also special diacritical marks are used that one needs to know to understand pronunciation. In the absence of such marks, one must be aware already of where they should go to know how to pronounce a word correctly—something that, for foreigners at least, only comes with time and experience.

The Serbian Cyrillic alphabet originally derives, as do other Cyrillic alphabets, from the ninth-century Byzantine monks Cyril and Methodius. Their labors saw the creation of a script, Glagolitic, that was later adapted by their follower Saint Kliment of Ohrid, in Macedonia, who created the Cyrillic alphabet. The alphabet was based on Greek, adding extra letters to represent sounds that do not exist in the Greek language, such as "ch," "sh," "dj," and so on. The Serbian Cyrillic alphabet contains thirty letters in all.

When written in the Latin alphabet, Serbian employs a few diacritical marks, the correct understanding of which will greatly assist the reader in pronouncing names mentioned throughout this book. Serbian Latin script is read almost completely exactly as it appears to English speakers, save for the letters *c*, pronounced like the "ts" in *cats*, and *j*, which is pronounced as a *y*. The letter *h* when encountered in Latin script should be pronounced more roughly, identical to the "ch" in the Scottish word *loch*.

Diacritical marks appear in seven cases, and always above, never below the letters. The letter *č* is pronounced "ch" as in *cheese*. The letter *š* is pronounced "sh" like *sheep*. The letter *đ* (upper case *D*) has a "dy" sound, akin to the English word *verdure*. The letter *ž* is pronounced like the *s* in the English word *pleasure*—however, the compound letter *dž* is pronounced as the *j* in *just*. Finally, the letter *ć* is pronounced as the "tch" sound in the word *future*.

Most of the regions of Serbia and Montenegro have their own local dialects, such as Vranski (the dialect of south Serbia, named after the town of Vranje). There are relatively minor differences between standard Serbian and Crnagorski (Montenegrin, or the adjective derived from the proper name *Crna Gora*, or Montenegro), though it even seems to be essentially one of pronunciation. This occurs according to a system. The Serbian word for *where*, *gde*, becomes *đe* when spoken by a Montenegrin. And a Serbian *e* as in the word *reka* (river) becomes elongated by Montenegrin speakers, similar to the case of Croatian/Bosnian, becoming *rijeka*, though this does not affect all words equally (e.g., the word *selo*, or "village," is pronounced identically by Serbs and Montenegrins). However, the Montenegrin government since 2007 has been pushing for ways to make the language still more distinct—with the discussion of adding three new letters to the Cyrillic alphabet being one of the proposals. The idea was spearheaded by the late Professor Vojislav Nikčević, a Montenegrin linguist who died in 2007 at the age of eighty-two. However, the controversy will continue long after his passing, it seems.

THE LAND

Everyone agrees that Serbia borders on Macedonia to the south, Bulgaria and Romania to the east, Hungary to the north, and Bosnia, Croatia, and Montenegro to the west. Everyone also agrees that Montenegro borders on

In its very name—meaning "Black Mountain" in Italian (Serbian equivalent, Crna Gora), Montenegro evokes its rugged geography. Mountains extend from its highland interior straight down into the Adriatic Sea, as shown here. Courtesy of Patrick Horton.

Albania to the southeast, Serbia to the east, and Bosnia and Croatia to the west. However, there is also the vexed issue of Kosovo, the nominally southwestern Serbian province inhabited primarily by ethnic Albanians that declared independence on February 17, 2008. Both Serbia and Montenegro border Kosovo, though Serbs do not recognize the legitimacy of the new state (at the time of this writing, the vast majority of world nations did not recognize an independent Kosovo either).

Serbia and Montenegro boast some of the most spectacular terrain in Europe, ranging from deep gorges and craggy peaks to forests, great fertile plains, and rivers, most famous among the latter being the Danube. While Montenegro's Adriatic coast is relatively short, it is a stunning one, with sandy beaches, olive groves, and cliffs.

For reasons of their geographic placement, Serbia and Montenegro also enjoy a varied climate. In the northern sections, especially the plain of Vojvodina, a Continental climate prevails; this involves hot, humid summers, cold winters, and adequate rainfall. Further south, this climatic zone merges with a sultrier Mediterranean one, with hot, dry summers. The Adriatic climate along the Montenegrin coast keeps temperatures slightly more mild and the air fresher than elsewhere. However, except for on the coast, snowfall can be substantial in winter.

Serbia

Despite millennia of civilization, Serbia still retains its forests and is a leading world producer of fruits such as plums, raspberries, and strawberries. It contains four national parks: Fruška Gora in the north, Kopaonik and Tara in the west, and Ðerdap in the east. There are several other nature reserves (amusingly referred to as "nature parks" or "nature reservations"), which comprise lakes, forests, and mountains.

Topographically, Serbia is essentially divided between the rich plains of its breadbasket in the north, Vojvodina, and a mountainous center and south bisected by a flat interior and south, the Pannonian Plain. This plain serves as part of the main north-south transport corridor from Central Europe to the Aegean, skirting the Morava River south to the Vardar River Valley, and continuing into Macedonia and then Greece. East of this rise the limestone ridges of the Stara Planina (Old Mountain), also known as the Balkan Mountain, which continues on from southeastern Serbia into Bulgaria; this range also boasts the highest peak in Serbia, Midžor (2,169 m). Swinging from the northwest to southeast are the Dinaric Alps, location of some of Serbia's most famous mountains: Zlatibor (1,469 m) and Kopaonik (2,017 m), both of which are popular ski resorts. And the southern Carpathian range emerges from Romania in the northeast and stretches toward the Stara Planina in the south.

Serbia also is known for its river systems, chief of all the great Danube, which forms parts of its borders, beginning with Croatia in the west and then veering straight across upper Serbia, dividing Vojvodina from Serbia proper and meeting the River Sava in Belgrade. The Danube then continues eastward and runs a jagged course southward, forming the border with Romania; it exits precisely at the point where Serbia, Romania, and Bulgaria meet, continuing eastward toward the Black Sea and forming the entire border between the latter two states. The entire length of the Serbian Danube is some 588 kilometers. Some 92 percent of Serbian territory belongs to the Danube drainage basin.

Another Serbian river forming a partial border is the Drina, which runs along the western border with Bosnia. The Tisa in the north is another major river, along with the aforementioned Sava and Morava, the last being the only one contained almost entirely on Serbian territory. While Serbia has few major lakes, it does have plenty of bubbling geothermal waters, which are used in numerous health spas spread around the country.

With its identity shaped by its geographical placement along the Adriatic Sea, Montenegro has always counted on fishing to enhance its sustenance. The picture shows traditional Montenegrin fishermen at work in 1920. Courtesy of Library of Congress.

Montenegro

As its name implies, Montenegro's territory of 13,812 square kilometers comprises almost all mountains, with an attractive 294-kilometer Adriatic coastline forming the country's western maritime border. This coastline runs from Croatia to the north, through Montenegro, and into Albania in the south. One of the most beautiful bays in the Mediterranean is at Montenegro's northern tip, at the winding Boka Kotorska Bay. This body of water penetrates deep into the interior, shielding the towns of Kotor, Tivat, and Herceg-Novi. Similarly aqueous is Montenegro's southern border, near the sandy beach at Ulcinj. Here the Skadarsko Jezero (Lake Skadar), the Balkans' largest lake at 40 kilometers long, runs into the River Bojana, which empties into the sea. Two-thirds of the lake belong to Montenegro and one-third to Albania.

Montenegro's capital, Podgorica, and other major towns such as Cetinje, Nikšić, and Bijelo Polje are located further inland. The Zeta Plain, near Lake Skadar, the Zeta Valley, and the Nikšić Plain are lowland areas suitable for growing crops. Indeed, a major reason for Montenegro's historical poverty, martial orientation, and clannishness owes to its geographical situation

Montenegro's numerous waterways include the largest lake in the Balkans, Lake Skadarksa, which forms the natural border with Albania in the south. Photograph by Rafael Estefania.

between towering mountains and ravines. The most notable of these are the steep Dinaric peaks of Orjen (1,894 m), Lovcen (1,749 m), and Rumija (1,595 m), which rise majestically out of the sea at Kotor. Beyond this range are the mountains of Durmitor (2,522 m), Komovi (2,487 m), and Sinjajev-ina (2,277 m), predominantly composed of limestone. The highest peak in Montenegro is Bobotov Kuk (2,522 m) in Durmitor in the west.

Montenegro's mountains are cut sharply by gorges and fast-flowing rivers, making it a favorite destination for kayaking and white-water rafting. The most notable mountain rivers are the Ceotina, Morača, Tara, and Piva rivers. The canyons gouged out of the mountains by the last three are up to 1,200 meters deep, making them among the world's deepest gorges. Along with Lake Skadar, Montenegro has a handful of elevated inland lakes, the biggest being Lake Plav, a popular weekend destination.

POPULATION

According to the 2002 census, the population of Serbia (excluding Kosovo) is 7,498,001 people. It is one of the most ethnically diverse countries in Europe, especially considering its relatively small size. Ethnic Serbs, most of them Orthodox Christian in religion, form the majority, at 82.9 percent. The country's Muslim minorities include Albanians, concentrated in the southwestern Preševo Valley near Kosovo, and Bosniaks, largely settled in the western district of Raška (also known by its Turkish name, *Sandžak*). This region is shared with Montenegro, and the Muslim population thus spills across the border.

Serbia's most multiethnic population is found in the northern province of Vojvodina. This is the legacy of pre-Yugoslav days when the area was the property of the Austro-Hungarian Empire, and large settlements of Germans and Hungarians arrived. Today, the Hungarian minority remains the largest, at almost 4 percent. Smaller ethnic populations include Ukrainians, Ruthians, Germans, Macedonians, Romanians, Slovaks, Bulgarians, and Croats. Interestingly, some 80,721 people (1.08 percent of the population) declared themselves Yugoslavs in 2002, most of them nostalgic elders.

Montenegro's population numbers about 620,000 people, according to the 2003 census. Here estimating identities is trickier; while Montenegrins have always been a breed apart, and recognized thus, the recent politics of ethnic nationalism that accelerated independence in 2006 has been reflected in censuses, with 43 percent declaring themselves Montenegrins and 32 percent declaring themselves Serbs. Combining these totals, as is proper considering their shared Orthodox Christian culture, results in a 75 percent Serb/Montenegrin population. Minorities include the Muslim Bosniaks of Raška/Sandžak (7.8 percent of the population) and Albanians (5 percent), mostly concentrated in the southeast near Albania and Kosovo. Other minorities in Montenegro include Croats, Roma, a few hundred Macedonians, Slovenians, Hungarians, Russians, Italians, and Germans. However, in summer, the huge influx of tourists brings a bigger international presence, and it is not unlikely that within a few years Montenegro will have a notable Western expatriate community.

Another minority in Serbia and Montenegro are the Roma, known to Westerners as Gypsies. While the former name is considered politically correct, the latter carries with it a certain evocative feeling and it is unlikely that popular concepts like the Gypsy brass band or Gypsy wedding will ever be sacrificed for cultural sensitivity. As elsewhere in the Balkans, the Roma live on the margins of society, deliberately (though sometimes not) excluding themselves from mainstream society. They tend to live in shantytown settlements and are accustomed to a transient lifestyle sustained by frugality, begging, and odd jobs. However, depending on where they live, Roma families can be more or less integrated into society. In rural areas and the smaller towns, integration is usually more successful.

HISTORY

Unlike most European countries, Serbs and Montenegrins are not quite finished making history. After Communism, most former Soviet and former

The two small islands off of Perast, Sveti Giorgi and Gospa od Škrpjela (Our Lady of the Rock), are both decorated with tiny chapels, commemorating legendary miraculous events. In Orthodox Christianity, special care is taken to build churches and religious arts in sacred places, often with appreciation for the natural beauty of the landscape. Photograph by Rafael Estefania.

Yugoslav states settled down into predictable patterns of political behavior and embraced the joys of consumerism. Serbia and Montenegro only formally split up after a Montenegrin referendum in 2006, thus extinguishing the last flicker of the former Yugoslav flame. However, drama continues as Serbia continues to protest, supported by stronger allies like Russia, against the independence of its southwestern province, Kosovo. Although this book cannot provide detailed coverage of Kosovo, the importance of what Serbs consider their spiritual heartland is inescapable, and as such it appears often in any discussion of Serbian history, religion, and thought.

Early History

Serbian tribes came to the Balkans with the Slavic migrations of the sixth and seventh centuries. However, they had been around much longer. The name *Serboi* (Serbs, in the Greek nominative plural case) is mentioned by ancient writers Tacitus (around A.D. 50) and Pliny (around A.D. 70), referring to a barbarian tribe located in Sarmatia on the Lower Volga River. The Serbs and other Slavic tribes would migrate to the Balkans from this area, in what is today southern Russia and Ukraine.

The Slavic tribes settled a Balkans devastated by previous barbarian invaders and their battles with the Romans. They both intermingled with and replaced preexisting populations, such as the Vlachs (descendents of Romanized Thracians and Dacians and ancestors of modern Romanians), Illyrians, Greeks, and Macedonians. The Serbs arrived in waves, from the early to mid-seventh century, and they were similarly converted to Christianity in waves between the seventh and ninth centuries. The recorded history of Serbs is therefore intrinsically bound up with their experience of Christianity.

The crucial element for the formation of a Serbian national identity and state, as with Bulgaria, was the Serbs' eventual conversion to Orthodox Christianity by the Byzantine Empire. With its capital in Constantinople, Byzantium represented what had been the Eastern Roman Empire after the empire split in the fourth century. During what is known as Western Europe's Dark Ages, the Byzantines (who referred to themselves as *Romaioi*,

The former Roman fortress of Kalemegdan sprawls across a sweeping bluff, overlooking the convergence of the Sava and Danube rivers that divide Belgrade. It is a popular spot for a stroll or a picnic, and has outdoor tennis courts and soccer fields used by athletic Serbs. Photography by the author.

or Romans), played a vital role in preserving the literature, philosophy, and sciences of ancient Greece and Rome. Despite the frequent struggles for independence and challenges to Constantinople's authority coming from the Balkan Slavs, these peoples would be permanently drawn into the orbit of Byzantine culture. Roman Catholicism, meanwhile, would eventually win the battle for influence along the northern and western extremities of the Balkans in Hungary, Slovenia, and Croatia.

The first Serbian states were Raška (also known as Rascia), under Časlav Klonimirović in the mid-tenth century, and Zeta (also known as Duklja) in Montenegro, under the Vojislavljević clan. With the rise of the powerful commercial empire of Venice, Roman Catholicism acquired influence over the Montenegrin Adriatic coast and, for a time, further inland. In fact, the first Montenegrin king of Zeta, Mihailo, was crowned by the pope in 1077. However, the constant threat of the Bulgarians in the south became the most urgent problem, obliging the Serbs to seek protection from Byzantium, itself engaged in recurring wars of attrition with the Bulgarians throughout the ninth and early tenth centuries.

The Height of Serbian Glory: From the Nemanjići to Tsar Stefan Dušan

Serbia's greatest period begins in 1166, when the young ruler Stefan Nemanja beat his brothers for rule in Raška. Beginning what became known as the Nemanjić dynasty, Stefan deftly allied with Byzantium while also fending it off, simultaneously expanding Serbian territory. Holding the title of *veliki župan* ("Grand Župan," or prince), Stefan expanded to the east and south, annexing Zeta and sections of the Adriatic coast.

By 1265, the Nemanjići emperors had created one of the most powerful states in the Balkans. Marriage alliances with the Hungarian kingdom allowed Serbs to expand to the north, in Bosnia, the region of Mačva, and Belgrade, creating the Kingdom of Srem in 1282. The Serbian kingdom became a full-fledged empire beginning in 1325, when the shrewd King Milutin made full use of medieval diplomatic practices; one was dynastic marriages (he himself was married five times, to Byzantine, Hungarian, and Bulgarian princesses). Like Stefan Nemanja, Milutin was renowned for his religious endowments, such as Kosovo's magnificent Gračanica Monastery, the cathedral in Hilandar Monastery on Greece's Mount Athos, and even Jerusalem's Saint Archangel Church. Milutin would be proclaimed a saint for these works.

Milutin was succeeded by his son Stefan Dušan, whose reign proved the high-water mark of medieval Serbian cultural and political life. Stefan expanded Serbian territory to the east and south, conquering Niš, Macedonia, and mainland Greece. Stefan's lasting contribution to Serbian medieval architecture is the Visoki Dečani Monastery, in western Kosovo's Metohia (literally, church lands) region. This monumental structure, set amid wooded hills, exemplifies the spirit of Serbian-Byzantine medieval Orthodox architecture and, as one of the few Serbian shrines to escape destruction by Kosovo Albanians since 1999, is all the more important today.

Tsar Stefan Dušan, an enlightened ruler, also created in 1349 a legal code unique among contemporary European states, the *Dušanov Zakonik* (Dušan's Code). In 1346, Tsar Stefan was crowned emperor of the Serbs and Greeks by the first Serbian patriarch in Constantinople; with the restored Byzantine Empire besieged by Turks, he sought a more prominent role in defending Christendom. In fact, before his sudden death, Stefan Dušan and the pope were planning a new crusade against the Turks. However, in December 1355, Serbia's greatest ruler died at the age of forty-seven, probably from being poisoned.

The Ottoman Conquest

With Stefan's death, power struggles among the nobility aided the fortunes of the growing Ottoman Turks, who had emerged from Central Asia onto the Anatolian plain in the late eleventh century and steadily spread across Byzantine lands. Although Constantinople and various other Greek-populated areas would hold out for another century, the Balkans rapidly fell into Turkish hands, owing to the disunity and mutual infighting of Christian leaders.

As an emergency situation built up, the two most powerful Serbian princes, the brothers Mrnjavčević, led a large army through Bulgaria to take on Turkish forces at Adrianople (modern-day Edirne, Turkey) in 1371. The Turks launched an unexpected nighttime raid that destroyed the Serbian army near the River Maritsa (the Battle of Maritsa). However, the Turks would be heavily defeated at the 1386 Battle of Pločnik. Three years later, a definitive battle unfolded when Serbian leader and Knight Miloš Obilić led his forces into battle on Kosovo Polje (the Plain of Kosovo).

The 1389 Battle of Kosovo looms larger than any other in Serbian popular history. Although Serbia was not completely subjugated for some time after it, this battle is considered the turning point in the war against the Muslim invaders, and so it has considerable symbolic significance. It also represents the end of Serbian rule over Kosovo, the disputed province that contains (or contained, until Kosovo Albanian destruction of approximately 150 churches and other cultural sites dramatically changed the province beginning in 1999) some of the most important artistic and architectural achievements in Serbian history.

In the battle, the troops of Prince Lazar, Serbia's strongest ruler, were allied with other Serbian and Bosnian lords. The Serbs were heavily outnumbered, Lazar died in the fighting, and they eventually had to retreat. However, for the only time in history, an Ottoman sultan (Murad I) was killed in battle. In revenge, Murad's son Bayezid killed most of the captive Serbian nobles. Later, popular legends and epics claimed that Vuk Branković, another Serbian lord, betrayed the Serbs by retreating unexpectedly. However, there is no evidence for this, and historians today believe that the legend was circulated as anti-Branković propaganda by Lazar's widow, Milica, and her son, Stefan Lazarević, who defeated Branković for rule over Serbs by allying with the Turks. Serbia became an Ottoman vassal state. Nevertheless, these murky events have enhanced over time the mythological significance of the Battle of Kosovo, introducing oft-referenced (and oft-repeated) themes of the hero and traitor into the Serbian national narrative.

Faced with an increasingly bleak Turkish onslaught, Serbian populations began moving northward out of Kosovo and southern Serbia. Under Stefan Lazarević, the capital was relocated north to Smederevo, a purpose-built fortified town. Smederevo finally fell in 1459, though Zeta in Montenegrin held out until 1499. Nevertheless, as Montenegrins like to point out, their mountainous country was hardly controlled by the Turks. A restored Serbian principality, existing as a Hungarian dependency, occupied parts of today's Vojvodina, northern Hungary, and Romania. This principality held out until 1540, when it succumbed to the Turks.

Serbia and Montenegro under the Turks

Under Islamic law, Jews and Christians such as Serbs and Montenegrins were considered protected people and not obliged to perform military service. They were allowed to keep their religious and social customs. However, this hardly meant that life was easy for the non-Muslim masses (the so-called *rayah*), essentially second-class citizens. Along with onerous tax burdens, non-Muslims also had no legal right to testify against Muslims. Further, they were obliged to dismount from horseback when passing a Muslim, and they could not construct churches higher than mosques; the biggest and best churches were often turned into mosques. This institutionalized imbalance lead to outrageous excesses and abuses by Muslims, especially brutal in border areas (Serbia and Bosnia) and during times of uprisings. It is no wonder that many Bosnian Serbs converted to Islam to improve their lot in life.

Most resented was the blood tax. Turkish authorities would assemble the healthiest and most able children of the local *rayah* and kidnap them for the sultan's pleasure, their parents powerless to defend them. Boys would be converted to Islam and then trained to become Janissaries, the elite guard of the sultan. Girls were sent to the harem. While a few such Janissaries were noted for helping their home territories once in power, the majority of them were known for their avarice and cruelty, terrorizing local populations and becoming a law unto themselves; indeed, the Janissaries eventually become such a threat to the sultans that the whole corps had to be purged in bloody fashion. But not only did the Janissaries and officials persecute non-Muslims. The new "winners" in society, Muslim converts from Bosnian Serbs and Albanians, took advantage of their privileged position in numerous violent and humiliating ways. The Ottoman Empire could not have functioned without input from all its constituent peoples, however, and the sultans recognized talent where the saw it. They understood the native diplomatic skill of many Serbs, and over the years a number of them became ministers and diplomats in the sultan's court.

Revolt and Relocation

Nevertheless, the institutionalized oppression of the Serbs and crushing taxation inspired frequent rebellions. Popular frustrations and local leaders' ambitions were often exploited by greater powers to serve their own conflicts with the Ottomans. Hungarian kings encouraged Serb refugees to immigrate into their territories, seeing them as a shield against the Turks. Serbs joined Hungarian forces, unsuccessfully, in the 1526 Battle of Mohács. Hungary lost its independence, and the Austrian kingdom assumed the burden of preserving Christian Europe. Serbs played crucial roles in Austria's wars against the Ottoman Empire. During the Austro-Turkish War of 1593–1606, Serbs in Banat rebelled. Ottoman Sultan Murad III crushed the revolt and tragically burned the sacred relics of Saint Sava. In a second rebellion, in Herzegovina, the Serbs were again left to their fate once Turkey and Austria made peace.

The momentous Great War of 1683–1690, pitting Turkey against the Holy League (Austria, Poland, and Venice, supported by the pope), proved disastrous for the Serbs. With Serbs convinced that the Holy League might finally deliver their freedom, they rebelled against the Turks in Montenegro, Dalmatia, Macedonia, Raška, and Kosovo. Nevertheless, the war ended with Austrian withdrawal; faced with the choice of staying behind to suffer certain Muslim revenge killings or evacuating to a Christian state, many Kosovo Serbs fled with the Austrian army. Now known as the Great Migration of 1690, this organized relocation saw the permanent exile of thousands of Serbs led by their patriarch, Arsenije Čarnojević. This migration was arguably the single most significant in Serbian population decline in Kosovo, and it has been captured for posterity in a moving epic painting, the *Seoba Srbalja* (Migration of the Serbs) by Paja Jovanović (see chapter 9, "Art and Architecture").

The Serbian Uprisings and Establishment of an Independent State

By the late eighteenth century, Ottoman power was declining, something that made Muslim treatment of Christians only more savage. This naturally inspired more revolts, not only in Serbia but also in Greece, which fought its War of Independence (1821–1829), and then in Bulgaria. However, the Serbs beat them both: the first Serbian uprising occurred in 1804, led by the legendary character of Black George, or Karađorđe Petrović (1768–1817), a brawny bear of a man whose deeds are commemorated in folk song. The direct cause of the rebellion was a Janissary revolt against the sultan that involved massacres of Serbs and mass executions of Serb leaders. The angered, mostly peasant rebels succeeded in winning key battles, recovering Belgrade and nearby areas. Karađorđe joined Russia to make war against the Turks, but by 1812 Russia had made peace, and Serbian nobles like Karađorđe were forced to flee to avoid Turkish counterattacks.

In 1815, the second Serbian uprising, led by another Serbian prince, Miloš Obrenović, forced the Ottomans to recognize Serbia as an autonomous principality within the empire. However, Obrenović also ordered the execution of the popular Karađorđe when returning from exile in 1817, allegedly on Ottoman orders. Thus began the long decades of strife and enmity between the Karađorđević and Obrenović dynasties, which would last until a palace coup brought the former to power in 1903. Today, the heirs of Black George continue to be recognized as the rightful royal family in Serbia.

This sudden independence inspired other Serbs to rebel. In 1848, Serbs living in the southern Vojvodina region of the Austro-Hungarian Empire proclaimed an autonomous province. However, Vienna declared it a province within the empire, the Vojvodina of Serbia and Tamiš Banat. This internal fiefdom survived only eleven years, being abolished in 1860. Only in 1918, with the destruction of the Austro-Hungarian Empire, would Vojvodina join Serbia.

Although the Turks kept military control of Belgrade until 1867, their influence gradually waned, except in the Raška/Sandžak area and Kosovo, where Turkish and Albanian Muslim abuses of Christian Serbs continued unchecked. In Serbia itself, the real struggle for control was between the Karađorđević and Obrenović dynasties. A principality, or *kneževina*, after 1817, Serbia became a kingdom in 1882, following the 1878 Treaty of Berlin that carved up the Balkans after the Russo-Turkish War. Naturally, the two leading dynasties in Serbia sought to take power for themselves, frequently feuding and intriguing with foreign powers in the process.

Montenegro's Rise and the Balkan Wars

This situation was made more complicated by the improbable rise of little Montenegro, whose prince, Nikola I, had grand ambitions for expanding his tiny principality and becoming, however unlikely it seemed, a major player in the Great Powers diplomacy of the time. From 1815 to 1852, Montenegro had been ruled by a Vladika, or metropolitan-prince; since such religious leaders could not marry, the hereditary position passed from uncle to nephew. Petar II Petrović Njegoš (1813–1851) the last *vladika*, was acknowledged as a man of wisdom and strength, and he remains the country's greatest poet (see chapter 6, "Literature"). Under Njegoš, reforms in education and society were undertaken, such as schooling for girls and an attempt to rein in the destructive blood feuding of the various Montenegrin clans, which had a very long history.

Known as fierce warriors, and especially acclimated to fighting in their harsh mountain homeland, the Montenegrins had for centuries kept a part of Serbdom essentially free of the Turks. Their leaders thus aroused great admiration among European observers sympathetic to the Christian cause. The most clever, charismatic and successful of these leaders was Prince (and finally, king) Nikola I (1860–1918), who in true Byzantine style managed to profit from, and evade, the competing powers of Italy, Russia, Austria, and Serbia, using marriage alliances and crafty diplomacy to make his little Balkan principality the apple of desire in numerous powers' strategic and economic aspirations. Above all, what he sought was the social validation of being a king (and, if possible, king of Serbia as well) and to recover the large sections of the Adriatic coast then in Austrian hands, including the strategic Bay of Kotor.

In 1912, the stage was set for a massive regional conflagration after an unresolved, multisided guerrilla war in Macedonia inspired Greece, Bulgaria, Serbia, and Montenegro to join forces to drive the Turks out of Europe. As could be expected, the Montenegrins declared war first. The Serbian army of Petar Karađorđević, who had recovered the throne from rival Milan Obrenović in 1903, swept successfully across the plains of southern Serbia and Macedonia, driving the Turks south. The Greek fleet, meanwhile, was recovering Turkish-occupied islands. The Bulgarians fought ferociously in Macedonia and Thrace, and the Turks were indeed being pushed out of Europe almost entirely. However, as the alarmed European Great Powers watched the traditional balance of power shifting, the Balkan allies disputed rights to Macedonia, leading to the Second Balkan War (1913), in which Bulgaria was soundly beaten. In the end, Macedonia was partitioned between the Greeks,

Through clever politicking and creation of marriage alliances between his daughters and powerful European royal families, Montenegro's King Nikola (1841–1921) achieved a prominence, both personally and for his small country, entirely disproportionate to its size, guiding Montenegro through numerous crises and both the Balkan Wars and World War I. King Nikola (seated right) with the royal family. Courtesy of Library of Congress.

Bulgarians, and Serbs (the modern-day Republic of Macedonia comprises the territory awarded to Serbia in 1913 and subsequently part of Yugoslavia).

World War I and the Kingdom of Serbs, Croats, and Slovenes

Austro-Hungary was especially concerned by Serbia's great gains, fearing that they would inspire Serbs in Habsburg-occupied Bosnia, Croatia, and Montenegro to rebel. Although popular history has it that the outbreak of the First World War can be attributed to the rash misdeed of a young Bosnian Serb fanatic, Gavrilo Princip, the conflagration cannot be blamed simply on any one man. Princip's assassination of Austrian Crown Prince Franz Ferdinand on June 28, 1914, did dramatically worsen relations between Austria and Serbia; however, the former had clearly been seeking a way to negate any possible Serbian threat for years before that.

When the Austro-Hungarian Empire declared war on Serbia on July 28, 1914, a chain of similar declarations erupted as the European alliance system followed its fatal course. However, the first Austrian assaults at Cer in Vojvodina were repelled vigorously by the spirited Serb defenders, temporarily making the better-equipped and larger Austrian army the laughingstock of Europe. The infuriated Austrians, this time with stout assistance from the Germans, invaded Serbia again. Then the opportunistic Bulgarians invaded from the south. Yet the Serbian kingdom did not surrender. Rather, King Petar won great respect when he personally led his ragged troops across the mountains of Albania in winter 1915. Reaching the Adriatic coast, the king, his family, and the surviving soldiers were evacuated by ship to the Greek island of Corfu. After recuperating, they reached Thessaloniki in Northern Greece, where they were united with their British and French allies. The combined troops held a line against the opposing Bulgarian, Austrian, and German ranks on what is essentially the border between Greece and Macedonia and Bulgaria today.

Finally, the Serbian and French troops broke enemy lines in September 1918 and moved swiftly through the Macedonian territory they had so recently won from the Turks. Within two months, all of the occupied Serbian territories had been liberated. The Austro-Hungarian Empire did not survive the war, and the restored Serbian monarchy joined the newly freed territories of Croatia, Slovenia, and Bosnia to create the Kingdom of Serbs, Croats, and Slovenes, a parliamentary monarchy.

The almost six years of fighting had devastated Serbia. Not to mention the losses sustained in the Balkan Wars, Serbia suffered in World War I alone some 1,264,000 casualties—more than half of the male population. Whole villages and towns had been destroyed. At the same time, the newly incorporated territories were too much to administer; not all Slovenes and Croats

The retreat of the Serbian army through the mountains of Albania to the sea in winter 1915–1916 ranks as one of the most heroic feats of endurance in modern European history. Despite thousands falling to starvation, the elements, injuries, and Albanian bands, the army survived to fight another day, led in person by 71-year-old King Petar. Courtesy of Library of Congress.

were keen on joining a Belgrade-centered monarchy, having just been freed from Austrian domination. The same went for the Bosnian Muslims and Albanian Muslims in Kosovo, horrified at the thought of losing their previously guaranteed Ottoman institutional privileges. However, the monarchy by and large dealt with the Muslims cautiously, not wishing to agitate them.

The new state expressed a concept—Yugoslavism—that had captivated intellectuals since the mid-nineteenth century. It was predicated on the shared cultures, but most fundamentally on the similar languages, of the three main component nations. A union of South Slavs had never before been possible, and few had a realistic understanding of its potential. Unfortunately, the economic disparities between north and south (a wealthy Slovenia and poor Kosovo and Macedonia), plus the Catholic-Orthodox divide between people in close proximity, such as Croats and Serbs in Croatia, worked against the new state. And the Serbian leadership also tended to centralize power, abetting rival ethnic nationalists. The 1920s government of Prime Minister Nikola Pašić was considered heavy-handed, intimidating ethnic minority parties and seizing opposition pamphlets. Pašić was a capable leader; however, he also alienated many. During the 1920s, ethnic tensions simmered, in Croatia especially, where an anti-Semitic, far-right political movement was challenging the more popular Croat Peasant's Party of socialist-populist leader Stjepan Radić. In his party alone were Croatian Orthodox Serbs and Catholic Croats starting to cooperate. However, in June 1928, Montenegrin parliamentary deputy Puniša Račić shot and fatally wounded Radić during a parliamentary session, thus ending any Serb-Croat rapprochement and promoting the rise of the Croatian right wing.

World War II and Ascendancy of the Partisans

After the assassination of Stjepan Radić, King Aleksandar I Karađorđević banned nationalist parties to try and subdue tensions. However, as Great Power intrigue returned to the Balkans, Hitler's Germany, Italy, and the Soviet Union all jostled for power. Yugoslavia was a coveted prize for them, and ethnic separatists were ready to act as well. In 1934, the king was assassinated in Marseille, France, by Bulgarian nationalists aided by the up-and-coming Ustaša, a Croatian fascist group. In the run-up to war, Serbian Prince-Regent Paul followed Bulgaria, Romania, and Hungary in signing a treaty with Hitler. However, Serbs protested vociferously, and Paul was exiled; his nephew King Peter II took his place. A furious Hitler decided to invade. His forces were able to occupy Serbia with far less difficulty than had their ancestors in 1914; the difference was air power. In the April 1941 bombing of Belgrade, still commemorated every year, some seventeen thousand civilians were killed and untold damage was done to the city's great architecture and civil infrastructure.

Yugoslavia soon surrendered. King Peter II and the royal family fled to London, where he was treated as a hero for daring to oppose Hitler. The king led a Yugoslav government-in-exile for the rest of the war from Britain.

The Axis Powers quickly carved up Yugoslavia into zones of occupation. Serbia was occupied by the Germans. In Bosnia and Kosovo, Serbs were controlled by Mussolini's troops. Hungarians allied with Nazi-controlled Vojvodina, beginning an occupation of terror that involved hanging Serbian civilians from light posts. Serbian-held Macedonia was occupied by both Bulgaria and Italy in its western, Albanian-populated areas. Italy also controlled Albania and much of Montenegro. Slovenia was divided between Germany and Italy.

The Nazi occupation of Serbia was grim. In Serbia, the Nazis set up several concentration camps, such as Banjica and Sajmište near Belgrade, in which some forty thousand Jews (90 percent of the Serbian Jewish population) were murdered, as well as resistance fighters such as the Communist Partisans. In the infamous Kragujevac massacre (October 20, 1941), which occurred in the central Serbian town of the same name, the Germans killed fifty Serbs for every one German who had been killed by Serbian rebels.[1] Meanwhile, the Germans and Italians provided support for the fascist Ustaša regime, which set up the independent state of Croatia. Under Ustaša rule, Serbs, Jews, Gypsies, and other non-Croats were subjected to treatment that can objectively be described as genocide. At Croat-run death camps such as the one at Jasenovac (located in today's Croatia), hundreds of thousands were tortured and exterminated in ways that shocked even Hitler's lieutenants.[2]

The Ustaša official policy toward the Serbs—"kill a third, deport a third, and convert a third"—was notably supported by the Catholic Church, and after the war some of the most important Croat war criminals were evacuated to South America through the same infamous Vatican "ratlines" used to save Nazi leaders responsible for the Jewish Holocaust.[3] The Albanian ultranationalist groups who briefly annexed Kosovo to Albania, under the encouragement of Italy and the Nazis, also participated in the Holocaust and the extermination of Kosovo Serbs, so that by war's end the latter became a minority in their historic heartland.

The major resistance groups that emerged to fight the Nazis and their allies were the Serbian Četniks under Draža Mihajlović, who remained loyal to King Aleksandar, and the Communist Partisans of Josip Broz Tito, whose members came from all ethnicities in Yugoslavia. Some were ideologues, but many were just bewildered, forcibly conscripted villagers. The eventual victory of Tito's forces might have seemed sure, considering that the various ethnic nationalist movements would cancel one another out, but for much of the war this was not the case. Many allied governments, especially the British, were sympathetic to the royalists, and the Serbian king made a constant case for his cause while in London throughout the war.

The Četniks also won the gratitude of the Americans when Mihailović's men performed the single largest airlift of downed Allied fighters, some five hundred American airmen who had been shot down over Serbia by German gunners while attempting to bomb oil fields in Nazi-allied Romania. At considerable risk to themselves, Četniks fighters and ordinary Serbian villagers took in the American soldiers, protecting them from the Germans until the U.S. Air Force could organize secret flights to evacuate the troops. Some of the veterans of this operation lobbied the U.S. government for decades to acknowledge Mihajlović's great deed. However, foreign policy always seemed to dictate against such an acknowledgment.[4]

The Allies, however, eventually switched their support to the Partisans for primarily pragmatic reasons: they simply saw that Tito's forces had a better chance of winning than did the Četniks. In addition, key advisers in the British Foreign Office had strong sympathies for Communism in theory and deliberately, if quietly pushed a policy favorable to Tito's cause.[5]

As 1944 finished, the Red Army liberated Serbia, and by May of the next year Allied forces and Partisan ones were united in Hungary, Austria, and Italy. The Germans were finally expelled at the Battle of Srem, with the help of Soviet airpower, and the Partisans hunted down the last of the Ustaša in the aftermath of the fighting. As in World War I, Yugoslavia's human and economic losses were among the greatest of all European countries. Some 1.7 million people lost their lives in the conflict, a figure that equaled almost 11 percent of the total population, while economic and infrastructure damages were estimated at $9.1 billion.

Serbia and Montenegro during Tito's Yugoslavia

World War II in Yugoslavia ended with the victory of the Partisans and their wily and charismatic leader, Josip Broz Tito (1892–1980), an ethnic Croat who was determined to restore the fractious country along ideological rather than nationalist lines. However, Tito was even more of a centralist than either Pašić or King Aleksandar I had been. His reign—a lifetime one, as it turned out—involved cultivating a robust cult of personality. Dissent was banned, and the Communists shot many who disagreed with their ideology and imprisoned others without trials. Several thousand Yugoslavs, many Serbs, were killed following the war. Any possible threats to the new order were eliminated, such as General Draža Mihailović, the Četnik resistance hero who was hung by the Communists in on July 17, 1946.

Tito changed the structure of the country as well as its name, which became the Socialist Federative Republic of Yugoslavia. Belgrade was still the capital, but six constituent republics were created: Serbia, Croatia, Slovenia, Montenegro, Bosnia-Herzegovina, and Macedonia. Two autonomous provinces were also created, Kosovo and Vojvodina, both in Serbia. Since other autonomous provinces could have been created in several instances in other republics, critics considered Tito's action against Serbia as part of an acknowledged policy that stated "a weak Serbia makes for a strong Yugoslavia." Nevertheless, Serbia's indisputable leading role as the largest Yugoslav republic meant that Serbian Communists would wield significant power.

The upheaval of war and the imposition of a new political structure radically affected the old order, especially as far as religion and property ownership were concerned. The Catholic Church, Orthodox Church, and Islamic communities in the various republics were kept in check, and, though religion was not banned, it lost its former hold on life. Meanwhile, the agricultural reforms conducted after the war resulted in the wholesale theft of land from the Yugoslav peasantry, who were forced into collective agriculture or relocated to drab new apartment blocks in the cities. However, Communism had some benefits, such as increased education and equality for women.

Despite the postwar division of the world's powers into capitalist and Communist camps, Tito's Yugoslavia was considered more or less a pro-Western country. Ever since the comrade in chief's 1948 break with Stalin, it had steered a careful course between East and West, largely due to the acumen and charm of Tito himself. The motto according to which he ruled Yugoslavia was one of brotherhood and unity, the ideal being a system of self-management as distinct from both hard-core Communism and rampant capitalism. Tito's unique Socialist system combined just enough of a market economy with just enough of a state-owned system so as to ensure a continuous stream of generous loans from both the West and the Soviets, thus keeping the Yugoslav boat afloat for decades. However, what really stood out for admirers of Tito's country was that its foreign policy provided a model as an alternative to the harrowing mutually assured destructiveness of the Cold War. The championing of a so-called non-aligned movement brought Tito many allies from the developing world and allowed him to portray himself as a bona-fide statesman on the world stage. Unlike the hardline Communist countries and the NATO states, Yugoslavia had no overt enemies.

However, internal ethnic unrest materialized in protests in 1968 and 1974, when a new constitution was introduced. It allowed for more decentralization in both the republics and in Serbia's autonomous provinces, a result that encouraged separatist movements supported by strong diaspora groups in Western countries, and even by the secret services of the United States, Germany, and other Western allies. Only in the case of Bosnia, where future president Alija Izetbegović was agitating for an independent Muslim state based on the models of Pakistan and Iran, were political goals being sought through a rival ideology alone.

In the end, Yugoslavia became a victim of its own apparent success. When Tito died in 1980, guaranteed leadership died with him, though his cult of personality would linger on in the increasingly meaningless slogans that schoolchildren were told to recite, such as *Za Domovinu, s Titom, napred* (For the country, with Tito, forward!) and *i po Titu, Tito* (And after Tito . . . Tito!). The latter bit of wishful thinking illustrated the inescapable problem of continuing a confederation previously held together by easy loans from abroad and the iron fist of one leader.

Post-Tito Yugoslavia created a new rotating presidency between the republics, though the one-party system remained intact. Nevertheless, significant changes began to occur. The more developed and Western-oriented republics of Slovenia and Croatia went toward market-based reforms, while Serbia and Montenegro clung to their state-owned system. In Kosovo, meanwhile, Albanian separatists took to increasingly violent protests, resulting in new police crackdowns. Wealthy Slovenes decried the fact that their tax money was being hemorrhaged in Belgrade's unsuccessful efforts to bring Kosovo into the twentieth century. Rival ethnic groups in Bosnia eyed one another uneasily. Inflation soared as foreign creditors began to call on their loans. The stage was set for a showdown, though most people could not imagine it, even up until the end.

Serbia during the Wars of Yugoslav Secession

Ethnic nationalism also began to assert itself in Yugoslavia, though this was complicated: whereas Slovenians, Croats, Macedonians, Bosnian Muslims, and Kosovo Albanians all wanted independence, most Serbs and Montenegrins in Serbia and other republics wanted to remain part of Yugoslavia. And so an up-and-coming politician from Yugoslavia's Socialist Party, Slobodan Milošević (1941–2006), maneuvered his way into the Yugoslav presidency and became associated in the (especially Western) imagination with Serbian nationalism. However, Milošević and his allies were more interested in personal enrichment, and they cynically manipulated national fervor for their own ends. Under Milošević's tenure, Yugoslavia, especially Serbia, became internationally isolated. Yugoslavia was strapped for a few years by a United Nations–enforced economic embargo, and economic mismanagement added to the woes of the average Serb. During the "transition" decade of the 1990s, an authoritarian government in Belgrade stifled dissent, and Serb paramilitaries and politicians were accused of committing or condoning war crimes in the wars in Croatia and especially Bosnia. A new gangster culture sprang up, sustained by popular culture, which glamorized violence and organized crime.

In 1995, Milošević reached the apex of his international stature as a diplomat when Western leaders praised him for his role in influencing the Bosnian

Serbs to sign a peace treaty with their Muslim rivals, overseen by U.S. officials in Dayton, Ohio. The Dayton Agreement authorized a federal state consisting of two main entities, the Republika Srpska (Serb Republic) and the Muslim-Croat federation. The Yugoslav civil wars had been especially brutal, contradictory, and complex. All sides committed atrocities against the others, and ostensible enemies secretly collaborated when they thought they could make a profit. Much of the wars were characterized by subterfuge, hidden assassins, and civilian massacres. However, while Serbia was never an active participant in these wars, it was increasingly singled out by Western media and governments as the primary supporter of them. In actual fact, it was a very selective image, as the Croats and Bosnian Muslims had long before hired American public relations coverage to push their side of the story. The Serbs did not pay this modern war tax, and they paid the price for it.

And so, by the time the war finally came to Serbia, with NATO's seventy-eight-day bombing campaign in the spring of 1999, President Milošević was being depicted in the media practically as another Hitler. Since 1997, an ethnic Albanian paramilitary group financed primarily by narcotics and diaspora remittances, the Kosovo Liberation Army, had been fighting a guerilla war with the Yugoslav army in several villages in western Kosovo. The Clinton administration decided to turn this localized conflict into a major global issue, opening a Pandora's box that is having, and will have, repercussions well into the future in other separatist areas of the world. After NATO started bombing, hundreds of thousands of Albanians fled to Montenegro, Albania, Macedonia, and indeed, to Serbia proper. NATO perversely justified its humanitarian intervention on a crisis that it had created itself.

Serbia suffered tremendously during the NATO bombardment, which targeted factories, schools, markets, television stations, bridges, and even the Chinese embassy in Belgrade. NATO proved inept at defeating the Yugoslav military, destroying a measly thirteen tanks at a cost of approximately $13 billion. Critics mocked the all-powerful alliance's failure to defeat a small, economically crippled country, and U.S. administration hawks called for a ground campaign that NATO was deeply afraid to undertake.[6] In the end, the alliance forced Milošević to capitulate only by causing unbearable civilian suffering and threatening to destroy Belgrade completely. NATO and the United Nations took over in Kosovo, where returning Albanians undertook a wave of revenge attacks on the helpless Serb minority. Since then, more than 150,000 Serbs have left Kosovo, while a similar number lives on in enclaves protected by international troops. Although the Kumanovo Agreement that ended the NATO bombing stipulated the return of Serbian police to Kosovo and no independence for the province, Western governments have failed to honor any of their promises.

Serbia and Montenegro after Milošević

On October 5, 2000, recent presidential election winner Slobodan Milošević was toppled following massive public demonstrations. The public anger was the expression of popular frustration with Milošević's rule, and it had been organized and shaped by a Western-backed youth group, Otpor. Milošević's election opponent, the lawyer Vojislav Koštunica, was brought to power, promising to set Serbia and Montenegro on a pro-Western course. Parliamentary elections, held in December, were won by a coalition led by reformer Zoran Đinđić, a longtime critic of the Milošević regime. In April 2001, Đinđić had an important role in getting Milošević shipped off to The Hague Tribunal in the Netherlands to stand trial for war crimes in the recent wars.

Many believed that Đinđić had had to call on the "heavies" among Serbia's criminal underworld to obtain this result, and that he had in any case links with organized crime bosses whom he subsequently pledged to rid the country of. It was thus not a surprise when, on March 12, 2003, Đinđić became the latest in a long line of political assassinations, murdered on the steps of the parliament by a member of Milorad Ulemek's Zemun Clan crime syndicate. The reach of this powerful mafia boss, nicknamed "Legija," was long, and in the resulting massive police sweep numerous high-profile individuals were arrested. Finally, it seemed that Serbia was taking steps to reign in an underworld that had been linked to several political assassinations in the years leading up to the killing of Đinđić.

The year 2003 also saw a transformation in relations between the final two Yugoslav republics, which were repackaged as an entity called the State Union of Serbia and Montenegro. This arrangement, dubbed dysfunctional from the start by the Western media, survived until May 21, 2006, when Montenegro held a successful referendum for independence. However, ties between the two countries remain strong, owing to their cultural, social, and geographic closeness. The situation with Kosovo is, however, more turbulent. On February 17, 2008, Kosovo's Albanian government declared its independence, sparking protests from Serbia. Kosovo's minorities, especially Serbs, do not feel secure to live in (or return to, in many cases) an Albanian-run independent Kosovo, and Serbia has continuously refused to give up its historic heartland. Although Serbia was powerless to stop the declaration, it (and powerful supporters like Russia) has sworn to block Kosovo's entrance into key international institutions. By the summer of 2008, only around forty countries had recognized Kosovo. While Kosovo will not be returned to Serbia, it also will not easily function as a normal sovereign state. The result is likely to be continued instability and the increasing role of organized crime in Kosovo Albanian politics and society.

Serbia proper, on the other hand, seems to be improving. Despite chronic Western concerns over the views of its main politicians and continued charges that Serbia has not complied fully with the Hague Tribunal, this has not scared off major foreign investors from both the West and Russia. They realize that all politics aside, Serbia will remain the motor of the Balkans, with a relatively large and well-educated population standing astride the major trade and transport route from Central Europe to the Aegean.

Montenegro, meanwhile, is finding its way through tourism. Even before its independence referendum, foreigners had been snapping up property on its gorgeous Adriatic coast. Since then, it appears, the coast is almost entirely in foreign hands, first and foremost Russian ones. However, this reliance on tourism could have unwanted effects. Some observers believe that the overdevelopment of the coast will reduce its long-term attractiveness and ecological condition. At the same time, the clear imbalance in wealth between the coast and the mountainous north seems to only be increasing. The mountain areas have a lot to offer in the tourism field as well, but so far they have grown at a more modest rate.

Ulcinj, a coastal town in the southwest of Montenegro, is one of the country's best-known holiday destinations, and one of relatively few places here to boast a long, sandy beach. Its old town features a castle overlooking the water from a high bluff. Photograph by Rafael Estefania.

NOTES

1. Carl Savich, "The Kragujevac Massacre," July 12, 2004, http://www.balkanalysis.com.

2. Numerous books and articles have been published about Jasenovac. Probably the most comprehensive collection of Web resources are found at the Web site of the Jasenovac Research Institute, http://www.jasenovac.org/.

3. See Vladimir Dedijer, *The Yugoslav Auschwitz and the Vatican* (New York: Prometheus Books, 1992).

4. See Gregory A. Freeman, *The Forgotten 500: The Untold Story of the Men Who Risked All for the Greatest Rescue Mission of World War II* (New York: NAL Publishing, 2007).

5. See Sebastian Ritchie, *Our Man in Yugoslavia: The Story of a Secret Service Operative* (New York: Routledge, 2004).

6. See John Norris, *Collision Course: NATO, Russia and Kosovo* (Westport, CT: Praeger, 2005).

2

Religion and Thought

Only unity saves the Serbs.

—Serbian national motto

I won't tell you my nationality, otherwise you will call me a Serb nationalist.

—Aleksandar Baljak, Serbian aphorist

My father was an atheist and he always described himself as a Serb. OK, maybe we were Muslim for 250 years, but we were Orthodox before that and deep down we were always Serbs, religion cannot change that. We only became Muslims to survive the Turks.

—Emir Kusturica, film director[1]

THE SERBS AND Montenegrins are a very spiritual people, though it may not seem so at first or may not always manifest as expected. The first key to understanding this is to gain an understanding of Orthodox Christianity, which to many American Catholics and Protestants might sound like a somewhat exotic sect. Truth be told, some 250 million people worldwide consider themselves part of the greater Orthodox family, in which distinct churches exist, generally according to nationalities or nation-states. For now, at least, the Serbian Orthodox Church has authority over the flock in Serbia and Montenegro, as well as Bosnia and Herzegovina and Croatia. Although the Serbian Orthodox Church has attempted to establish a presence in neighboring Macedonia by controlling a handful of opportunist priests, the Macedonian Orthodox Church and the Macedonian people have resisted this strongly.

Orthodox worship differs markedly from Catholic or Protestant worship. Masses are led by priests, usually bearded, who swing censers full of pungent incense while singing out prayers in the style of Byzantine chant. In most churches, worshippers stand in the open center of the building or along the walls in high chairs that can support the arms but are too high and narrow for sitting. The whole experience is much more free-form and arguably more focused on individual spirituality than the organized Catholic or Protestant style of service. And of course, there are the artistic differences: whereas the latter churches can seem aesthetically bleak and even empty, Orthodox churches are full of vividly painted icons, frescoes, and elaborate wood-carved iconostases behind the altar. The total effect of an Orthodox ceremony thus becomes a very vivid and sensual experience.

Fundamental to understanding the differences between Orthodoxy and other Christian churches is the central role of icons. These painted images of Jesus, Mary, and the saints, the unique gift of the Byzantine tradition, are understood as a channel to the divine. According to Orthodox dogma, praying before an icon allows the worshipper to make an intimate and direct connection with God. The artistic features of iconography—one-dimensional figures with haunting eyes that seem to follow the observer, no matter where he or she observes from—make this form unique. Today, icon painters in Serbia and other Orthodox countries carry on a tradition almost two millennia old.

FROM PAGANISM TO A PATRIARCHY

The momentous division of the Roman Empire into eastern and western halves and the creation of the eastern capital of Constantinople by Emperor Constantine the Great in A.D. 330 institutionalized the progress of a church that was divergent in several respects from the Roman Church. The latter used Latin, whereas the former increasingly used Greek. The Roman Church was more logical, Scholastic, and concerned with law, such as in the writings of St. Augustine. The Eastern Church, on the other hand, nurtured doctrines more mystical and stemming ultimately from the Platonic and neo-Platonic philosophical movements of the Hellenistic world. The Eastern Church also took a decentralized approach to ecclesiastical power, stressing the equal nature of the various patriarchs (in those early days, there were many in Anatolian and Near Eastern cities, though they would not survive the Turks), whereas the bishop of Rome—that is, the pope—was championed as the single leader of Christendom in subsequent centuries in the Latin West. These differences, which essentially involved minute doctrinal differences and the issue of papal supremacy, eventually led to the ostracism of the two halves of the greater Christian church.

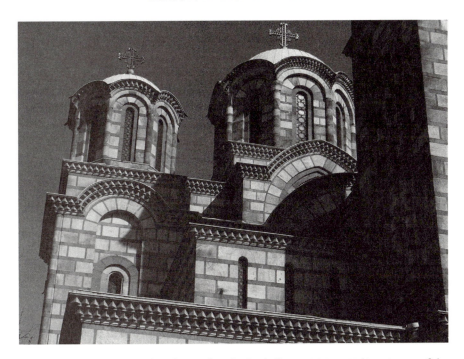

The domes of St Mark's Church in Belgrade. Built from 1931 to 1940, it is one of the holiest places in Serbia. It was built in a neo-Byzantine style and contains the remains of legendary fourteenth-century ruler Emperor Stefan Dušan. Photography by the author.

The Serbian and other Slavic tribes that migrated to the Balkans in the early Byzantine period were pagans, and a number of pre-Christian practices seem to have survived in religious and other festivals and ceremonies, not only after their conversions to Christianity but also right up until the present day (for more information, see chapter 4). Christian missionaries baptized the Serbs and Montenegrins, who became Orthodox Christians under the spiritual tutelage of Byzantium (despite that some of their early rulers were crowned by the pope). The missions of the brothers Saints Cyril and Methodius in the ninth century laid the foundations for a written Slavic language (known today as Old Church Slavonic). The possibility to instruct the flock in their own language consolidated the power of the new churches in Bulgaria, Russia, and Serbia and helped them resist Roman efforts to win them over to Catholicism and Latin instruction.

Like Byzantium, medieval Serbia and Montenegro were military theocracies, and though they are today democratic, parliamentary states, the role of the church in politics and in fostering a sometimes militant nationalism remains strong. The great thirteenth-century ruler of Raška, Stefan Nemanja, oversaw the endowment and creation of numerous monasteries, a Byzantine practice that conferred great prestige upon the benefactor. Among these lasting endowments were monasteries that today rank among the most important in Orthodox lands: the Đurđevi Stupovi Monastery, Studenica Monastery, and Hilandar Monastery on the monastic peninsula of Mount Athos in today's Greece. To be allowed to create a monastery on the holy mountain, the most sacred monastic community of all, was a mark of prestige that indicated the growing importance of the Serbs in the Orthodox world. To this day, Serbian monks inhabit Hilandar and maintain the traditions of Stefan Nemanja's time along with Greek, Bulgarian, Russian, and other monasteries.

The prominence of Raška in the Orthodox world was elevated further by the successes of Stefan Nemanja's youngest son, Rastko. After becoming a monk and taking the name of Sava, he became determined to spread Christianity among the Serbs. Sava's brother Stefan Prvovenčani was crowned king by Pope Honorius III in 1217, some thirteen years after the Crusaders' sack of Constantinople and imposition of Latin rule. For his part, Sava succeeded in winning autocephalous status for the Serbian Orthodox Church, becoming its first archbishop in 1219. Byzantium's misfortune was Serbia's gain, although significantly Serbian religion, art, and culture remained within the Byzantine Orthodox sphere.

Under Tsar Stefan Dušan (ruled 1331–1355), Serbia's place in the Orthodox hierarchy became more prestigious still when the archbishopric of Peć was raised to the rank of patriarchate. However, the church's power ebbed following the Turkish invasion, with the result that a successor to Patriarch Arsenije II (d. 1463) was not elected. Thus de facto abolished, the Serbian Orthodox Church became subservient to the (Greek-controlled) ecumenical patriarchate in Constantinople. However, the Serbian patriarchate was restored by the greatest of Ottoman leaders, Sultan Süleyman the Magnificent, in 1557. At that time, the Serb Mehmed Paša Sokolović was actually grand vizier (prime minister) of the Ottoman Empire, and his brother Makarije was elected to resume patriarchal duties in Peć. However, later Serbian uprisings backed by the church led the Turks to once again abolish the patriarchate in 1766. It passed again under the control of Constantinople, which was heavily influenced by Greek moguls—the so-called Phanariots. The Greek patriarch was allowed to begin proselytizing to the Slavs, sending Greek priests into the villages of Macedonia, Bulgaria, and Serbia, a custom that was greatly resented by locals. The Serbian church's autocephalous status was only restored in 1879, the year after Serbia's recognition as an independent state. The Peć patriarchate was finally reestablished in 1920, following the expulsion of the Ottomans.

FROM WORLD WAR II TO THE LOSS OF KOSOVO

The empowerment of the fascist and stridently anti-Orthodox Ustaša revolutionary movement in Croatia during World War II, and the similar control of Islamist fascists in Bosnia and Kosovo, had ill results for Serbs and their church. Numerous bishops and priests were killed, while hundreds of churches were destroyed or desecrated. The Ustaša's Vatican-supported policy of "kill a third, deport a third, convert a third" was carried out, and forced conversions of Serbs to Catholicism did occur. Under Tito's Communist Yugoslavia, religion was restricted or heavily managed, and as the most powerful group, the Serbs were singled out for the worst abuses. Church property was confiscated, religious teaching was prohibited in schools, and priests were persecuted in various ways. On the other hand, Tito built more mosques for Bosnian Muslims than had existed previously, a tactic designed in part to win approval among his new "non-aligned" Arab allies.

With the end of Yugoslavia, the Serbian Orthodox Church was able to reassert itself aggressively in public life, just as Catholicism and Islam were doing in other Yugoslav republics. The increasingly prominent political role of the church alarmed both local and foreign observers, however, who saw it as another weapon of warlike nationalists. To a great extent, the Serbian opposition to giving up the overwhelmingly Albanian-populated province of Kosovo has owed to religious sensibilities: the patriarchate of Peć, Visoki Dečani Monastery, Gračanica Monastery, and other of the Nemanja rulers' greatest endowments are located in Kosovo. Moreover, since 1999, Albanians have damaged or destroyed approximately 150 Serbian churches and holy places, some dating back to the thirteenth and fourteenth centuries. Usually, former church sites are used as garbage dumps or paved over to conceal any trace of former Serbian presence. This fact has added more fuel to the fire and convinced Serbs that Albanians are intent on perpetrating a total cultural genocide in the very place of greatest spiritual significance to them, Kosovo.

It is often hard for outsiders to understand the meaning of Kosovo to the Serbs; to do so would first require an understanding of the place of religion in society, in terms of both individual experience and as a tool of collective social organization. So much of Serbian identity is bound up with religious experience and religious history that an attack on a piece of architecture can be considered an attack on an individual or group. This often seems to come in spite of, not because of, their spiritual leaders. Serbs and Montenegrins remain well aware of the politicking and sometimes even profiting that church figures have regularly been accused of and tend to look at the church as an institution at arm's length.

RELIGIOUS PRACTICE TODAY

Religious practice in the newly independent Serbia and Montenegro has generally seen a revival of the forms of religion present before Communism, and specifically in the same ethnic groups where they had traditionally existed. Thus, while more than three-quarters of Serbs and Montenegrins are Orthodox Christians, the Bosniak and Albanian minorities are generally Muslim. Most of the Roman Catholic population is made up of Hungarians in Vojvodina (4 percent of the population), with small numbers of ethnic Albanians in Montenegro and Croats in Vojvodina and Montenegro also professing Catholicism. Only about 1 percent of the population is Protestant, but numerous different denominations are represented. The few survivors of the local Jewish population, descendents of Sephardic Jews forced to emigrate from Spain during the Inquisition in 1492, live largely in Belgrade.

One issue that has been frequently brought up by human rights crusaders and unrepresented religious groups is the difficulty with which new sects can operate. Montenegro's 2003 constitution, for example, stipulated the Orthodox Church, the Islamic Community, and the Roman Catholic Church by name as traditional religious groups. The religious leaders of Serbia's and Montenegro's traditional creeds naturally take a dim view on the idea of sharing the flock with newcomers, and thus legal difficulties have been established for other groups—most of them different Evangelical groups or sects—that would like to proselytize to the Serbs.

The issue has been complicated by sporadic violence perpetrated against newer faiths, usually by nationalist youth, sometimes recruited from the sports hooligan groups of the major cities. A small number even belong to neo-Nazi groups. Attacks, often in response to a provocative event or inflammatory newspaper articles, have occurred most often in Vojvodina, where nationalists have attacked Protestant groups as well as churches and cemeteries belonging to Croat and Hungarian Catholics. In the aftermath of the March 17–19, 2004, riots in Kosovo, in which fifty thousand Albanians targeted Serb areas and burned thirty-five churches, the main mosques in Belgrade and Niš were attacked as a form of symbolic revenge, though both the government and Orthodox Church leaders condemned it. Nevertheless, while relations between the different religious groups are usually cordial, the severe political and economic pressures that Serbia and Montenegro have recently endured have created an atmosphere in which extremists can express their fear of the other through violence.

Extremists of a different sort have made headlines in the shared Sandžak region of Serbia and Montenegro. Here, as in neighboring Bosnia, Bosniaks radicalized by foreign Islamist ideologies have been active in promoting the

Saudi Arabian Wahhabi version of Islam, an archaic and puritanical practice at odds with the traditional Ottoman-style Islam of the Balkans. This challenge, funded from outside and typically attracting the poor and uneducated, has caused regular incidents within the Islamic community as Wahhabis challenge the official leadership for control. So far, the extremists have not been able to appeal in great-enough numbers to affect society at large, but several high-profile incidents, like the Serbian police raid in April 2007 that discovered a mountainside terrorist-training camp near the Sandžak city of Novi Pazar, indicate that Islamic extremism still remains a danger.

For visitors to Serbia and Montenegro, understanding etiquette in relation to church, monastery, or mosque is useful. When entering a mosque, one must take off his or her shoes, usually placing them on a rack off to the side built for the purpose. Taking photographs inside is usually allowed, though it is considered polite to wait until prayer time has finished before entering and snapping away. In Orthodox churches and monasteries, on the other hand, taking photos or video inside is most often prohibited, though it is allowed outside the church or within the monastic grounds. It is also frowned on to enter a church in "immodest" clothing, and the larger churches do indeed offer frocks or long pants for visitors who are dressed too skimpily.

When entering a church, Serbs and Montenegrins cross themselves, and do so again when leaving, and they always make sure to exit the doorway walking backward, so as to not turn their back on the inside of the church. Inside the church, guests usually make the rounds to various icons set on display and along the walls and altar. The practice is generally to cross oneself and kiss the icon before or after praying. Some people also leave a few coins or small notes on the icon as a gift to the church. In most churches there is a person at a booth or table near the front (usually an elderly woman) selling candles, icons, crosses, and other paraphernalia. Serbs and Montenegrins usually light a candle for their loved ones, and often for their whole family. The lit candles are placed together with other ones in tall racks, either having metal holes for placement, or sand. It is important to know that lit candles on the lower tray section of the racks are for people who have died, whereas the upper trays are reserved for the living.

THOUGHT

It almost goes without saying that Serbian philosophical thought is rooted in the church and in Scripture. The retarding influence of the Ottoman Empire, which kept Serbia and Montenegro cut off from the West for well more than four hundred years, partially accounts for the failure of Serbs and Montenegrins to participate in the same intellectual processes that occurred in

Western Europe from the Renaissance to the Enlightenment. Serbian thought has developed unique characteristics as a result of this historical experience and the social abreactions it brought on.

Over the long and difficult centuries for Serbia and Montenegro, there have been certain maxims and ways of acting that have been constantly invoked. Invariably these are nationalistic or patriotic in character. The most famous (and formulaic) is the phrase *Samo sloga Srbina spasava* (Only unity saves the Serbs), which is a national motto that is overtly a patriotic call to unity and covertly a lament over the Serbs' chronic inability to make a united front against their enemies, whether politically or militarily.

Here, historical wrongs and perceived wrongs play a big part in keeping the tradition. The potency of such slogans comes partially from images like the 1389 Battle of Kosovo, when internal division among the Serbs allowed for an Ottoman victory. However, it seems that the power of the saying is all too often invoked as a lament: all too often discord and disunity have characterized the Serbian position or actions. Reminding the Serbian people that only through unity will they succeed in their goals tacitly implies that this unity does not exist.

The saying, however, is not a saying per se, as people do not speak it to one another aloud—that would seem silly. The only case in which they would do so would be as a wry, ironic statement when faced with a situation of obvious disunity or discord. Rather, it is a pictorial representation that presents the concept. The way that the slogan is traditionally depicted merges the concept seamlessly with religion: the symbol of *Samo sloga Srbina spasava* is a Serbian cross with four large *C* letters (*S* in Cyrillic) in each of the quarters of the cross, all opening outward.

This form is called an *ocila*, and it has an interesting history. While the twelfth-century Saint Sava is sometimes given the credit for inventing the slogan, it is likely that, at least as a visual symbol, it derives from the Byzantine coat of arms, which featured a similar cross filled out with the Greek letter *B*, representing the imperial motto *Basileus Basileon Basileuon Basileusin* (King of kings, ruling over kings). The *Samo sloga Srbina spasava* phrase is almost never written out as such, but the cross-and-letters symbol is widely seen, often as graffiti, in Serbia and in other Serb-populated areas of the Balkans.

SATIRE AND APHORISM

A more irreverent means of surviving hard times for the Serbs has been through black humor. As elsewhere in the Balkans and Central Europe, Serbs enjoy collective commiseration without losing their cool through satire and witty aphorisms. These aphorisms are typically deadpan one-liners that have a double meaning or complex association of not only language but also terminology alluding to historical or current events. The aphorism has been a part of Serbian literary thought and social criticism for decades. The forerunners of today's Serbian social critics took aim at numerous aspects of society that seemed ridiculous or dehumanizing. In the beginning, the main target was the so-called better life promised by the Communists. By quietly mocking the empty ideals of their rulers, the Yugoslav people could, to some small extent, restore their sense of individuality, dignity, and sanity.

As in other countries that were swallowed up by Communism after World War II, organized sarcasm became a self-defense mechanism against the pointless rhetoric and irrational policies of the government. However, ironically, the very possibility of some amount of aphoristic resistance could take place only in environments that were relatively relaxed, such as Poland and especially Yugoslavia. In the 1960s an informal movement sprang up and became known as the Belgrade Aphoristic Circle. Originally based on the example of a few dissident writers, the group became a genuine grassroots phenomenon, with hundreds of amateur aphorists soon taking part. The need to avoid the ever-vigilant government censors influenced the format of expressed thought, requiring trenchant social critiques to be made indirectly, allusively, and subtly.

The death of Tito in 1980 provided fertile ground for satire, though the machine of state repression also became weaker and increasingly incapable of withstanding the numerous challenges rising up against its authority from all sides. And in those days, it was almost as if the system had devoured, or had been devoured by, the satirical establishment. Indeed, some of the "real" government policy slogans—such as *i po Titu, Tito* (And after Tito ... Tito!)—sounded almost like something a clever aphorist might have come up with to mock the uncertainty and shadow puppetry at work in the country during the 1980s. But they were not made in jest. Such statements expressed the crisis of confidence that was gripping the country after the passing of its lifelong leader.

After the 1980s, Serbian aphorisms had to rise to the new challenges posed by nationalism, war and sanctions, the ever-elusive civil societies, mafia rule, peacekeeping missions, economic transition, and the wonders of democracy. These all became very rich feeding grounds for aphorists who had been starving from the stupidity and brigandage of the Milošević years. For these people, even being able to make clever quips was a form of empowerment, and it became an especially important social self-defense mechanism. However, in the 1990s, Serbs simply were no longer in a position of criticizing their government; now, with the media-propagated images of Serbs as enemies of the West, the challenge was even more complicated. Yet we should not say that Serbian aphorism has reached its apogee; indeed, as Aleksandar Baljak, considered one of Serbia's best aphorists, memorably quipped: "Our best aphorisms were created in difficult times, but for our modern satire—better days lie ahead."

Boris Mitić, a Serbian aphorist and documentary filmmaker on the subject (his film is called *Aphocalypse Now!*), has much to say about aphorism—and not only pure aphorisms but also some of the logic behind them. Explains Mitić:

An aphorism, as defined and practiced in Serbia, is a short, sharp, linguistically effective sentence or two, which imperatively contains an unexpected twist and which describes in a most striking, clairvoyant way the hidden truth of some common social matters or states of mind. What makes Serbian aphorisms different from classic proverbs is their multilayered, open-ended nature, their surprisingly creative wordplays, their unpretentious individualism and their killer dose of black humor, satire and merciless sarcasm that still conveys a strong humanistic message. In a time when the human rights industry has become nothing more than a big fundraising competition which benefits only the most shameless hustlers and whiners, our frail civilization deserves to have empowering tools that are freely available to all. . . .

I myself have systematically collected aphorisms for the last ten years. Whenever I wonder why I am still living in this crazy country after years of civil wars, domestic repression and international satanization, I turn to my collection of aphorisms for reassuring consolation and a 100%-proof optimism fix. . . . All of a sudden, a wasted childhood becomes an asset; terminal living in Serbia—a privilege. From this perspective, Serbia stops being a traumatized, post-war country lost in transition, and turns into a stylish crossroads full of off-beat characters trying to contribute to a better understanding of this world by making up great lines.[2]

The younger generation of satirists today has special respect for elder statesmen of the genre who, like Rastko Zakić, faced persecution and censorship from the Communists back when it was dangerous to speak freely. Zakić was the most censored satirical writer in Communist Yugoslavia—seven of his books were actually banned. After being hauled into court because of his aphorisms, Zakić was told by the secret police that he could be cleared of all charges if he would spy on his fellow aphorists. The police were very surprised when he agreed—on condition, of course, that they give him a special police uniform. Recalled Zakić, "I didn't refrain from answering their madness with greater madness."[3]

Typical fodder for aphorisms has always been politics, war, corruption, and any notion of progress, whether in Communist or Democratic society. There are numerous examples in each category that have been thought up by members of the Belgrade Aphoristic Circle including Baljak, Mitić, Zakić, and more. These aphorisms reflect the perception of contemporary realities. For example, the feeling that Serbia is constantly threatened by the West to give up territory (Kosovo), individuals (alleged war criminals to The Hague Tribunal), and policies has sparked aphorisms such as "I can't work any longer for Serbian diplomacy—my knees hurt," by Belgrade psychiatrist Slobodan Simić.

The Kosovo situation is summed up in an admirably complex aphorism by Aleksandar Baljak, who alludes to two long-discussed concepts in one breath. The first is the argument that giving Kosovo independence for its Albanian majority is like "letting the genie out of the bottle," or something that will spark other secessionist movements elsewhere in the world. The second is the United Nations' and NATO's promises that they can guarantee freedom of movement to the Serbian minority in Kosovo—something that has been manifestly and demonstrably proved false over the past few years, as Serbs there have frequently come under attack and intimidation by Albanians. Baljak aphorizes thusly: "We are calling on the ghost to return inside the lamp. His freedom of movement will be guaranteed."

Government and governmental corruption are two other favorite topics of Belgrade satirists. Zoran Rankić has a memorably succinct line: "The best government is always the one that has yet to come, provided that it never comes." And on the other theme, Momčilo Mihajlović quips, "The Minister was astonished when he found out that he was receiving a triple salary. He immediately drew up a budget to start an investigation." And then there are the aphorisms that seem to sum up the whole Serbian experience of an uncertain and potentially disastrous "transition" period in one uproarious moment. This is the case with Božo Marić, who cracks, "Finally, a light at the end of the tunnel. And not one, but two!"

Serbian aphorisms and black humor are almost always funny when read in translation, though they are usually better in the original. Most often, this is because there is some linguistic value (e.g., rhyme, idiom) or because of an innate allusion to another literary object. Often these types of things emerge from slogans. An example was the popular take on the Serbian nationalist slogan of the 1990s, *Srbija do Tokija*, which means "Serbia (continues until) Tokyo." With the severing of the other Yugoslav republics, the secession of Montenegro in 2006, and then the independence of Kosovo in 2008, the allusive, almost-rhyming old phrase *Srbija kao Nokia* seems more appropriate. The phrase means "Serbia (is) like Nokia"—just like the phones produced by the Finnish company, Serbia comes in a newer and smaller model every year.

Cutting Serbian aphorism does not work everywhere, however. Some people just don't get it. When Aleksandar Čotrić, a former politician and prolific aphorist, recently published a book of aphorisms in Sweden, it failed to stir any interest—because, he quips, "Everyone there is too happy."

YUGOSLAV PHILOSOPHY: THE PRAXIS MOVEMENT

Despite its often repressive and dogmatic nature, the Communist Yugoslavia of Josip Broz Tito also created an opportunity for innovative thinkers and succeeded in putting Yugoslavia on the map of international philosophy. This occurred during the 1960s and 1970s, with a movement linked mainly to academics in the universities of Belgrade and Zagreb in Croatia, the Praxis school, which sought to bridge the gap between theory and practice in Marxism—a line of inquiry that often got its leaders into trouble with the authorities.

The major figures in the movement included Serbian professor and philosopher Mihailo Marković, and Croatian colleagues such as Gajo Petrović and Milan Kangrga. From 1964 to 1974, the informal group of eight founders published the Marxist journal *Praxis*, at the time considered one of the world's leading sources of thought for Marxist theory. The journal was published both for an internal Yugoslav edition and an international one, and famous philosophers from Western universities contributed to it and attended the group's popular Korčula Summer School, held each year on the beautiful Croatian Adriatic island of the same name. Some of the eminent outsiders included Jürgen Habermas, Richard Bernstein, Ernst Bloch, Eugen Fink, and Erich Fromm. The Yugoslav thinkers drew their inspiration from these luminaries as well as from the German critical theorists of a generation before and, of course, from Marx.

For the Western thinkers involved, Yugoslavia represented an intriguing mix of two worlds, somewhere between the capitalist West and Communist East, and as such, its philosophers seemed worth hearing out. Tito's authorities were not as happy to do so, however, as the Praxis thinkers consistently criticized what they considered the Tito regime's "modified" brand of Marxism-Leninism as put into practice by the League of Communists of Yugoslavia. The topics covered by Praxis theorists were impressive—typically ranging from aesthetics and civil society to history, to creativity, technology, and existentialism—but they were all based on, or revolved around, a premise that Communist rulers in Yugoslavia and the Soviet Union found hard to swallow: that Leninist and Stalinist theory had been a bad-faith interpretation of original Marxist theory, suited for political pragmatist use and not impervious to criticism. It was thus no surprise when the League of Communists of Croatia organized to close the summer school in 1966 (it resumed the next year) and that the authorities finally stopped *Praxis* magazine in 1975, one year after the passage of the controversial new Yugoslav constitution.

A new condition of repression for intellectuals soon set in. In January 1975, Mihailo Marković and seven colleagues (Ljubomir Tadić, Zagorka Golubović, Svetozar Stojanović, Miladin Životić, Dragoljub Mićunović, Nebojša Popov, and Trivo Indić) were expelled from Belgrade's Faculty of Philosophy following a decision of the Serbian Assembly. The Praxis thinkers were considered enemies of self-managing socialism and professional anti-Communists by an increasingly paranoid Titoist regime. The Praxis members tried but failed to relaunch their magazine and reopen the Korčula Summer School, and it would not be until 1981 when the magazine would finally reappear—this time published abroad, at Oxford University in England. The first co-editors of the relaunched magazine, now called *Praxis International,* were Richard Bernstein and Mihailo Marković.

In his work, Professor Marković upheld the school's essential critiques of Leninism, Stalinism, and Yugoslav Communism for failing to honor Marx's original philosophy. In his many books, Marković often was concerned with the themes of human alienation and dynamism. He also referred often to the need to return to the source (i.e., the writings of Marx himself). One could thus point out Marx's demand for social critique and how this naturally implied the necessity for greater freedom of speech. Marković spells out his ideas in the important text *From Affluence to Praxis,* the preface of which was penned by the eminent philosopher Erich Fromm. According to Fromm, the Praxis school's main concern was to "return to the real Marx as against the Marx equally distorted by right wing social democrats and Stalinists."[4]

Although Yugoslavia is long gone, the influence of the Praxis school remains today, especially in the work of critical theorists and Western Marxists. *Praxis International,* the second coming of the original *Praxis,* continued to be produced until 1994, when it was given a new name, *Constellations: An International Journal of Critical and Democratic Theory.* However, the magazine still functions at a high level, attracting important figures from left-wing academic philosophy to read and write in its pages. The efforts of those Serbian and Croatian theorists in the 1960s, many of whom traveled and taught subsequently in Europe and the United States, significantly helped to restore the study of Marx and to keep alive some of the most interesting lines of thought of the World War II–era critical theorists, combining dialectical and humanist approaches with a political and social context that was, for its time, considered advanced and ever so experimental.

MODERN SERBIAN PHILOSOPHY

Many of Serbia's most eminent modern philosophers, like Mihailo Marković (b. 1926), participated in the Praxis movement or in similar initiatives. The larger political context proved impossible to escape. After earning

The Serbian parliament building in Belgrade is one of the most distinctive and tradition-laden structures in the city. It is the focal point of Serbian political life, where ideas are debated and legislation is passed. Photography by the author.

a Ph.D. in philosophy at the University of Belgrade, Marković continued his studies at University College London, where he studied logic under the great British philosopher A. J. Ayer. After Marković became a professor of philosophy back at the University of Belgrade, he would make waves with his first book, *Revision of the Philosophical Bases of Marxism in the USSR* (1952). It was the first major critique of Stalinist ideology in Yugoslavia, coming in reaction to the Informbiro's resolution condemning the Yugoslav Communist regime. Marković, who took part in the partisan war effort to liberate Yugoslavia during World War II, has remained close to the political fray throughout his life. Most recently, in the 1980s and 1990s, he was a prominent supporter of the late Slobodan Milošević, serving as vice president of his Socialist Party of Serbia until 1995, when he became more critical of the party.

Along with his works on logic and critique of Stalinism, Mihailo Marković produced ten other major works between 1957 and 1997. An eight-volume anthology of selected works was released in 1994. A contemporary of Mihailo Marković, Milan Damnjanović (1924–1994) was a philosopher specializing in aesthetics. He spent his career as a professor at the Faculty of Fine Arts of

Belgrade University, and he founded or was active in academic societies for aesthetics in Serbia, Greece, the United States, and various European countries. Damnjanović wrote nine major works, ranging from the 1970s *Aesthetics and Disappointment* to the 1990s *Dealing with Multiplicity*.

One of the most original and well-known modern Serbian philosophers is Mihailo Đurić (b. 1925), a former professor at Belgrade University's law faculty. Đurić took a more classical focus in his study, rooting his inquiry in ancient Greek culture, philosophy, and law. Like the Praxis philosophers, Đurić also fell afoul of the Yugoslav authorities in the early 1970s, but for a different reason. In 1972, he was expelled from the university and sentenced to nine months in prison for criticizing the constitutional amendments of 1971 and for opposing the demolition of a chapel dedicated to Montenegrin national hero Petar Petrović Njegoš on Mount Lovćen. His removal from the law faculty in 1973 ended a twenty-year tenure there. After being released from prison, the philosopher was employed by Belgrade's Institute of Social Sciences, returning to Belgrade University only in 1989. In the interim, he also served as a visiting professor at several German universities, and this experience helped direct Đurić's work over the second half of his career, which was concerned with the German philosophers Friedrich Nietzsche and Martin Heidegger.

Đurić wrote several books in both German and Serbian that considerably improved the understanding of these thinkers in Serbia. He also stressed the common areas between them. In 1984, Đurić released his *Niče i metafizika* (Nietzsche and Metaphysics), followed two years later by *Izazov nihilizma* (The Challenge of Nihilism), again focusing mainly on Nietzsche and his philosophy. However, in his 1999 study *O potrebi filozofije danas: Filozofija između Istoka i Zapada* (On the Need of Philosophy Today: Philosophy between East and West), Đurić considers Nietzsche through the lens of Heidegger, creatively expanding on his interpretation of Heideggerian epistemology and his reading of Nietzsche. Most recently, Đurić has gone back to some of the Greek themes that marked his work in the 1950s and 1960s with his *Krhko ljudsko dobro: Aktuelnost Aristotelove praktičke filozofije* (The Fragile Human Good: The Contemporary Importance of Aristotle's Practical Philosophy), released in 2002.

NOTES

1. Quoted in Fiachra Gibbons, "I Will Not Cut My Film," *Guardian*, March 4, 2005.

2. For Boris Mitić's thoughts and his film on Serbian aphorisms, see his Web site, http://www.dribblingpictures.com. He is also the creative director of the Kosovo Compromise Web site, http://www.kosovocompromise.com, which has provided

rational discussions of the entirety of the Kosovo problem and arguments for and against its independence. The aphorisms mentioned in this chapter, and many more, can be found on these Web sites.

3. Dan Bilefsky, "Dark One-Liners Shine a Light on the Mood of Serbs," *New York Times*, December 2, 2007.

4. Erich Fromm, foreword to *From Affluence to Praxis*, by Mihailo Marković (Ann Arbor: University of Michigan Press, 1974), vii.

3

Marriage, Gender, Family, and Education

The teacher in Yugoslavia is often a hero and fanatic as well as a servant of the mind; but as they walked along the Belgrade streets it could easily be seen that none of them had quite enough to eat or warm enough clothing or handsome lodgings or all the books they needed.

—Rebecca West, *Black Lamb and Grey Falcon*

Serbia and Montenegro, especially the latter, are family-oriented, tight-knit societies. While urbanization and modernization have naturally lessened historic clannishness, as did the experience of Communism, it can still be said that they are, like other Balkan countries, much more focused on maintaining familial relations, ceremonies, and frequent visits to extended family than people are in the West. In part because of the revived prominence of religion in daily life—the factor that accounts for most of the ceremonies and holidays that bring people together—Serb and Montenegrin family members see much more of one another than do the typical American family's members and kin.

Part of this, however, is economic; young people in Serbia and Montenegro are often forced to live with their parents and even relatives because of the poor economic conditions. (There is, it should be noted, no real stigma or pressure associated with doing so, unlike in the United States.) Still, the strain of war and especially the crippling economic sanctions of the 1990s have wreaked havoc over society, affecting everything from outward migration (the well-known brain-drain syndrome) to fewer marriages, high divorce rates, and fewer children being born—sadly, Serbia has one of Europe's highest abortion rates. And, though there has been little research carried out on the topic so far, the promotion of a gangster culture during the 1990s, with the help of wartime nationalism and vapid, scantily clad Turbo-folk singers, seems to have further affected traditional societal values in a negative way. As in Russia, the Orthodox Church even has started to offer financial incentives to encourage women to have more children, with little result so far. While things are definitely improving in the absence of war or sanctions, it will be some time before Serbia recovers fully.

Things are better when it comes to education. During Communism, the enforced participation of women in not only schooling but also skilled labor dramatically improved the status of women in society, particularly in once-tribal Montenegro. Serbs, who count the legendary Croatian-born Serb Nikola Tesla as one of their own, have shown marked aptitude for economics and the sciences, and foreign firms offering high-tech, high-finance, and skilled industry positions in Serbia today frequently point to the availability of a skilled labor pool to justify their investment decisions. While Serbia and Montenegro continue with their education reform programs to bring education in line with European Union accession requirements, they are confident that the "raw materials," or the students themselves, have the native capabilities that so often come to the surface in countries where success (and even survival) is not something to be taken for granted.

MARRIAGE AND POPULAR CULTURE

A Serbian or Montenegrin wedding is a legendary event, involving copious amounts of feasting, drinking, and dancing, usually accompanied by a traditional music group and freewheeling Gypsy brass band. However, the 1995 wedding of Turbo-folk singer Svetlana Veličković, nicknamed "Ceca," and paramilitary leader Željko Ražnatović, nicknamed "Arkan," seemed to many to represent the debasement of the institution and all that was wrong with Serbia in the 1990s. The lusty, busty queen of a genre known for its shallow lyrics belted out to exotic, pseudo-traditional riffs while marrying the embodiment of armed Serbian nationalism—it was not just a wedding, but a statement about the values that were being wedded, at least in the mind of tabloid popular culture. Indeed, many were fascinated with the spectacle, and while some met it with revulsion, others met it with admiration. When the wedding footage was subsequently released on videotape, it sold one hundred thousand copies—a record for Serbia. Today, you can still find DVD copies of the celebrity wedding for sale among street vendors in Serbia and throughout the Balkans. However, Ceca's marriage was cut short in January 2000 by an assassin's bullet that ended the short and violent life of her husband.

The weddings and marriages of most Serbs and Montenegrins, however, are altogether less dramatic than that of Arkan and Ceca. For the most part, Serbia and Montenegro remain traditional societies in the sense that men do little housework and are expected to be the breadwinners of the family. However, social scientists have commented on the effect of the wars and impoverishment of the 1990s as causing a kind of emasculation, whereby men began to lose confidence in their traditional roles and responsibilities because of their inability to fulfill them. This may have something to do with the unfortunate continuing trends toward domestic violence.

While there is no consistent short-term trend up or down, statistics regarding marriage and divorce point to a long-term decrease in the number of marriages performed in Serbia each year and a rise in the number of divorces. In 1991, there were some 45,145 weddings conducted and requests for 8,018 divorces. By 2001, there were 41,406 weddings and 7,835 registered divorces. While the number of marriages in 2006 (39,756) marked a slight gain over the previous year (38,846), it is still far below the numbers from when Serbia was more prosperous in the pre-sanctions period. The number of divorces in 2006 also increased over those of 2005, from 7,661 to 8,204.[1]

The rise of Turbo-folk culture has had an impact on the way women perceive themselves and their role in society, though this is hard to calibrate. Branislav Dimitrijević, the Serbian cultural analyst at Belgrade's Museum of Contemporary Art, believes that Turbo-folk culture "is one of the most interesting phenomena in Serbia." Dimitrijević believes that Turbo-folk represents a way of coping with hard times and presents an idealized image of women, as well as the expensive luxuries an ideal woman can enjoy:

Turbo-folk has been usually associated with Serbian nationalism—and not even nationalism, but war-mongering ideology. You have war in Bosnia, you have economic sanctions, and then you have Turbo-folk, with these nice girls, with these big cars, and with this kind of glamorization of reality that never existed, in a sense. But the thing is that this iconography, in a very vulnerable society, really is very dangerous for this society.[2]

Fortunately, at present there seems to be a move away from the licentiousness and vapidity that has characterized the genre in recent years. A sign of a change in thinking occurred in 2008, when Belgrade's Pink Television, long the standard-bearer of Turbo-folk culture and one of the major exhibitors of videos and concerts featuring its singers, requested female performers to "dress up" a bit, ruling out the most scantily clad costumes. This, observers say, is part of the station's attempt to become a serious news provider, under the direction, reportedly, of a Washington public relations firm. Nevertheless, a notable segment of the population still enjoys singing along with

Turbo-folk songs, and television stations and producers continue the phenomenon of "creating" stars out of thin air, taking any attractive young woman or man and putting him or her in front of the cameras to sing. They seem to have ultimate power to decide who will "make it" in the business (though most careers are notably short).

CLAN, FEUDS, AND THE CONCEPT OF *INAT*

Things have improved somewhat for Montenegrin women since 1875, when the British traveler James Creigh noted in horror how "wild Montenegrins, carrying long guns, and wearing knives and clumsy pistols, drive their heavily-laden women up and down, as if they were pack mules."[3] The Black Mountain's ancient martial tradition indeed made life especially difficult for women, who were not only burdened with the family but also expected to work the fields and carry heavy loads; for the men, fighting or resting in the rare moments when they were not fighting was sufficient. A famous image captured in books and engravings shows a Montenegrin man riding a horse up a steep mountain path while his wife trudges along in front, pulling the horse by a rope.

Montenegrin traditional society was historically organized according to a clan structure, ultimately led by a ruler known as the *vladika* (*metropolitan*), who had both spiritual power as the bishop and political power. The leaders of the various clans elected the *vladika*, whose dual responsibilities were, historians believe, a direct result of the Ottoman stipulation that only religious, not political, leaders could lead subject peoples.[4] Since bishops could not marry, the hereditary title would pass from uncle to nephew. This system of government lasted from 1516 to 1852, when the country became a secular principality. This sort of society, dominated by male-led clans and a childless male ruler, obviously limited the input and value of women.

The colorful—and to many outsiders, incomprehensible—trait that marked Montenegrin life under the clans was an honor system in which blood vendettas were often carried out against perceived offenders (this system survives today only in northern Albania). Although deplored for its apparently senseless and wanton violence, the blood feud system actually equipped them to live without submitting to outside forces, with tightly controlled freedom in a system that had clear and recognizable rules governing individual behavior and relations with the other clans. As the foremost expert on the subject, Christopher Boehm has noted, "When political and military unity became crucial to biological or political survival . . . they were able to join forces and to fight effectively together their enemies, the Turks."[5]

Instead of organizing as simple nuclear families, as in the West, traditional Montenegrin and Serb kin were organized into extended family groups in which all relatives lived under the same roof—and, especially in poor rural areas, on the same floor. Unsurprisingly, throughout the nineteenth century, families' uncommon bathing and close proximity to livestock created conditions for illnesses, and the lack of modern medical facilities or access to doctors meant that they had to rely on folk medicine and herbal remedies. Traditional Serb and Montenegrin families were therefore characterized by many children and many deaths.[6]

The Serbian equivalent of the Montenegrin familial structure was the *zadruga* ("compound" or "community"), which typically was set on farmlands and housed many family members. Since the menfolk were often away, doing hired labor or conscripted into one of the country's endless wars, women had to take over the work of the husband as well, making for a very difficult life for Serbian women. However, the proximity to many relatives also meant that any individual encountering a financial problem or illness could count on an extended support network. Even today, things like retirement homes are rare in Serbia and Montenegro, where people are brought up with the idea of caring for their parents and grandparents into old age. The modern-day version of the *zadruga*, therefore, has become a multilevel home that houses various generations of the same family on different levels, structures that are large enough to require labor and funds to build them over a period of several years. This practice continues, however, more or less only in rural areas.

While clans and blood feuds are now things of the past, some of the old spirit remains in Serbian and Montenegrin families today, something that affects everything from everyday life to politics. When working abroad, Montenegrins especially are known to be close-knit; they gravitate toward one another outside the country and provide mutual assistance. Political clannishness remains as well. Serbs in Kosovo, in probably the most extreme example, are told how to vote and which party to support according to where they live or the most eminent political personality in charge. Even prominent politicians in Belgrade are often referred to in public as belonging to a clan or tribe; the same goes for organized crime syndicates, which have their own rules and codes of honor. While there are no blood vendettas anymore, in Serbia, Montenegro, and elsewhere in the Balkans, a spirit of begrudgery, gossip, and jealousy, tend to underlie social perceptions, with the result that people sometimes would rather see their neighbor fail than succeed themselves.

This tendency has something to do with the famous Serbian concept of *inat*, a word with complex meaning that can be translated as a combination of stubbornness, spite, defiance, and devil-may-care, whatever-the-consequences disdain. Serbs consider having *inat* a good thing, a mark of strength in the face of overwhelming odds. The concept probably arose as a form of psychological defense to Turkish oppression. In recent times, the NATO bombing of 1999 provided a perfect opportunity for Serbs to show off their *inat*, as when Belgrade residents responded to the attacks by holding rock concerts and wearing shirts displaying target symbols on their backs. When defying blackout orders and leaving the lights on at night, thereby increasing the chances of being bombed, Serbs responded, "How else could the NATO pilots see us giving them the finger?"[7] Sometimes this *inat* merged seamlessly with the famous Serbian concept of black humor (see chapter 2, "Religion and Thought"), as when the residents of the town of Zrenjanin learned that theirs was the only town of any importance to have been left off NATO's bombing list. They promptly put up a billboard reading, "NATO, why don't you hit us? We are not contagious."[8]

WOMEN, WORK, AND FAMILY

While Tito's Communist regime unquestionably improved the ability of women in Serbia and Montenegro to work meaningful jobs and advance in their careers, it also meant an added burden, as Communist legislation did not extend into the home, where men continued to escape from chores and housework. Women thus became not only mothers and housewives but responsible for their professional activities as well.

Today, women make up 42 percent of Serbia's overall workforce and hold 25 percent of senior management positions, according to government figures. Women are roughly equally employed in both the private and the public sectors. In 2002, women constituted some 37.8 percent of total employed people in Serbia, while in Montenegro the number was even higher, at 39.9 percent.[9]

Serbia's 2001 labor law prohibits discrimination against job seekers on the basis of gender. It also mandates 365 days of maternity leave. Montenegro also passed a labor law in 2003 guaranteeing more fairness in the workplace for women. The government of Montenegro also has a Gender Equality Office, as does the autonomous Serbian province of Vojvodina; both are involved with formulating government policy and advising on gender issues.

Women still face numerous obstacles in workplace advancement, which is preventing more women from assuming more senior decision-making roles. In addition to women's family responsibilities, experts also report continued wage discrimination in favor of men, negative stereotypes from men, lack of sufficient child-care facilities, and psychological barriers such as a lack of self-confidence, assertiveness, and ambition or motivation among women.[10] However, in Serbia and especially in the much smaller Montenegro, where the population is slightly more than six hundred thousand, having "connections" is often vital for getting a good job, which means that one cannot be sure of success based on merit or skills alone.

The post-Communist transition period, characterized by war and economic and political torpor, has had a marked influence on family structures and childbearing in Serbia and Montenegro. As elsewhere in Eastern Europe, many young people continue to emigrate, if possible—especially the most skilled or educated who can find good work abroad. Others become discouraged from getting married and having children because it seems just too expensive. The Milošević years brought great strain and uncertainty, fostering pessimism amongst Serbs that has yet to wear off, though Montenegrins on the coast at least are starting to see greater wealth and optimism as a result of the tourism boom of the past few years.

From 1990 to 1998, the Serbian birthrate had declined by 15 percent, making it the lowest since the end of World War II. Along with the economic ruin brought by sanctions and hyperinflation, fears of conscription encouraged up to three hundred thousand young men to leave the country during the 1990s. Although Yugoslavia once had the highest living standard of any Eastern European country, the reversals of that decade influenced young women to not have babies. Also, rumors spread that NATO's bombing of fuel facilities and chemical factories had created toxic radiation in the air and water supply, convincing many young women not to have children or to have an abortion. Although the government claimed the danger was false, speculation had its effect.[11]

Along with the deliberate decrease in reproduction, Serbia has also witnessed a sharp increase in abortions, which are available cheaply and easily. Abortion laws in Yugoslavia were liberalized in the 1970s, a result of the high number of deaths caused by illegal abortions. In 1977, a law was passed stating that a woman's right to choose was in fact a human right. Today, the decision to terminate a pregnancy is often influenced by economic fears as well as the concern that a couple or family cannot provide well enough for a child. As one Belgrade obstetrician told the *New York Times*, "In this culture, if you cannot pamper your children, it is better not to have them."[12] Today, it is believed that approximately 150,000 pregnancies are terminated annually in Serbia, placing the country near the top among European nations.[13]

More alarming, however, is that local experts claim that young women consider abortion an acceptable and normal form of contraception. Recent statistics indicate that between six thousand and seven thousand pregnancies are terminated annually; this number accounts only for underage girls (fifteen to nineteen years of age). In Serbia, the same studies show, only 5 percent of women use contraceptives, making abortion an option to avoid pregnancy. These figures show that "young people obviously do not understand abortion as a serious surgery."[14] It has been documented that serious complications arise in every tenth abortion in Vojvodina, every fifth in Belgrade, and every third in Central Serbia. Interestingly, research has shown that Serbian women, regardless of age, education, profession, or marital status, turn to abortion more often than contraception.

The decision of women in Serbia not to use modern contraception has numerous causes. According to the social scientist Mirjana Rašević, these include "insufficient knowledge of contraception and abortion, a belief that modern contraceptive methods are harmful to health, and a number of psychological barriers, also those arising from relationships with partners. Additionally, the liberalization of the abortion law occurred at a time of decreasing birth rate and a very modest presence of modern contraceptive methods. Also, there are few organized efforts to promote sex education, as well as limitations in the family planning programme."[15]

EDUCATION

The roots of education in Serbia and Montenegro lie in the efforts of the church, first during the medieval kingdoms and then under Ottoman rule. Especially during the latter period, schools organized secretly during periods of Muslim oppression were vital to maintaining learning and literacy in rural areas. As elsewhere in medieval Europe, manuscript copying and the study of the Gospels and theology constituted much of higher learning in Serbian lands, though the nobility and their families were given increasing chances to travel and study abroad. The first universities in Serbia were the Catholic ones at Titel and Bač in Vojvodina, starting in the twelfth century. As the Serbian kingdom of Raška grew in power in the thirteenth century, Orthodox priests began to operate schools of higher learning in monasteries endowed by great kings, such as Sopoćani, Studenica, and the patriarchate in Peć (Kosovo). In 1869, in Montenegro's provincial capital of Cetinje, a Russian-backed school for girls was opened—one of the first such schools in the Balkans. The oldest modern university in Serbia was set up at Sombor, in Vojvodina, by the region's Austro-Hungarian rulers in 1788. Then, in 1808, Serbs in Belgrade established the first university in that city. Called at first the Great Academy, it would form the basis for the present-day University of Belgrade.

Educational Structure

The educational system in Serbia and Montenegro has been modified several times since the end of Communism and is undergoing still more change to bring it in line with European Union standards. It runs from *vrtić* (kindergarten) through *osnovna škola* (primary school), a choice of three kinds of secondary school, and *univerzitet* (university). The first is not compulsory, and since it is open to children as young as two years old, it functions more like day care for working parents than like school, especially for very young children. Still, in a country where family ties are the norm, this exposure to other children from an early age and on a regular basis further assists the socialization process. Primary school (for children aged seven to fifteen) is compulsory, and is followed by secondary education, which lasts for three or four years, depending on the subject. The curricula in Serbia and Montenegro are adopted by the ministers of education, with the consent of each country's national education councils.

Something that American students might find unusual about elementary and high school in Serbia and Montenegro (as in other former Yugoslav countries) is the "shift" system. Because of the lack of sufficient space in the schools of larger towns and cities, students inevitably have to study in shifts—a first group occupies the school from 7 A.M. to 1 P.M., with a second taking its place from 1 P.M. to 7 P.M.

High school in Serbia is divided into three categories. The equivalent of an American high school is the *gimnazija*, which teaches a variety of different subjects. The second, *stručna škola* (professional secondary school), offers a combination of a specialization in a certain subject (say, economics) and various other subjects. Both of these last for four years. Third is the *zanatska škola* (vocational school), which is for three years and does not offer the chance to continue into higher education. The pressure is on from a very early age, as the students' final elementary school exams determine which of these three schools they can attend: while theoretically, students have freedom to choose which kind of school they will attend, only those with the highest marks can attend *gimnazija* or *stručna škola*, whereas those with the lowest results are usually forced into *zanatska škola*.

In comparison to American public schools, those in Serbia and Montenegro force students to learn a huge array of subjects, for better or for worse. Students learn foreign languages from elementary school, and physics, chemistry, and trigonometry starting at the age of fourteen. The typical *gimnazija* general education includes approximately ten to thirteen different subjects on a regular basis, including French, Latin, English, philosophy, and psychology. Students have complained that the workload is both too strenuous and too superficial, leading to apathy and preventing in-depth knowledge in many areas.

The opposite of this course of studies is the *zanatska škola*. While the vocational education program does not make the students particularly well rounded, it does produce an individual with a bankable skill, a benefit for someone looking for work in states with high unemployment. Finally, another interesting facet of this system, and one rarely studied, is the tendency toward gender inequality in different courses of study, both at the high school and the university levels; whereas the hands-on vocational subjects attract mostly boys, girls predominantly undertake subjects like language and literature.

Higher education in Serbia includes university higher education (arts and sciences faculties). In the old days of Communist Yugoslavia, only state universities were allowed to operate. After the end of Communism, in the 1990s, private universities were allowed to open for the first time. Among the local business moguls to open a university were the Karić brothers, two of the wealthiest businessmen and owners of BK Television. They also ran the Karić Foundation and were active in politics.

For students who do not want to do an entire university degree, there is the option to attend *viša škola* (something like junior college in the United States), a two-year faculty. For example, while one can be a nurse with only a high school degree, to become a head nurse requires at least a *viša škola* degree. Thus, this option appeals to those who are set on a certain career path and want to do the minimum amount of study to start working more quickly. The program usually runs for two to three years, finishing with a diploma *višeg obrazovanja* (diploma of higher education, or bachelor's degree), accompanied by a professional title (e.g., senior nurse, senior medical technician, senior designer). Nevertheless, most young people who elect to continue their education beyond secondary school will choose to go to *univerzitet* (university), where classes begin in October and end in June or July.

Within the *univerzitet*, students are associated with a specific *fakultet* (faculty). The meaning of this word is not the same as in English, in which it refers to the group of professors teaching; rather, it is more like the English word *department*. For artists and graphic designers, there are also *umetnicke akademije* (art academies). The diplomas offered for higher education degrees in Serbia include the diploma *visokog obrazovanja*, the degree of *magistar nauka* (master's degree), and finally, the *doktor nauka* (Ph.D.). For aspiring lawyers in Serbia, the first degree to be earned is the diploma *pravnih nauka*.

The foremost university in Serbia is, of course, the University of Belgrade, established in 1808, which has thirty-one different faculties and approximately ninety thousand students. Other major public universities in Serbia include those at Niš, Novi Sad, Kragujevac, and Novi Pazar. Following the NATO bombardment of Kosovo and the expulsion of the Serbian administration from there, the existing University of Priština has been relocated to the northern, Serb-inhabited side of the northern Kosovo city of Mitrovica. Degrees earned by students there are recognized throughout Serbia. The Albanian leadership in Kosovo has since opened its own rival University of Priština.

Belgrade also hosts specialized public universities, such as the University for the Arts and the Academy of Criminal and Police Studies. Private universities in the Serbian capital opened in recent years include Megatrend University, Singidunum University, and University Braća Karić, led by the megarich businessman, politician, and media mogul Bogoljub Karić (the name of the university means "Brothers Karić").

Novi Sad in Vojvodina also hosts a large number of private universities today, including the Economics Academy, Union University, and European University. Novi Pazar in the Raška/Sandžak region of western Serbia is home to the International University. Private faculties that do not belong to any of these universities include the Information Technology Faculty in Belgrade, as well as the Faculty for Management, the Faculty of Sport and Tourism, Faculty for European Law and Political Studies, and Faculty for Law and Business Studies. These last four are all located in Novi Sad.

All told, some 58 percent of all university graduates in Serbia today are female. In 1990, 8,123 of all Serbian graduate students were female; in 2006, however, that number reached 17,702, more than double, though the total number of graduate students in the country increased only 48 percent during the same period. This may indicate that women recognize the value of continuing their education more than men do.

Montenegro's national university is located across fives campuses, with the largest one in the capital, Podgorica. The others are in Cetinje, Nikšić, Kotor, and Herceg Novi. Altogether, the campuses offer studies in fourteen faculties. Some 10,600 students were enrolled at the University of Montenegro as of 2005. A new Montenegrin private university that opened in 2006 is the Mediterranean University, with faculties located in Podgorica and the coastal town of Bar. The subjects of study are business, language, information technology, visual arts, hotel management, and tourism.

In addition to studying at home, a large number of Serbian students are also electing to go abroad to study, some in Western Europe but many in Greece, a historic friend and ally. The port city of Thessaloniki, an eight-hour drive from Belgrade, hosts numerous private colleges. An increasing number offer affiliate degrees with (especially British) universities in Europe offer degrees with their own prestigious name on it, but all studies are undertaken at the university in Greece—a handy way for the mostly Western European colleges to make money.

PROBLEMS IN THE EDUCATIONAL SYSTEM

The Serbian educational system is one of the largest in the entire public sector. In 2001, it comprised more then 1,400,000 students and about 120,000 teachers and other employees, meaning that more than 20 percent of the population was involved with it directly.[16] Owing to Serbia's recent history of international isolation, economic impoverishment, and war, the educational sector has suffered heavily. This turbulent recent history has meant serious problems for an overstressed system and an undermaintained educational infrastructure. Problems also include the demoralization of teachers by political interference and low earnings, and the alienation of students by stagnant curricula and indifferent teaching methods. It is also to be remembered that, during the 1990s, Serbia was forced to take in almost 700,000 refugees from Bosnia and another 250,000 from Kosovo. Incredibly enough, the NATO bombing in 1999 also targeted schools.

Some of the longer-term imbalances in the Serbian system are population disparities between the fairly densely populated central and northern regions and the more sparsely populated south and southeast. As a result, more than 50 percent of primary schools cater to fewer than fifty students each. In general, only 7.6 percent of students use more than half of all schools, whereas 91.5 percent of students use the other 48.5 percent of schools. In addition, more than 12 percent of primary schools in Serbia have only a single teacher to take care of all four grades; these same schools have an average of eleven students per school. On the other hand, in the large cities, such as Belgrade, Novi Sad, and Niš, it is not uncommon to find schools with two thousand to three thousand students.[17]

Further problems involve dilapidated infrastructure. More than 25 percent of Serbian schools lack a sewage system or have problems with their heating, and more than 50 percent lack proper water supply or telephone lines. All of these conditions make it difficult for children to pay attention to their studies. The salaries of teachers and other staff are, on average, low in both absolute and relative terms. In October 2000, net salaries of educational sector employees in Serbia were US$33 per month, or US$365 per year, for a 71 percent decline since 1989.[18] Because of these oppressive conditions, many teachers are forced to work a second job to make ends meet.

The need to integrate with European Union practices has set Serbia and Montenegro on a further reform course, known as the Bologna process.[19] Named for the Italian city where the accord was signed in 1999, this reform process aims to create a European higher education area, standardizing academic degree requirements standards and ensuring that quality standards are compatible throughout Europe. In Serbia, implementation of the reforms began in 2005. The objective is to transform the existing academic degree into a baccalaureate while also shortening the programs of study from four years to three. The Serbian version of a master's degree (*magistratura*) is achieved after an additional two years of study (medical studies still require five or six years). The Ph.D. (*doktorat*) remains unchanged.

The major innovation of the Bologna reforms was to add a new, credit-based system (European Credit Transfer System, or ECTS) to guarantee that students who achieved successful results in their education could apply their credits toward further studies in other European universities. A more immediate benefit of this system is that it rewards attendance and activity in class; under the old system in the state universities, students had to pass only a specific number of exams to graduate. Adding the facts that rote memorization played a large part in teaching, and the ill-paid professors were disinterested or demagogic, it is not hard to see how students' attendance and participation faltered.

While implementation of the new system should be a welcome reform, students have protested rising tuition costs that seem to be accompanying it. Further, Serbia's nonparticipation as of yet in the ERASMUS program (a system of university exchanges throughout Europe) means that Serbian students have limited ability to transfer to European universities, thus limiting the usefulness of whatever ECTS credits they accumulate.

GAY RIGHTS

Gays and lesbians in Serbia and Montenegro do not stand out. There are still widespread stereotypes and phobias about "alternative" lifestyles, and right-wing nationalist youth groups, some associated behind the scenes with religious bodies, have been known to threaten or even attack gay-themed gatherings. However, major cities like Belgrade and Novi Sad do have gay or gay-friendly bars and cafés, and the average Serb or Montenegrin is no more disturbed or outraged by homosexuality than is the average American.

The struggle to gain rights for gays and lesbians has been patchy, and changes have occurred more quickly in some places than in others. In the Serbian autonomous province of Vojvodina, homosexuality was legalized in 1980, some fourteen years earlier than in the rest of Serbia. The age of consent was set at fourteen in 2006. The church, of course, has constantly opposed such decisions. However, there still seem to be firm limits to the amount of liberalization the Serbian state can handle. For example, the Serbian constitution passed in November 2006 bans same-sex marriages and civil unions. Gays are not permitted in the army, though it seems that in practice, a "don't ask, don't tell" policy similar to the American one is in operation. However, gays are still harassed, which has even included beatings by right-wing youth groups. The European Commission has also recently criticized Serbia for discrimination against people of different sexual orientation. While Serbian legislation protects the rights of gays and lesbians in labor circumstances, it does not provide protection against hate speech or sexual orientation–based abuses.

In May 2008, an anti-homosexual extremist group in Serbia vowed to attack gays and lesbians arriving for the EuroVision Song Contest, hosted in Belgrade that year. Thousands of gays and lesbians from around Europe, media reports claimed, were planning to arrive in Serbia's capital for the annual display of kitsch and silliness that transfixes 300 million European television viewers each spring. Although the threat failed to materialize, it did reveal before a large international audience that Serbia has a long way to go in terms of enforcing charitable behavior for all.

The situation for gays and lesbians in Montenegro is even more difficult. Although the country decriminalized homosexuality back in 1977, long before Serbia did, there is no recognition of same-sex couples. A traditionally "macho" culture, Montenegro does not have much tolerance for openly gay behavior, meaning that groups have made less progress than in Serbia and tend to operate much more quietly. Gays and lesbians continue to face harassment, have even been targeted by the police (though mostly in the past), and have encountered negative stereotyping. The gay scene in Montenegro remains small and discreet.

NOTES

1. Figures courtesy of Serbian State Statistics Office (http://www.webrzs.statserb.sr.gov.yu).

2. Matt Prodger, "Serbs Rally to Turbofolk Music," BBC, January 11, 2005.

3. James Creagh, *Over the Borders of Christendom and Eslamiah: A Journey through Hungary, Slavonia, Servia, Bosnia, Hercegovina, Dalmatia, and Montenegro, to the North of Albania, in the Summer of 1875* (1876; Chestnut Hill, MA: Adamant Media Corporation, 2005), 246.

4. Elizabeth Roberts, *Realm of the Black Mountain: A History of Montenegro* (Ithaca: Cornell University Press, 2007), 115.

5. Christopher Boehm, *Blood Revenge: The Enactment and Management of Conflict in Montenegro and Other Tribal Societies* (Philadelphia: University of Pennsylvania Press, 1984), 245.

6. Dejan Ćirić, "Spells, Herbs and Surgery: Medical Care in Provincial Balkan Town in the 19th Century," January 9, 2008, http://www.balkanalysis.com.

7. Scott Taylor, *Inat: Images of Serbia and the Kosovo Conflict* (Ottawa: Esprit de Corps Books, 2000), 69. This firsthand journalistic account of the experience of being inside Serbia during the bombing provides numerous examples of *inat* in action and offers a unique and informed view of the conflict in general.

8. Michael Dobbs, "Serbs' Bulls-eyes Defy, Mock NATO—Targets Express Common Will," *Washington Post*, April 9, 1999.

9. Statistics compiled from the International Labour Organization (http://www.ilo.org).

10. Jelena Smiljanic, "Obstacles Women Face in Trying to Advance at Work in Serbia," University of Belgrade Seminar Paper, 2005.

11. Blaine Harden, "Crisis in the Balkans: Population; Stresses of Milošević's Rule Blamed for Decline in Births," *New York Times*, July 5, 1999.

12. Ibid.

13. "U Srbiji godišnje oko 150.000 abortusa," *Beta*, September 25, 2007.

14. Ibid.

15. Mirjana Rašević, "Abortion Problem in Serbia," Institute of Social Sciences, Demographic Research Center (Belgrade), 2006.

16. Jasna Aleksić, "Development of Education National Report of the Federal Republic of Yugoslavia-Serbia," International Bureau for Education, UNESCO (Belgrade), 2007.

17. Ibid.

18. Ibid.

19. See the official Web site of the European Union for more information (http://europa.eu.int).

4

Holidays, Customs, and Leisure Activities

I just wanted to hit it as hard as I could. My father said I should try to keep it inside the lines, but I wasn't interested in that for a while.
—Ana Ivanović, Serbian tennis champion[1]

No matter where you may be, for Christmas Eve you should be home.
—Traditional Serbian saying

We express our joy and sadness with the trumpet, we are born with the sounds of the trumpet, and also buried with sounds of the trumpet. . . . Those that can't understand and love Guča, can't understand Serbia.
—Vojislav Koštunica, former Serbian president and prime minister[2]

SERBS AND MONTENEGRINS must be among the world's most athletic nations—not incidentally, they are also among the tallest. Dating back to the days of Yugoslavia, Serbs and Montenegrins have been a major force in international sports such as basketball, tennis, and water polo, playing at high levels in European leagues; numerous Serbian basketball players have also made careers in the American National Basketball Association.

The continuing nature of this sporting success may be considered all the more remarkable considering the experience of harsh economic sanctions during the 1990s and the effects of war, all of which have taken a toll on infrastructure, athletes' salaries, and the ability to undergo training at levels equal to those in more developed countries. On the other hand, perhaps these

Belgrade's central pedestrian thoroughfare, Knez Mihailova, runs from the Hotel Moskva down to Kalemegdan fortress. Lined with stylish shops and trendy cafés, the street is buzzing with life day and night. Photography by the author.

existential traumas have also given the Serbs more tenacity and grit than athletes not raised in the pressure cooker of modern Balkan life.

At the same time, Serbs and Montenegrins also love to relax, usually over coffee with friends or by partaking in the nightlife of major cities such as Belgrade, Niš, and Novi Sad or at Montenegro's coastal holiday resorts. At least among fellow people of the Balkans, Montenegrins enjoy the dubious honor of being the world's laziest people. As elsewhere in the Balkans and Mediterranean Europe, friends can sit over a beer or coffee for hours, enjoying life at a relaxed Old World pace no longer found in the more hectic societies of Western Europe and America.

You will also encounter (mostly) old men whiling away the afternoons over games of chess in places like Belgrade's Kalemegdan Fortress park. During leisure time, families and couples can often be found making the time-honored evening stroll along the riverbanks, through parks, and on the (usually historical) pedestrian central streets of major towns and cities. During summertime in Belgrade, locals flock to the Danube River beach (Ada Ciganlija) for sunbathing and swimming, while riverboat bars and

Originally a humble fishing village in the fifteenth century, Sveti Stefan since the 1960s has become Montenegro's most exclusive resort, a place where the rich and famous can enjoy pampered seclusion within magnificent stone walls and houses on the sea. Courtesy of Patrick Horton.

restaurants are also popular. And the Adriatic coast of Montenegro is now squarely on the international tourist map, with Serb and Montenegrin vacationers being joined by increasingly posh foreign visitors in the country's chic new hotels and resorts.

Serbs and Montenegrins are also a very festive people, and their yearly calendar is chock-full of religious and other holidays, each accompanied by its own unique tradition and customs. These holidays have interesting regional and local variations that maintain unusual traditions. The majority of Serbs and Montenegrins are Orthodox Christians, meaning that holidays follow the Orthodox calendar, though there are other Christian groups, Muslims, and small Jewish populations as well, each with its own traditional festivities.

HOLIDAYS

Along with Russia, Belarus, and Macedonia, Serbia and Montenegro still retain the pre-Gregorian Julian calendar for marking religious holidays, which puts Christmas thirteen days after Christmas in the United States and means that there are two New Year's holidays to be celebrated—December 31 and the old calendar's New Year's Eve thirteen days later.

Owing to the strong role of tradition and the Serbian Orthodox Church, it is not surprising that most holidays in Serbia and Montenegro are based on the religious calendar. The major holidays, as in other Christian countries, are Easter and Christmas. Personalized holidays, the "name days" associated with the individual saint for which one is named, are also common and akin to a second birthday. When a name day is associated with a patron saint of a village, town, or the nation, it becomes a feast day with a much wider celebration. The feast day of a specific family is called a *slava* and is widely celebrated.

Both name days and feast days fall in the category of the *slava*. In difficult premodern times, when most of the population survived via farming and lived in chronic poverty, these holidays marked the few regularly scheduled festive occasions—no doubt part of the reason why Serbs and Montenegrins celebrate them so vivaciously.

Christmas

Christmas in Serbia and Montenegro is refreshingly noncommercial, as the exchange of presents is not a major part of tradition. However, as it is associated with Saint Nicholas, who is for Serbs the patron saint of children, children may receive some small gifts. The humorous name for Santa Claus here, as in other Slavic countries, is Deda Mraz (Grandpa Frost). Christmas is more of a holiday to bring family together and enjoy copious amounts of eating and drinking. Decoratively, while some now place a small Christmas tree in the house or a wreath on the door, the real Christmas tradition for Serbs and Montenegrins is to place a sprig of oak leaves above the door of the home.

In the old days, on Christmas Eve, the head of the household would go to a forest to cut the *badnjak* (oak). The tree would be taken to the church and ritually blessed, then taken home, where the branches would be cut off. The tree, with a bit of wheat and other grains thrown in, would then be burned in the fireplace. This ritual undoubtedly derives from pagan times and is considered a sacrifice to God, a request for good luck in the coming year. Nowadays, people no longer go to the trouble of cutting down a tree, as they would rather take down a bit of oak leaves from a nearby tree (or even buy such sprigs from street vendors where no trees are readily available). On Christmas Eve, people go to church in the afternoon. The priest burns a branch of an oak tree in keeping with tradition. After the ceremony, worshippers go home for a special dinner. The meal is always made without meat, eggs, or dairy products, usually consisting of fish, beans, and different kinds of bread.

The main tradition during this Christmas Eve dinner involves a special loaf of flat baked bread, the *česnica*, prepared by the matriarch of the house. Baked inside the bread is one small coin, which everyone hopes to get in his or her piece. The oldest person in the house breaks off the pieces by hand, dispensing them according to a tradition: the first piece is always for God, the second for the house, and then the people in the family from oldest to youngest. (In villages, a piece is also reserved for the household's livestock.) The person who finds the coin in his or her piece is, tradition maintains, blessed with luck for the whole year to come. But before that, the oldest person stands and blesses the house (the blessing is called *zdravica*). In the most traditional and rural version, the toastmaster can go on for a long time indeed.

Christmas (*Božić*, or God's Day), falls on January 7. A wonderful tradition in Serbia and Montenegro involves children. Very early in the morning on Christmas Day, the children of the village, neighborhood, or apartment building go door-to-door waking everyone up by singing songs and banging on the doors. They sing funny carols, and the fairly groggy people inside give them nuts, candies, and a little money.

After that, worshippers may go for a morning mass. People salute each other with the greeting *Hristos se rodi* (Christ is born), to which one answers, *Vajstina se rodi* (Truly he is born). After that, a special afternoon lunch is held, usually with roast suckling pig, plenty of wine, and *sarma* (cabbage stuffed with ground meat and rice). Plenty of sweets like baklava, small cakes, and candies also line the table. Another snack is *koljivo*, a sweet cake made of wheat with spiritual, ritualistic value (one crosses oneself before eating it). The two days after Christmas are also celebrated with almost the same intensity as Christmas. More of the same eating and drinking follows.

Easter

Easter (*Uskrs*, or Ascension Day) is the major religious holiday in Serbia and Montenegro. The beginning of Lent, forty days before Easter, is called *Pročka*, or the Day of Forgiveness. On this day, families hold a special dinner in which the younger people ask their elders for forgiveness. It is something seen as particularly fitting in the case of young sons-in-law with their new "parents"; though this act was probably once a heartfelt and significant gesture, it is largely a symbolic one today.

Fasting for all of Lent is not as widely practiced as it used to be, though many still manage to do without meat, eggs, and dairy products during the final week before Easter. This week is well structured and full of events. On Palm Sunday (*Cvetnice*), people go to church and begin the real preparations for Easter. During Easter Week, the churches are frequented continuously by a stream of worshippers who come to light candles and pray.

A tradition that still endures, mostly in rural areas, takes place four days after Palm Sunday. Very early in the morning on Holy Thursday (*Veliki Četvrtak*), the woman of the house wakes up early in the morning to paint hard-boiled eggs. It must be done before sunrise, the tradition goes, to prevent the sun from seeing the eggs. While in the past all of the eggs were supposed to be red, nowadays a more liberal and creative style is followed along with making the red ones, with a blend of colors used to make beautiful designs.

The next day, Good Friday (*Veliki Petak*), is a solemn affair in which people attend church, accompanied by much priestly chanting and incense. In the middle of the church a table stands with a red cloth draped over it; children go under the table and make a special wish. Despite the general solemnity of the day, people are kept busy preparing for Easter by making candies and getting the food prepared for the coming days.

Holy Saturday (*Velika Subota*), the day before Easter, provides a second opportunity for errant egg painters to finish the job. People also come and go from church during the day, with the real ceremony starting after 11 P.M. Before midnight, the priests come out of the church and, with the assembled worshippers, circle the church three times. At midnight, the church bells start ringing loudly and everyone cheers the victory of Christ over death. People hug and greet one another with the phrase *Hristos vaskrese* (Christ has risen). The response is *Vajstina vaskrese* (Truly he has risen). The same greeting is used throughout the day on Sunday.

With midnight marking the arrival of Easter Day, people can begin cracking eggs. This is one of the most entertaining aspects of Orthodox Easter. Challengers face off to see whose egg is stronger, cupping each firmly in their fist with only the top or bottom sticking out. Each gets a chance to crack down on the other's egg, and the person with the egg that doesn't crack is the winner. There are no Easter-egg hunts as in the United States, and the sweets are refreshingly homemade. Serbs and Montenegrins generally do not give presents, as Americans have begun to, for Easter.

The best part of Easter is the great feast, usually centered around copious portions of roast lamb. Also, people visit one another's houses, ensuring a great series of eating and drinking. The day after Easter is likewise Holy Monday. The days from Good Friday to the second day of Easter are not workdays.

New Year's Eve

Serbians enjoy the New Year's holiday (*Nova Godina*) in much the same way as do Westerners, with fireworks displays and gregarious drinking, feasting, and dancing. An increasing number, however, now go on trips abroad to sunnier locales or to one of Serbia's ski resorts to enjoy a romantic getaway from the usual.

An interesting twist to the New Year's holiday is that it repeats, thanks to the enduring Julian calendar, on January 13 with the so-called *Srpska Nova Godina* (Serbian New Year, also known as *Stara Nova Godina*, or Old New Year's, in some regions). The date may have originally derived from pagan tradition, as small villages here (and elsewhere in the Balkans) still hold colorful costumed carnivals, accompanied by much feasting and music, on and around this date. In pre-Christian times, the carnival would have represented an annual winter cleansing, to drive away evil spirits and warm up the bleak winter.

Name Days and Feast Days

The Orthodox calendar is full of dates associated with saints. Since most people are given fairly traditional names by their parents, almost everyone has a second birthday to look forward to when the time on the calendar comes, though not everyone celebrates. While an individual's name day might be celebrated by a small group of family and friends, larger celebrations, feast days, are held on the name days of a select few saints. Most every village, town, or city has its patron saint, and Serbia and Montenegro themselves have major patron saints. The unique Serbian custom of the *slava* refers to the celebration of a family's own special protector saint; this saint is inherited from father to son, and celebrating it is one of the main annual events that brings all of the family together.

On a national level, the events accompanying saints' feasts are similar to those of name days, though on a much grander scale. The most important such feast day for Serbs takes place on January 27 with Saint Sava's Day (*Savindan*). It commemorates Saint Sava, the founder of the Serbian Orthodox Church, and as such is widely celebrated. Another major religious holiday that reveals the close ties between spirituality and nationhood is that of Saint Vitus's Day, or the Day of the Fallen (*Vidovdan*), which commemorates the defeat of the medieval Serbian kingdom with the 1389 Battle of Kosovo against the Ottoman Turks. Taking place annually on June 28, *Vidovdan* is commemorated with church services.

National Holidays and Other Commemorative Anniversaries

Serbia has numerous national holidays that inevitably mean a day off from work or school. On February 15, Statehood Day (*Dan državnosti—Sretenje*) is celebrated. Curiously perhaps for Americans, May Day or Labor Day (*Dan rada*) is an important spring holiday in Serbia and Montenegro and elsewhere in the Balkans as well. Maybe it has something to do with the countries' recent Communist past, but *Prvi Maj* (May 1) is a holiday that people spend a bit of time preparing for, usually trying to plan long weekends around it. There is no particular way to celebrate, though generally, as an expression of the unequivocal start of spring, it is not surprising that most people try to be outdoors—whether enjoying the nature around their town or village or heading to the coast for a bit of relaxation. Eight days later, on May 9, is Victory Day (*Dan pobede*), another holiday but a workday.

FESTIVALS

Serbs and Montenegrins hold festivals for all kinds of things, from beer and sausages to music and dance. The intensity of their enjoyment is complemented by the offbeat contests, side events, and general merrymaking that ensue.

Music Festivals

Since the 1990s, Serbia has begun to come into its own in terms of popular music festivals, and Montenegro, flush with money from foreign investors in the tourism sector, now hosts high-profile summer concerts featuring well-known foreign and Balkan singers. The major Serbian popular music festival is EXIT, held at Petrovaradin Fortress in Novi Sad each July (see the festival's official Web site at http://www.exitfest.org). It was originally organized by three university students as a form of protest against the Milošević regime in 1999, but since then has gone comfortably mainstream. The festival, now the biggest in Southeast Europe, draws huge crowds from the Balkans (and further afield) in Europe for six days of partying and music on several stages. Some of the major acts to have played the EXIT Festival in recent years include Franz Ferdinand, Billy Idol, the Pet Shop Boys, the White Stripes, Lauryn Hill, and the Beastie Boys. In 2007, EXIT was named the Best European Festival at the U.K. Festival Awards, and it is now written into every informed media body's calendar listing of annual music festivals on the continent.

Novi Sad also features another, though smaller and more discerning, music festival held annually: the Novi Sad Jazz Festival (the jazz festival's Web site is http://jazzns.eunet.yu/index.htm). It has been held since 1999, when the local cultural center was big enough to host it, but the festival has grown substantially in recent years, with first-rate international jazz musicians like Jimmy Cobb, Al Di Meola, Keith Copeland, and Kenny Garrett gracing the stage along with Serbian and other European jazz ensembles.

Another much more traditional kind of annual musical gathering is the famous Guča Trumpet Festival, held each August in the village of Guča, near the small city of Čačak in west-central Serbia (the Guča Trumpet Festival's official Web site is http://saborguca.com). Also known as the Dragačevo Assembly, this truly extraordinary happening involves three days and dozens of freewheeling brass bands. The first festival in Guča—under the grandiose full name Dragačevo Assembly of Trumpet Players—was held on October 16, 1961, in the village churchyard. Today it is a riotous event of barbeques, beer, and cacophonous music, in which the bands ramble aimlessly through the village, all playing at the same time, for whatever donations the increasingly intoxicated festivalgoers thrust into their trumpets and tubas. Attending the Guča Trumpet Festival is certainly one of the most unique and extraordinary experiences one can have in Serbia. A somewhat dazed British observer described the experience like this: "A man is hanging from a tree pouring beer over a brass band beneath him, and a chef is carrying the carcass of a pig across a makeshift dance floor.... As entire pigs and sheep rotate on spits above open fires, the bands target the customers, swooping on tables and blasting the diners with a cacophony of sound. The audience shows its appreciation by plastering Serbian dinar notes on the sweat-streaked foreheads of the musicians. It goes on late into the night, and starts again first thing in the morning."[3]

The Guča festival has grown wildly in popularity in recent years, leading some veterans to grumble that modern organizers have failed to "keep it real." Some 300,000 visitors, an ever-increasing number from abroad, bear down on this otherwise sleepy town of 2,000 people for the festival, where more than three tons of bread are consumed, 250,000 servings of meat are eaten, and more than 700,000 pints of beer are drunk. The official festival begins with an opening concert on Friday, followed by Saturday-night celebrations, and, finally, Sunday's competition. The prize for winning is the coveted golden trumpet, "an award that more often than not will lead to a recording contract and enough wedding bookings to keep the winning band busy for months."[4]

Trumpet music is embedded deep in the Serbian consciousness, deriving first from the military brass bands that arose in the nineteenth century (Prince Miloš Obrenović, leader of the second Serbian uprising of 1815, ordered the formation of the first military band in 1831). Brass bands, and specifically trumpet music, traditionally accompany every major event in a Serbian person's life, from births, baptisms, and *slavas* to weddings, festivals, and funerals.

It is considered a great honor for brass bands to be invited to the festival, and there are indeed competitive heats held during the year to separate the pretenders from the contenders. To date, the trumpeter to have met with the greatest success—so great, in fact, that he stopped competing out of mercy—was Boban Marković, a Serbian Roma (Gypsy) from the unassuming southern town of Vladičin Han. In 2001, he became the first musician ever to receive the highest mark from every jury member at the festival. The man who put Serbian brass band music on the map internationally, Goran Bregović, has also appeared at the festival in recent years. Most of the approximately 1,500 musicians are Roma—a traditionally musical people who perform impromptu and organized brass concerts around the Balkans, particularly popular at weddings.

Other Festivals

Serbia has several more impassioned and offbeat festivals. For example, the country is well known for its meat festivals. The annual *kobasicijada* (sausage festival), held for almost thirty years in the last week of February in the northern village of Turija, made headlines in 2004 when organizers claimed to have created the world's longest sausage.[5] According to a contemporary news report, "Twelve butchers used the meat of 28 pigs, 40 kilos of paprika, 50 kilos of salt, two kilograms of pepper and five kilograms of garlic to make a sausage 2,020 meters long."[6] Although the chefs had been preparing the sausage for four days in eager anticipation of some outside acknowledgement, it was drolly noted that "unfortunately, the representatives of the *Guinness Book of World Records* did not come to register the new world record for the longest sausage." Among other larger-than-life festivities, the event features contests for long jumping, fastest sausage eating, and a contest to crown the fattest visitor to the festival. Of course, lots of music, dancing, and beer round things out.

Another major meat festival held since 1988 is the Kačarevo Bacon Festival in the town of the same name. Considered by locals as a sort of Olympics of bacon eating, it is indeed an event that would have Homer Simpson salivating. The origins of the festival are quite humorous: one winter's eve in January 1988, local farmers got into an argument over the best way to smoke meat and make good bacon. When they could not solve their differences verbally, the men invited friends and neighbors to come to taste their specialties in hopes of winning the debate. The very popular Kačarevo festival has seen its share of oddities over the year, none perhaps more so than local Rača Vulanović's artwork—the world's first bacon sculpture. Five tons of bacon went into the sculpture, which towered twelve meters (thirty-six feet) high. Everyone knew Serbs were prone to doing things big, but even this was something special!

More food and drink festivals occur in Belgrade, where the annual Beer Festival has attracted considerable attention since 2003 (see chapter 5, "Cuisine and Fashion"), as well as the *roštiljijada* (barbecue week) held every September in the central Serbian town of Leskovac. This town is famous for its grilled meats both in and beyond Serbia. During the event, the main boulevard is closed, becoming a pedestrian-only zone replete with grill stands and tented, temporary restaurants. Visitors come from far and wide, and of course there are the contests and feats of strength—such as the contest to make the biggest *pljeskavica* (a Serbian hamburger).

LEISURE ACTIVITIES AND SOCIAL CUSTOMS

Serbs and Montenegrins spend a lot of time enjoying—passively by whiling away the hours in a café or enjoying nightlife—as well as actively through recreational sports. Reading is popular in Serbia, and especially in Belgrade, known regionally for its annual book fair. This pastime has historic roots; some of the best bookshops in the old Yugoslavia were in Belgrade. Until recently, when they started to be "discovered," Belgrade featured a number of "secret" bars, hidden away in the basements of buildings or flats, with no visible markings, where groups of friends in the know would congregate for private drinking sessions.

Greetings in Serbia, as in other Orthodox countries, are accomplished with a handshake and kissing three times on alternating cheeks—a reference to

The Ruski Tsar, one of Belgrade's most historic cafés, cultivates an old-world ambience and is a great place for an espresso and people-watching just off the pedestrian Knez Mihailova Street. Photography by the author.

the Holy Trinity. The same follows upon departures. Serbs say *Drago mi je* (Nice to meet you) to new acquaintances, and when sitting in a house or public place and others enter, those seated customarily rise to greet those who are entering. Since you will frequently find yourself eating and drinking with Serbian hosts, it is worth remembering that you must look a person in the eyes when saying *Živeli* (cheers). The full explanation for this custom is: *kad se kuca u oči se gleda, radi običaja i radi reda*, which can be translated as, "When you clink (your glass), you should look the other person in the eyes, because of the tradition and order." The host or hostess will ensure that your glass is topped off when you have finished it, so to gulp it down too fast could be considered bad manners; at the same time, not drinking enough might be seen as lacking in conviviality.

Serbia and Montenegro's warmhearted people are known for their hospitality; as elsewhere in Southeast Europe, guests are usually offered far more than they can eat or drink, even if the hosts themselves are poor and go without. Traditional hospitality is especially strong in rural areas, and these are one of the last places in Europe where locals will invite you into their homes when a village lacks accommodation for visitors.

When invited into a Serbian or Montenegrin home, one can expect to be immediately given a cup of Turkish coffee (*Turska Kafa*), also called *Crna* (black) *Kafa* or even *Srpska* (Serbian) *Kafa*. A full spread of cheeses, smoked meats, and perhaps vegetable dips will be placed before you, often with sweets such as baklava, cakes, or *slatko* (sweet fruit preserves). Of course, a shot of *rakija* is always on hand, usually in the (often homemade) form of *šljivovica*, Serbian plum brandy. Guests visiting one another's homes usually bring a small gift such as a box of chocolates or bottle of wine.

If the visit involves a *slava* (the celebration of a family or individual's saint day), along with a small gift, the special greeting is *Srećna slava* (happy *slava*). When entering the house, guests are offered *pšenica*, a ceremonial sweet of wheat, honey, and nuts. After making the sign of the cross, the recipient takes a spoonful of the sweet and dips it in a glass of water before eating.

SPORTS

The Serbs and Montenegrins are on average some of the tallest people in Europe, and this, together with their natural athleticism, has helped them win European and world championships in several sports, in both the previous Yugoslav system and more recently as independent states. For a nation of only 7.5 million people, Serbia has produced a disproportionately large amount of sportsmen and sportswomen, and it continues to do so. With

This oštrač (knife sharpener) shown here working for customers in the Central Serbian city of Nis typifies Serbia and Montenegro's enduring tradition of artisans and craftsmen, who can still be found on the street corners and shops of these Balkan countries. Photography by the author.

the conflicts of the 1990s now far beyond, attention has turned to improving the infrastructure that will sustain training of world-class athletes.

Basketball

The Serbs are especially passionate about basketball and have been very successful at it over the years. As is generally the case in Europe, Serbian teams play with a more pass-oriented, team-first style of play and less razzle-dazzle than is usually the case today in the United States. The International Basketball Federation (FIBA), the world body governing international competitions, considers Serbia's national team the rightful descendent of the national teams of Yugoslavia and, subsequently, the short-lived Serbia and Montenegro state union.

This combined legacy is a very accomplished one. Yugoslav national teams won FIBA world championships in 1970, 1978, 1990, 1998, and 2002, also achieving second-place finishes in 1963, 1967, and 1974. Yugoslavia won its only Olympic gold medal in 1980, but it picked up numerous silvers at the games in 1968, 1976, 1988, and 1996, as well as a bronze in 1984. Yugoslav teams have been especially successful at the European Basketball Championships, winning it all in 1973, 1975, 1977, 1989, 1991, 1995, 1997, and 2001. Of course, all of this success has not been just the result of Serbian players (Croats, former Yugoslav partners, are also passionate about the game), but it does indicate a long standard of excellence.

In Serbia and Montenegro, the very competitive national leagues offer a high standard of play and are frequently watched by scouts from U.S. and other European clubs, with a result that Serbs and Montenegrins are represented on professional rosters far and wide. The major powerhouses on the Serbian scene are Belgrade's KK Partizan and Crvena Zvezda (Red Star), both formed in 1945. These teams have won numerous titles both nationwide and in European competitions, and American players attracted to European clubs sometimes wind up in Belgrade. Serbia and Montenegro's long basketball tradition has been marked by earlier generations of players. Sarajevo-born Aleksandar Nikolić (1924–2000) was one of the very first Serbian basketball stars, excelling both as a player and as a coach. He is considered so important to the development of basketball in Yugoslavia that he has won the name "Father of Yugoslav basketball." After moving to Serbia at a young age, Nikolić grew up, studied, and turned to basketball, playing professionally for Belgrade's greatest clubs right from the early days of their inception. He played for both Partizan Belgrade and Crvena Zvezda, as well as for Železničar Čačak and BSK Belgrade, winning the Yugoslav league title in 1947, 1948, and 1949. Nikolić also played for the Yugoslav national basketball team during the late 1940s.

However, it was as a coach that Nikolić had the greatest success, coaching the Yugoslav national team between 1951 and 1965, and again between 1977 and 1978. Under his tenure, Yugoslavia won numerous medals in international competitions, including golds at the 1977 European Championship and 1978 World Championships. One of Nikolić's contemporaries, Borislav Stanković (b. 1925) also played at a high level and is noted today for his forward-thinking ideas that Europeans should aspire to play in the American NBA. He has remained active as an administrator and organizer long after his retirement.

Among the second-generation Serbian standouts was Bosnian-born Dražen Dalipagić, one of Europe's biggest stars during the late 1970s and early 1980s. He led the Yugoslav national team to gold medals in both the Olympics and the World Basketball Championships, as well as three European titles. He remains one of the most celebrated athletes from former Yugoslav times. Today, the tradition remains strong, with Serbia's youth teams recently winning European and World titles, ensuring an ever-growing crop of young stars.

Serbian players have indeed made a big impact worldwide, with many playing for major clubs in Europe. Further, a number of Serbs have had, and continue to have, success in the American NBA. The most famous of these Serbian stars is unquestionably Vlade Divac. Born in 1968 in the town of Prijepolje, the 7′ 1″ center Divac was one of the dominant big men of the 1990s, but he was also known for his passing skills and outside shooting. While a player with Partizan Belgrade in 1989, he was drafted by the Los Angeles Lakers with the twenty-sixth overall pick. Mentored by legendary teammates Magic Johnson and Kareem Abdul-Jabbar, Divac became accustomed to the American style of play quickly and was named to the All-Rookie Team that year, his ebullient and easygoing personality also winning him friends despite the fact that he could not speak English at first.

Although a star, Divac was traded away to the Charlotte Hornets in 1996 for the draft rights to Kobe Bryant. After two seasons playing in Charlotte, Divac signed as a free agent with the Sacramento Kings, turning the Californian team into a perennial powerhouse over the next few years. Together with Chris Webber and fellow countryman Peđa Stojaković, the Kings proved serious challengers for the NBA title—losing twice in the semifinals to Bryant's Lakers. In 2004, when the Lakers had traded away star center Shaquille O'Neal in a desire to rebuild the franchise, Divac returned to his original team. However, injuries plagued Divac, and in 2005 he announced his retirement after sixteen years in the league. He remains one of only three players (along with Hakeem Olajuwon and Kareem Abdul-Jabbar) to amass 13,000 points, 9,000 rebounds, 3,000 assists, and 1,500 blocked shots in his career.

During and after his playing days, the affable and entertaining Divac has made frequent appearances in the media, films, and advertisements and is considered something of a national hero by most Serbs. He showed dedication to his native country by attempting to invest in various businesses, including his old basketball team in Belgrade, yet time and time again he was stymied by bureaucracy and suspected interference from protective government interests. Nevertheless, Divac continues to be active as a businessman and especially as a humanitarian figure in Serbia, with the opening of a foundation to help children in need. He has also given generously to supporting war refugees in Serbia. Like many Serb athletes, the war in Kosovo affected him deeply: in addition to having two sons, he and his wife adopted a girl whose parents were murdered by Albanian snipers.[7]

Serbia's second best-known basketball star in America, Predrag (nicknamed "Peđa") Stojaković, arrived a generation after Divac, drafted with the fourteenth pick by the Sacramento Kings in 1996. Although quite tall at 6′ 11″, he plays forward and is legendary for his three-point and free-throw-shooting percentage. After trades to the New Orleans Hornets and Indiana Pacers in

2006, Stojaković began to suffer injuries that have affected his productivity. However, his shooting touch and speed made a return in an exciting 2008 playoff run, a reminder of Peđa in his heyday.

Among the many other famous Serbian players to have made careers in the NBA are center Nenad Krstić (New Jersey Nets), power forward Darko Miličić (Memphis Grizzlies), Marko Jarić (Minnesota Timberwolves) and the relative newcomer, hulking 7′ 2″ Kosta Perović, who was drafted in 2006 by the Golden State Warriors. Another talented Serb, Vladimir Radmanović, currently plays for the Los Angeles Lakers.

Montenegro has offered fewer NBA players, and these have tended to identify themselves as ethnically Serbian. Former Montenegrin NBA players include Predrag "Peda" Drobnjak and Žarko Čabarkapa. The native Montenegrin star Aleksandar "Sasha" Pavlović, who plays alongside LeBron James on the Cleveland Cavaliers, continues the Serbian tradition of dead-on outside shooting.

Soccer

As everywhere else in Europe, soccer commands a loyal following in Serbia and Montenegro. The major towns and cities all have their own clubs, with the most famous soccer teams being Belgrade's Partizan and Crvena Zvezda. Soccer is a major sport in Serbia and Montenegro and, like everywhere else in Europe, attracts its share of hooligan fans. Partizan's fans are known as *grobari* (the gravediggers) and Crvena Zvezda's as *delije* (the heroes, or strong ones). Although these names and associations have become part of Belgrade pop culture, it should be noted that, despite the occasional confrontation, Serbian soccer fans are much less violent than English or Scottish ones.

Dozens of Serbian and Montenegrin soccer players have distinguished themselves over the years. A recent star and later coach and administrator, Dragan Stojković was known in Serbia by his nickname, "the Pixie." He played for the Belgrade club Crvena Zvezda and several European clubs before injuries led him to move to Japan, where a street is now named after him. Dejan Savićević was another star of the 1980s and 1990s to play for Crvena Zvezda. When he moved on to Italian powerhouse AC Milan, the Montenegrin star known for his poise and control won the admiration of club owner and future Italian president Silvio Berlusconi, who dubbed him "Il Genio" (the Genius). Savićević led AC Milan to three straight European Cup finals; in the club's 1993 victory, Savićević made one of the greatest plays of the year—a thirty-five-yard half-volley goal.

Water Polo

Along with basketball and soccer, the sport in which Serbs and Montenegrins have been traditionally most distinguished is water polo. Since the downfall of Yugoslavia, Serbia has had a fierce rivalry especially with Hungary and former Yugoslav teammates Croatia. Unlike in the United States, water polo is a widely televised sport in Serbia and Montenegro.

The sport was invented in the late nineteenth century for American and British private schools, meaning that these countries tended to win all of the early championships. However, once water polo became popular on the Continent, the balance of power shifted eastward. While Hungary has the longest and most distinguished record of success on the international stage, Yugoslavia and its two most accomplished sporting successor states, Serbia and Croatia, have done quite well also. The early roots of the game in Yugoslavia began in royalist times and included the annual event of the Kingdom of Yugoslavia Water Polo Championship, held from 1921 to 1940. Following World War II, the sport was revived, and Communist Yugoslavia excelled, winning Olympic gold medals in 1968, 1984, and 1988, along with the silver in 1952, 1956, 1964, and 1980.

Water polo is governed by the Fédération Internationale de Natation (FINA), the international swimming federation, and the very first FINA men's world water polo championship was indeed held in Belgrade in 1973, when Yugoslavia won the bronze. In 1978 and 1998, the country again took the bronze. In 1986 and 1991, Yugoslavia was world champion. Most recently, Serbia and Montenegro took the silver in the 2004 Olympic Games in Athens. The country also took the bronze in the FINA 2003 world championships and the gold in 2005.

The man considered by many to be the best water polo player of all time, Igor Milanović (b. 1965), comes from Belgrade. In 349 games for the Yugoslav national team, he scored an impressive 540 goals. Milanović led Yugoslav teams that twice won the Olympic gold medal, the World Championships, the European Championships, and the FINA Cup. He played the greatest part of his professional career for Belgrade's VK Partizan (1975–1988), later playing for several other Serbian and international teams until his retirement in 1996. Ten years later, he was inducted into the Water Polo Hall of Fame in Fort Lauderdale, Florida.

Among the many notable current Serbian players is Aleksandar Šapić (b. 1978 in Belgrade), considered by many the best offensive player in the world. After making his debut at only thirteen years of age, Šapić went through several clubs and helped the Serbia and Montenegro national team win gold at the World Aquatic Championships in Montreal, as well as the silver medal at the 2004 Olympics and a bronze at the 2000 Olympic Games. At the European Championships in 2006, held in Belgrade, Šapić won gold with the home team.

Šapić is known for playing with tenacity and fiery determination, which has sometimes led to altercations and fines. Šapić became the world's most sought-after player in 2005, when Russian water polo club Sturm gave him a record contract of $300,000 per season, making him the world's highest-paid player. This financial acknowledgment of the Serbian player's skill is borne out by his prolific and sustained scoring ability: every year since 1995, Šapić has been the league's leading scorer in whichever team or league he was playing in at the time.

Other currently active players who have helped Serbia achieve great results on the world stage, and who continue to excite fans in the Serbian and other European water polo leagues, include Aleksandar Ćirić, Danilo Ikodinović, Nikola Kuljača, Vanja Udovičić, and Vladimir Vujasinović.

Tennis

While Serbia, and Yugoslavia before it, have always contributed world-class tennis players, only recently have Serbs become well known on the world stage. The greatest Serbian-born player to date, Monica Seleš, is an ethnic Hungarian from Vojovodina. However, she developed her early skills before emigrating to America from then-Yugoslavia with a Serbian musician, Đorđe Balašević, who even built a court for her to practice on in his backyard. Seleš was dominant in the women's game during the late 1980s and early 1990s, and several times played for the former Yugoslavia in international matches. She has proved an inspiration for Serbia's younger generations of aspiring tennis players.

At the same time as Seleš, Serbian men's tennis came alive with Slobodan Živojinović, who represented Yugoslavia internationally and won two career singles titles, in 1986 and 1988, peaking at No. 19 on the international rankings and memorably defeating John McEnroe in the 1985 Australian Open. At the same time, Živojinović was famous for being married to Serbian Turbofolk singer Lepa Brena. He was more successful in doubles than in singles play, and in 1986 he was ranked the top doubles player in the world. Živojinović is now active in initiatives to improve training facilities for coming generations of Serbian tennis players.

Most recently, Serbian tennis has returned to world attention, with young Serbs, both men and women, challenging for major titles. The most accomplished current Serbian men's player is Novak Đoković, born in 1987 in Belgrade. Noted for his powerful serve, strong forehand, and slice backhand, Đoković achieved a remarkable victory in the Australian Open in January 2008. At just twenty years of age, he knocked off the legendary Roger Federer in the semifinals before winning the tournament, becoming the first player representing Serbia (as an independent state) ever to win a Grand Slam singles title. Đoković is also the youngest player (in the open era) to have reached all four Grand Slam semifinals. At the 2007 U.S. Open, he was runner-up and won four of the five Masters Series finals he reached. Đoković was also a semifinalist at the French Open in 2007 and 2008 and at Wimbledon in 2007. During 2008, he was ranked second in the world.

Đoković, whose family is originally from Kosovo, has also been associated with Serbian politics. After Kosovo Albanians' unilateral declaration of independence on February 17, 2008, Đoković spoke out against the decision, and two months later visited Serbs in the northern Mitrovica enclave of Kosovo to rapturous applause.[8] A second young Serbian player, Janko Tipsarević, was ranked No. 33 in the world in May 2008 at the age of twenty-four. He had won nine tournaments by that time and has represented Serbia in Serbia's Davis Cup play every year since 2000.

Serbia's modern female tennis stars have commanded even more attention, as with the Russian Anna Kournikova, both for their game and for their looks. Jelena Janković, a tenacious, hard-hitting player equally comfortable on all surfaces, reached the position of No. 3 in the world ranking after making it to the semifinals of the 2007 French Open. Notably, in 2007 she played more matches than any other player and still maintained her third-place ranking. Another Serbian female star, Ana Ivanović, has done even better, in June 2008 moving up to No. 1 in the world. She reached her first Grand Slam singles final in the 2007 French Open but lost to Justine Henin, later admitting that she was overwhelmed by the moment. However, on June 7, 2008, Ivanović had another opportunity; this time she won it all in Paris, defeating Russian Dinara Safina to win the French Open for her first major tournament victory. The ecstatic twenty-year-old described it as "a dream come true" but has indicated that she plans to keep her feet on the ground and not let the fame "change her." She views her success as a sign that young Serbian players will have something to strive for.[9] Like Jelena Janković, Ivanović is a hard-hitting player with excellent depth and a strong two-handed backhand. She is especially known for her astonishingly powerful 128-mile-per-hour serve.[10] Interestingly, she was inspired to play tennis after seeing countrywoman Monica Seleš on television—at the age of five.

With tennis now identified as a promising national sport, the government—and politicians eager to be seen with the young stars—is taking measures to correct some of the infrastructure flaws and lack of funding that have kept the country back and seen young talent go ignored. Slobodan Živojinović, the national star of the 1980s, told the British newspaper the *Guardian* of his dream of having "10 Serbian players in the world's top 10"—a typically grandiose expression of Serbian enthusiasm. According to the newspaper, Ivanović's finals appearance at the 2007 French Open led to "a 40% increase in participation levels" among Serbian youngsters, and television stations are suddenly fighting for rights to broadcast the sport. The president of the country's national tennis federation since 2003, Živojinović has guided plans to builds a national tennis center; today's current stars were forced to

With her triumph in the 2008 French Open, Serbian tennis player Ana Ivanović became world number-one at the age of 20. Along with tennis peers Novak Đoković and Jelena Janković, Ivanovic has attracted the world's attention to the quality—and good looks—associated with Serbian tennis. Courtesy of Manuela Davies, http://www.anaivanovic.com.

do their training as youngsters in a former swimming pool converted into a tennis court.

The privations of life in Serbia, and the aftereffects of war and economic sanctions, have indeed been referenced by the players themselves. "I think when you learn to fight for your position and you don't have anything given to you, or any financial help, that makes you stronger," said Jelena Janković to the newspaper. "You mature a lot faster and become very strong mentally, so when you come to a place where you have good courts and everything is given to you, you appreciate it more."[11]

Volleyball, Handball, and Other Sports

Other popular team sports in Serbia and Montenegro include volleyball and handball. Possibly because they are on average so tall, Serbs and Montenegrins are also great aficionados of volleyball, always fielding world-class teams. Most recently, Serbia's women's team took the silver medal in the 2007 European Championships.

Two of Serbia's best-known volleyball players are brothers: Nikola and Vladimir Grbić. Both played for Yugoslavia on the gold medal–winning national teams at the 2000 Olympics and the 2001 European Championships. Ivan Miljković is another leading volleyball player who played on those great teams, and he memorably scored the final point against Russia in the Olympic finals, falling to his knees in amazement. Like the Grbić brothers and other leading Serbian players, Miljković plays abroad (in Italy), where salaries are higher.

Handball is also popular in Serbia and Montenegro and elsewhere in the Balkans. Among the legends of Serbian handball is Zoran Živković (b. 1945), who played goalkeeper in Serbian handball leagues and is currently a noted coach. During his career, he made eighty-two appearances for the Yugoslav handball national team. As a player, he protected the goal for the Yugoslav national team's gold-medal performance at the 1972 Olympics, and as a coach also won gold for Yugoslavia at the Olympics in 1984, among many subsequent victories.

In other sports Serbs have excelled as well. Dragutin Topić set the junior world record in the high jump in 1990 before also winning the European Championships three weeks later. All in all, Topić has set five national high-jump records and won four national titles for Yugoslavia. One of the world's greatest female sports shooters of all time was Croatian-born Serb Jasna Šekarić (b. 1965). Three times elected world shooter of the year (in 1990, 1994, and 2005), she was also crowned "Shooter of the Millennium" in 2000 by the International Shooting Sport Federation. Over her long career, Šekarić has won ninety medals in competitions including the Mediterranean Games, the Olympics, the European and World championships, and the World Cup.

In addition to organized professional sports, Serbs and Montenegrins take an active interest in skiing, hiking, swimming, and playing pickup basketball or soccer with friends.

NOTES

1. Bud Collins, "Befitting the Royal Treatment," *Boston Globe*, June 8, 2008.

2. "Koštunica: ko ne razume Guču ne razume ni Srbiju," Radio Televizija Srbije, September 3, 2006.

3. Matt Prodger, "Serbian Town Has Much to Trumpet," BBC, August 7, 2005.

4. Ibid.

5. See the official Web site of the sausage festival at http://turija.co.yu/strane/kobasicijada/program.htm.

6. "Festival Claims World's Longest Sausage," Agence France-Presse, February 29, 2004.

7. Rick Reilly, "Vlade Divac's Private War," CNN/*Sports Illustrated*, May 25, 1999.

8. "Australian Open Champion Novak Djokovic Visits Serb Stronghold in Northern Kosovo," Associated Press, April 3, 2008.

9. Simon Dilger, "Ana in Dreamland," *Sky News*, June 8, 2008.

10. Peter Bodo, "When Ana Ivanovic Serves, You Better Duck," *New York Times*, June 3, 2008.

11. Stuart James, "Serbia Seeks to Build on a Rich Talent Pool," *The Guardian*, June 25, 2007.

5

Cuisine and Fashion

SERBS AND MONTENEGRINS are hearty eaters, and their cuisine, with its nourishing blend of Central European and Mediterranean flavors, is excellent. There are a wide variety of dishes ranging from breakfast pastries like Austrian-style strudels or Ottoman *burek* (a kind of flaky cheese pie), to healthy salads, numerous local cheeses, and copious amounts of meat of all kinds. Serbia and Montenegro are also well known for their drinks; fruit brandies, like the Serbian national aperitif *šljivovica* (from plums), are drunk on every occasion for which diners can create a good excuse to say *živeli* (cheers), which is frequently. Wines from the region, typically whites in the northern province of Vojvodina and reds in southern Serbia and Montenegro, are also robust and flavorful. There are also a handful of domestic favorites on the beer scene, such as Serbia's Jelen Pivo (Stag Beer) and Nikšićko, named after the Montenegrin town of Nikšić, where it has been brewed since 1896. Like everything else in these invigorating countries, portions are huge, and especially when visiting the hospitable homes of local people, saying no is not an option—so come with an appetite.

On the fashion scene, Serbia and Montenegro have distinguished themselves on the catwalks of New York, Paris, and Milan for their beautiful, long-legged models. While actually fashion designing is taking a while to reach the same level of notoriety on the world stage, there are numerous well-regarded Serbian and Montenegrin designers, and events like Belgrade Fashion Week, held every year in April, give them an opportunity to show off their latest creations.

FOOD

Serbian and Montenegrin cuisine is a rather unique one, owing to geography and history. While it is strong on meat, at the same time it is much more healthful than the heavy, vegetable-averse cuisines of more northerly Slavic countries such as Slovakia and the Czech Republic. With geography that mixes Continental and Mediterranean climates and terrains, Serbia and Montenegro offer a wide variety of natural, homegrown fruits and vegetables, plus a taste of seafood on the Montenegrin Adriatic coast. The historical influences on cuisine result from the distinct influences and experience of two empires: the Austro-Hungarian Empire, in the northern plains of Vojvodina, and the Ottoman Empire, which left behind spicy sauces and famous sweets like baklava. Other Balkan specialties from the region, like Greek and Macedonian dishes, fill out the rest of the traditional cuisine.

While people in Serbia and Montenegro enjoy eating out, they also tend to cook much more homemade food than do Americans, using old family recipes and fresh local ingredients. Some of the most commonly made foodstuffs occur as if by ritual, according to the season when the ingredients are freshest: for example, strawberry jam is always made in late May and early June, during the peak season for this abundant fruit, while *ajvar* (a sweet red-pepper sauce) is made in autumn, after the peppers have been harvested and hung to dry. A common sight in Serbia and Montenegro in the cold days of winter is the small outdoor oven with a stovepipe puffing out hot air and an old man or two sitting around to watch the *rakija* bubble. This becomes almost a pastime, when neighbors can gather and while away an evening cooking the next year's brandy while sipping that of the previous year.

The dining habits that today's Serbs and Montenegrins follow are those of the West, with three meals daily, though this has its own variations. Lunch is the largest, as in other Mediterranean countries, whereas breakfast tends to be the smallest; it was only introduced as a concept in the second half of the nineteenth century. While breakfast may be as simple as a piece of pastry or Continental breakfast, you will also see in any large town or city barbeque stands on the street; it is not uncommon to see Serbs in Belgrade munching on *pljeskavica* (grilled beef burgers) at eight o'clock in the morning! Serbs and Montenegrins also preserve another Mediterranean custom, the practice of having a long, leisurely dinner or drink (whether a coffee or alcoholic beverage), without looking at the clock or feeling the need to hurry.

Pastries and Breakfast Foods

Breakfast in Serbia and Montenegro can be larger or smaller, faster or slower, depending on the location, timing, and, of course, the dinner involved.

In the larger cities, where people often get something to eat on the way to work, lines form in the morning inside the *pekara* (bakery), usually a narrow shop with a very long counter and the day's specialties under big curving glass windows behind it. Most Serbian bakeries have a few seats or tables where people can sit or stand while eating, though many just get their breakfast to go.

The most popular offerings here include *burek*, a slightly greasy, golden-brown pie made of several layers of phyllo dough baked in the oven, with white cheese, spinach, or ground beef inside. *Burek* is made by a pastry chef who, like a pizza chef, kneads out the elastic dough into a flat, circular shape, slips it on his finger, and flips it in the air several times before folding the edges over repeatedly and placing the filling inside. Thus sealed up and brushed with cooking oil, the *burek* is cooked until golden brown and then served. The steaming pie is about three inches thick and as wide as a good-sized oven pan. It is cut with a large, rounded knife into quarters or eighths. The former will definitely fill you up, whereas the latter makes for a good and quick snack. A close relative of *burek* is the *banica*, almost the same but slightly flakier and less heavy. For a drink, *burek* is always accompanied by sour drinking yogurt. Serbs and Montenegrins might also eat such food in late shops after a night of drinking, because the grease in *burek* soaks up the alcohol, thus preventing a hangover the next morning!

Other popular breakfast foods available at the *pekara* include various kinds of sweet *pita* (pie). These include *pita sa jabukama* (rolled apple pie) and *pita sa višnjama* (cherry pie). Other quick breakfast snacks are quite light sugar doughnuts (*krofne*) and plain doughnuts with chocolate filling; other kinds of doughnuts are not traditionally made. During the Christmas season, street vendors cook doughy doughnut balls, which are then sold in small boxes to be eaten with chocolate syrup.

When Serbs and Montenegrins eat breakfast at home, it can range from simple Continental fare (cold cuts, olives, cheese, hard-boiled eggs) to *slanina* (bacon) or *kobasica* (sausage), accompanied by bread (usually a large and crusty loaf, almost never sliced sandwich bread) or pastries, and sometimes topped by *kajmak* (sour cream). Homemade breads range from *bela pogača* (white village bread) to *proja* (cornbread), and are accompanied by butter, jam, honey, or milk. *Kiflice* are small croissants, and *kačamak* is a flour-and-water kind of polenta. In Serbia, especially in northern Vojvodina, an excellent tradition of homemade sausage making is continued, and the very finely sliced smoked bacon (*pršuta*, prosciutto) can be fantastic. Finally, in addition to regular fried eggs, Serbs and Montenegrins make a delicious kind of omelette that involves sweet peppers and onion cooked together with scrambled eggs.

For an accompanying drink, anything from a glass of water or juice to tea and coffee is served. However, coffee prepared at home in Serbia and

Montenegro is almost always Turkish coffee (sometimes they call it "Serbian" to express national pride), which is widespread in the Balkans. Turkish coffee is made in a long-handled copper pot held over the burner or fire, in which water and a small amount of ground coffee and sugar are cooked. The result is a thick, black, and strong coffee with a slightly leathery head. For outsiders, it takes some getting used to, but most swear by it after a while. However, in cafés, most Serbs and Montenegrins now opt for espresso drinks of various kinds, espresso *sa mlekom* (espresso complemented by a dash of milk) being a particular favorite. Coffees are often accompanied by *kisela voda* (sparkling water), of which Serbia has several popular brands, the most famous being Knjaz Miloš (King Milosh), which is bottled deep in the Serbian mountains of Aranđelovac.

Soups, Salads, and Cheeses

Cuisine in Serbia and Montenegro is remarkably healthy partly because of the amount of soups and vegetables people eat. Soup is most often eaten at lunchtime, whereas salads are enjoyed at both lunch and dinner. There are two types of soups in Serbian cuisine: standard *supa* (soups) and soups with roux (browned flour); the latter are called *čorba* and are the more commonly ordered. These soups are simple but nourishing, featuring noodles with beef or chicken. Soups featuring vegetables include *čorba od zelja i sira* (soup with cabbage and cheese), *čorba od spanaća*, *koprive ili zelja* (soup with spinach, nettles, or cabbage), *čorba od boranije* (soup with green beans), and *paradajz čorba* (tomato soup). *Pasulj* (bean soup) is also popular. Slightly more high-brow (and expensive) are *riblja čorba* (fish soup) and *jagnjeća čorba* (lamb soup).

Serbs and Montenegrins eat many varieties of salads as well. They are typically eaten together with the main course. The most common salads include *srpska salata* (Serbian salad, a vegetable salad, usually served during summer with roast meat and other dishes, made from diced fresh tomatoes, cucumbers, and onions, usually seasoned with oil, salt, and commonly *feferon*, a local hot pepper similar to cayenne pepper), *ruska salata* (Russian salad, made with carrots, green beans, and mayonnaise), and *šopska salata* (made with sliced tomatoes and cucumbers and topped with slivers of soft white cheese). Simpler salads can also be made with anything from lettuce and cabbage to tomatoes, cucumbers, and carrots. Vegetable spreads, to accompany meals as a side dish or with bread and cheese, include the sweet red-pepper sauce *ajvar*, *ljutenica prebranac* (baked beans in sauce), and a hot pepper sauce. Stuffed vegetable dishes are also popular and diverse, from *punjene paprika* (bell peppers stuffed with ground beef and rice) and *punjene tikvice* (stuffed zucchini) to the famous *sarma* (stuffed cabbage with beef and rice).

In the great family of Serbian and Montenegrin cheeses, the major difference is between *sir* (white cheese) and *kaškaval* (yellow cheese). White cheeses are also divided by *kravlji sir* (cow's-milk cheese) and *ovčji sir* (sheep's-milk cheese). Goat cheese is more rarely encountered. Most villages claim to have their own local specialties, though they are often fairly similar in the end.

The Wide World of Roštilj (Barbecued Meats)

If there is one thing Serbs are especially renowned for, it is *roštilj* (barbecued meats), and they do eat a lot of them. Whole cities, such as Leskovac in central Serbia, are so famous for the quality of their grills that restaurants in other countries are named for them. And annual events like bacon and sausage festivals (see chapter 4, "Holidays, Customs, and Leisure Activities") are widely visited and popular. Grilled meats in Serbia and Montenegro are eaten for lunch or dinner (and as we have seen, even for breakfast) in both restaurants and as fast food from the ubiquitous street stalls with the smoke and smell of cooking meat emanating from within. In Belgrade, the hip Skadarlija district, known for its winding stone streets and arty vibe, is full of traditional restaurants serving *roštilj* dishes in the traditional way.

Rocky and rough Montenegro has historically offered few expansive tracts of farmland, so lamb and goat are more pervasive in the national cuisine, as is fish on the seacoast. The much larger and agriculturally well-suited Serbia, on the other hand, has historically been a center for cattle and pig farming, and during the days of the Austro-Hungarian Empire, Serbian farmers made fortunes on pig exports to the Habsburgs. In Serbia, therefore, beef and pork dishes are most common. *Karađorđeva šnicla* (breaded, rolled steak stuffed with cream cheese) is a Serbian classic, named for the 1804 revolutionary hero Black George. As elsewhere in the Balkans, grilled *ćevapčići* (seasoned, rolled patties of mixed ground beef) are a particular favorite, as is the aforementioned *pljeskavica*, which can only be described as a hamburger but is somehow much tastier. When cooked with yellow cheese, spices, and sometimes mushrooms inside, it becomes *gurmanska pljeskavica* (gourmet's *pljeskavica*). These two dishes are encountered much more often in restaurants or street stands than in home kitchens, as most people do not have at home the large, flat metal grills needed to cook them properly.

Serbs also enjoy a lot of pork dishes. Along with bacon and various types of sausages (*kobasice*), including blood sausage (*krvavice*), there is *praška šunka* (boiled ham) and *vešalica* (long strips or filets of smoked pork). Particularly harrowing for most delicate Western stomachs are *škembići* (tripe), *mućkalica* (intestines grilled in sauce), and especially the clear, jelly-like *pihtije*, a nutritious but very heavy wintertime dish created from low-grade pork meat, such as the head, shank, and/or hock. Some recipes also include smoked meat.

Meat for breakfast—and lunch and dinner as well—is popular in Serbia and Montenegro. Here an early-morning customer munches on a pljeskavica (hamburger) at this rostilj (barbeque) place in Belgrade. Such restaurants are plentiful and serve a wide variety of tasty beef, pork and chicken dishes. Photography by the author.

Other meat dishes are equally seasonal or foreign flavored. Roast lamb is the traditional dish for Easter, and roast suckling pig makes a very rich and lip-smacking meal for Christmas and wintertime in general. Wiener schnitzel (*Bečka šnicla*) provides a taste of Austria and Central Europe, while Hungarian flavors are found with the famous *gulaš* (goulash). One of the popular Mediterranean dishes in Serbia and Montenegro is *musaka* (a Greek casserole of minced meat, eggs, and potatoes). And skewered kebabs (*ražnjići*) are made by grilling chunks of pork or chicken, often with little strips of green pepper and onion between them; this is reminiscent of the Turkish shish kebab. In restaurants, where the selection is typically vast, large parties often opt for a big pile of *mešano meso* (mixed grill).

BEER AND WINE

In comparison to Germany, Belgium, the Czech Republic, and American microbreweries, Serbia and Montenegro do not make phenomenal beers, but they do have some good ones. The main problem true beer lovers will find here is that because of unadventurous local tastes and the frequently hot temperatures, there is not much variety: lagers and pilsners are almost exclusively the only types of beer made locally. However, Belgrade now offers a fun summer beer festival, which brings to one place lots of grilled meat (of course) and beers from around the world; it is believed that events such as this might provide the opportunity for American beers, currently very hard to find in the Balkans, to make an entrance into the bars and shops of Serbia. In bars, beer is available either in the bottle (*flaša*) or on tap (*točeno*).

Today, Serbia has fourteen breweries and Montenegro just one. This popular Montenegrin brew is Nikšićko, a product of the Trebjesa Nikšić brewery named for the inland town of Nikšić where it is located. This flavorful, slightly bitter lager has been produced in the town since 1896. Montenegrins were justly proud when Nikšićko bagged the gold medal at the prestigious Brussels Beer Fair in 2003. In addition to its flagship Nikšićko Pivo, the brewery has rolled out three new varieties: Nik Gold, a slightly stronger malt beer; Nik Cool, lighter than the original; and Nikšićko Tamno, a typically Balkan dark beer (meaning dark in color rather than robust in texture and taste). Trebjesa Nikšić beers are the most popular and most widely consumed beers in Montenegro and second in Serbia after Apatin's Jelen Pivo. Nikšićko beer is also now starting to be exported throughout Europe.

The most popular beer in Serbia and Montenegro according to sales is Jelen Pivo (Stag Beer). This light, refreshing beer is a typical lager, the "everyman's beer" that provides refreshment rather than nourishment, a good warm-weather brew. Jelen Pivo is crafted in Serbia's leading brewery, Apatinska Pivara, located in the Danubian town of Apatin in Vojvodina. This land of gentle rolling hills and fields is well known by brewers for the quality of the barley grown locally. Apatin is the second-oldest brewery in Serbia, with records attesting to its beer-marking activities as far back as 1756. It is suspected that the first brewers benefited from some "outside expertise," as it was founded just a few years after Austro-Hungarian queen Maria Theresa populated the area with Austrian and German settlers in 1748. Only the smaller Vršačka Brewery, founded all the way back in 1742, is older in Serbia. Today, Serbs and Montenegrins consume some 500 million liters of Jelen Pivo every year.

The second-largest brewery in Serbia is MB Pivara of Novi Sad, also in Vojvodina. This newcomer (established in 2003) on the scene has shaken things up with a wide range of different beers and has been helped immeasurably by savvy marketing and cameo advertising spots from Serbian celebrities. In 2006, MB made headlines by opening what it called the "largest beer saloon in South Eastern Europe" in Novi Sad, a beer hall with a capacity for 2,200 guests. With substantial investment from its owners, the brewery began almost immediately to export to fifteen European countries, and it boasts some of the most modern equipment of any brewery in Serbia.

The MB varieties include the light, mild, and foamy Pils Bier, the name alluding to the style, Czech pilsner, that was invented in the Czech town of Pilsen in 1840. The Serbian version does not live up to the original, but it is good nonetheless, especially on a hot summer's day. The brewery also produces a German-style pilsner (MB Premium Bier) that is slightly more bitter, full-bodied, and amber in hue. More adventurous than usual for Serbia, MB Brewery also introduced a top-fermented Dunkel, which combines some of the strong taste and full body of an English or Belgian ale or German *Alt* beer. The name *alt* in German means "old," and this style of beer is indeed older than lagers or pilsners and is produced in a different manner, using special brewer's yeast that ferments only under unique conditions, giving the beer a rich taste and aroma with a combination of fruity, bitter, and sweet flavors. Considering ingrained local tastes, MB has made the biggest gamble, however, with its Schwarz black beer, which combines chocolate and coffee tastes and is the closest thing Serbian breweries offer to a porter or stout—pretty good, but still not Guinness.

Along with these big three, Serbia has several other, smaller breweries, which also produce popular beers of more or less the same lager or pilsner style: some examples include Jagodinska Pivara from the town of Jagodina, just south of Belgrade; Weifert, which produces a velvety, sweet dark beer; and the country's oldest brewery, Vršačka, also in Vojvodina, which has won more than thirty gold, silver, and bronze medals for quality in the past twenty-five years.

It is interesting to note that beer consumption in Serbia and Montenegro has been on the rise over the past few years. Beer consumption in Serbia has risen appreciably, reaching 50 liters per capita in 2005. Since 2002 especially, there has been a boom in beer-related advertising as companies try to expand the industry among the existing market. This has been helped by the deep pockets of major foreign breweries that have invested in breweries here since 2003. MB has probably spent the most money on advertising in recent years, with an aggressive marketing campaign that featured a catchy, subtly nationalistic slogan; the brewery told Serbs in its ads that MB beers are *svetsko, a naše* ("the world's, but ours too"). A number of celebrities were used to build up the brand, including the actor Lazar Ristovski; the queen of Turbo-folk music, Ceca Ražnatović; and Italian former football referee Pierluigi Collina. Breweries have also built up their brands by being seen at "fun spots," such as sponsoring large outdoor concerts, sporting events, and other forms of mass entertainment.

The increased use of advertising and marketing to heighten the prominence of beer in the national consciousness has been made possible by the unlimited funds of foreign investors. Indeed, Serbian and Montenegrin breweries have attracted considerable interest from the biggest European corporate breweries, which began snatching them up not too long after the fall of Slobodan Milošević and restitution of Serbia as a democratic state. Things started moving in August 2003, when the Turkish brewer Efes announced it would take over 63 percent of Pančevo Pivara, investing 6.5 million euros. In October, Denmark's Carlsberg announced it would pay 26 million euros for 49 percent of Pivara Čelarevo. And then a day later, Belgian brewer Interbrew, the biggest brewer in the world, announced it was purchasing 50 percent of Serbia's oldest beer maker, Apatin. At the time, Apatin held a 39 percent share of the Serbian market and was valued at 262 million euros. These examples cheered the Serbian government, which, with a cofinancing grant from the Swedish government, declared plans to privatize three major breweries (Beogradska Industrija Piva, Vršačka Pivara, and Jagodinska Pivara) in February 2004.[1] And Trebjesa Brewery in Nikšić has also been bought by InBev.

The value of Serbia's breweries continues to rise as the heavy advertising continues to increases the beer-drinking market. In December 2007, when MB's owners decided to sell the four-year-old brewery, it already held 7 percent of the Serbian beer market, placing it fourth behind Apatinska Pivara, Carlsberg Srbija, and Efes Srbija. Dutch giant Heineken International bought the company in February 2008, thus ensuring that things will only get better for the brewery now renamed Brauerei MB.

New tastes are also being formed by events such as the Belgrade Beer Fest, held annually over three to four days in the summer at the foot of Belgrade's Kalemegdan Fortress, showcasing the products of various local and international beer producers.[2] The festival, which features live music performances each evening, has grown in size and popularity, going from seventy-five thousand visitors in 2004 to three hundred thousand visitors the next year, making it the second-most-visited festival in Serbia for that year. Another, smaller festival is the Dani Piva (Days of Beer), held since 1985 in the Vojvodina town of Zrenjanin and organized by the local brewery Zrenjaninska Industrija Piva.

Wine

The wine-making tradition in Serbia goes back at least three thousand years, and drinking wine was enjoyed and wine making supported by Roman emperors, medieval Serbian kings, Austro-Hungarian rulers, and various bishops (though not by the Muslim Ottomans in places they occupied). Although Serbia is not as well known for its wines as perhaps it should be, considerable efforts in the past few years have gone into developing the industry, with the government devoting resources and promotional campaigns to it.[3]

In Serbia, there are nearly 270 square miles of vineyards in the country, which produce about 430,000 tons of grapes each year, most by local wineries. It is not unusual for families in the countryside to have their own modest wine-making operation, creating wine just for their own enjoyment. Wine is a common accompaniment to meals, both at home and in restaurants.

The major varieties of wine produced in Serbia include the Belgrade seedless, Prokupac (an endemic grape), Sauvignon, Italian Riesling, Cabernet Sauvignon, Chardonnay, white and red Burgundy, muscat, Tamjanika, Krstač, Smederevka, and the famous regional Vranac. Rare varieties like the Krokan are also grown here. The oldest local grape varieties are the Prokupac and Tamjanika. The former, which produces a robust red wine, has been grown since the early Middle Ages; Tamjanika is a muscat from Southern France, introduced to Serbia more than five hundred years ago.

Serbian wines are also distinguished by regions. The most important one is that of Negotinska Krajina, near the town of Negotin, 250 kilometers from Belgrade on the eastern border of Serbia with Romania and Bulgaria. Here wine has been grown since Roman times, then on the quicksand soil surrounding the Danube. Approximately one thousand acres of vineyards currently exist here, bordered by two rivers (the Danube and Timok) and framed by the Miroč, Crni Vrh, and Deli Jovan mountains, part of the Stara Planina system. Old-time wine shops (*vinare*) are distinguished by their traditional stone-and-wood construction and serve excellent local food as well. The wine culture in the Negotin area also benefits from steady sunshine and a slight elevation (150–250 meters high) beneficial to the grapes. This region produces many kinds of wine, but it is most famous for the delicate, golden Bagrina white and fragrant reds like Prokupac and Burgundy.

The Vojvodina Plain also contains several famous vineyards. Vršac, one hundred kilometers northeast of Belgrade), is known as the "town of wine" for its sweet grapes, noted by Ottoman travel writer Evlija Celebija, which are even incorporated into the town coat of arms and on the facades of its traditional houses. Wines produced here are almost exclusively whites and include some rare local specialties like the Kreaca, made from an endemic and ancient local white grape. Vintners have also had good luck crafting imported flavors, and today Rieslings, Pinot Bianco, and Rhine white wines are among the best local offerings. An interesting fact about this area is that the small town of Gudurica is one of the most multicultural places in the world per capita; its 1,500 inhabitants come from twenty-two different nationalities!

Another Vojvodina wine area is found on the mountain slopes of Fruška Gora, southwest of Vršac; the Srem wine region is one of the oldest in Europe, dating back some 1,700 years to Roman times. Under Austro-Hungarian rule in the fifteenth century, some of the most notable local wines (like the Sremski Karlovci) were exported far and wide. This region has further historical interest for wine making, as the earliest known wine treatise in the Serbian language (*Iskusni Podrumar;* The Experienced Cellar Keeper) was written here in 1783 by a leading writer, Zaharije Orfelin (see chapter 6, "Literature"). The region's most unique, standout wine, Bermet, is a flavorful wine produced similarly to vermouth, but with a special blend of twenty different herbs and spices. Finally, in the far north of Serbia, near the Hungarian border at Subotica, is the unique Palić wine region, covering some twenty-four thousand acres. The soil in this area is composed of various sands and clay because it was, in prehistoric times, the bed of the long-gone Pannonian Sea. This unique soil composition makes excellent grounds for light, flavorful white wines, such as the Italian Riesling, Župljanka, and muscatel.

Another important Serbian wine region is near the Danubian town of Smederevo, just south of Belgrade. This capital of medieval Serbia has been richly endowed by rulers from Stefan Lazarević in the fifteenth century to Miloš Obrenović, leader of the second Serbian uprising in 1815. This area of rolling hills with loose, rich soil produces delicious, light table wines and blends. Another area that had long connections with Serbian royalty is the Oplenac wine country in leafy Šumadija, one hundred kilometers southwest of Belgrade. This area's abundance of grapes has long been noted, and its resurrection of a long wine-making tradition was enhanced by a unique historical quirk: the chief wine-cellar keeper of the Karađorđević dynasty, who emigrated to Canada in 1945, later sent the secret recipe for the best wine produced for the royal family back to one local vintner. Production of this wine, Trijumf (Triumph), resumed; composed of a unique blend of Sauvignon Blanc, Chardonnay, and Riesling, it is considered today one of the best Serbian wines.

The oldest attested wine making in Serbia, however, is that of the Župa region, 230 kilometers south of Belgrade. Wine is known to have been made here for at least three thousand years. The oldest written notice concerning wine here is the 1196 charter of Studenica Monastery, which, like other leading monasteries Žiča and Hilandar, all had extensive landholdings and wine-making operations in the area. The Župa region lies in a vale surrounded by mountains, and the climate is said to be similar to the French Bordeaux region. The sprawling vineyards here occupy 2,500 acres, and the variegated soil provides perfect conditions for growing grapes. The two oldest grapes in Serbia, Tamjanika and Prokupac, are grown here. Locals enjoy a harvest festival each summer in which the custom of running wine down the town fountain continues.

Wines from Montenegro are fewer, owing to the rocky conditions; however, some are known internationally. Krstač is Montenegro's top white grape and wine, while vintners also produce a hearty red Vranac made from a type of grape found in Montenegro and Serbia but especially in Macedonia. The most famous winery in Montenegro is Plantaže of Podgorica, known for its intense, ruby-colored Vranac. The prime wine-making region in the country is the Southeast, in the fertile area between the capital and Lake Skadar. The Serbian and Montenegrin wine industry has been growing significantly in recent years, with an annual international wine festival, In Vino, held in Belgrade since 2004. The best-known, world-class wine for export is the Terra Lazarica by Serbia's largest producer, Rubin, located in the central Serbian town of Kragujevac.

Liquor and Aperitifs

Making and drinking fruit brandies is a national tradition in Serbia and Montenegro, and whether one lives in the countryside or in the city, anyone with access to raw ingredients and an outdoor cooker can make his or her own. The aperitif for which Serbia is most famous is undoubtedly *šljivovica* (plum brandy, also written as slivovitsa or slivovitz in other Slavic languages). It is a member of the great family of *rakija* (brandies of high alcohol content) common to Central and Eastern Europe. *Šljivovica* is clear in color and strong—alcohol content may vary from 25–70 percent by volume, with the general bottle sold in stores coming in at around 40–45 percent. About 70 percent of Serbian plum production (424,300 tons per year) goes into making *šljivovica*. Major producers often age their *šljivovica* in oak barrels for between five and twelve years. In the old days, this aging process was also important for local producers and even families, as money was scarce, the economy unreliable, and the only thing that would appreciate in value with age was plum firewater.

Special drinking customs for *šljivovica* and other kinds of *rakija* are respected and closely followed. It is drunk from special small glasses, a bit larger than the average American shot glass, and the first sip is always accompanied by a round of *na zdravlje* (cheers). Serbian hospitality dictates that guests entering the home be offered a glass of *rakija,* and it typically comes at both the beginning and end of a meal. In restaurants, proprietors wishing to show their appreciation for the customers will often provide a round of *rakija* on the house after the meal.

Naturally, the widespread pride in plum brandy of Serbia and some neighboring countries has led to disputes over trademark, similar to the old Czech-American dispute over rights to the name *Budweiser*. After several nations laid claim to *šljivovica* as their own, in October 2007 the European Union ruled to create a compromise solution; *slivovitz* was chosen as a generic term, allowing individual nations to protect their own national brand by adding the name of their own country. Thus was born Serbia's first national brand, Serbian Slivovitz, or *Srpska šljivovica*.[4] Although it is common in several countries,

Serbs are adamant that *šljivovica* originated with them, and they like to think they have the plums to prove it (Serbia is the third-largest plum producer in the world).

Other kinds of *rakija* common in Serbia and Montenegro are *lozovača* (grape brandy), *viljamovka* or *kruškovača* (pear brandy), and *jabukovača* (apple brandy, like the French Calvados). And finally, the rarefied *pelinkovac* (a wormwood liqueur similar to but milder than absinthe). *Lozovača* is especially popular in Montenegro.

FASHION

From the old days to the present, clothing in Serbia and Montenegro has evolved but always been marked by vivid colors, rich texture, and an inventive range of embroideries. The countries also have distinctive traditional shoes, hats, and other garments that add a unique touch. The richly varied forms of traditional dress in Serbia and Montenegro are unique not only on national levels but also on regional levels within the two countries. Although no longer worn except on special occasions, traditional garb was worn in rural areas until the 1980s, and even today in the villages you will see old men and women in clothes that are not too far evolved from the kind of dress that was worn for hundreds of years in these countries.

Nowadays, Serbian fashion designers are starting to make an impression on the European design scene, helped, of course, by the tall and gorgeous models the country is also known for.

Traditional Dress

Traditional Serbian costumes, as with others throughout Europe, are no longer worn but are an essential part of folk culture and folk history. The clothing itself was varied, reflecting geographical location and climatic conditions, and accordingly made from different dyed fabrics, especially wool, hemp, and cotton. Decorative ornamentation was enhanced by vivid colors, often dyed into the yarns in the process of weaving. Clothing styles also varied between villagers and urban dwellers. In Serbian territories controlled by the Ottomans, clothing developed according to Turkish and oriental influences. However, in Vojvodina and along the Adriatic, where Italian and Austrian influences were strong, clothing was largely European in style. During the many traditional festivals, holidays, and folk dances held in the country each year, the old-style clothes are unhesitatingly brought out, ensuring that young generations can appreciate (and wear) the attire of their grandparents' and great-grandparents' days.

Serbia and Montenegro have rich traditions of traditional clothing. The women depicted in this historic image from 1939 are wearing the traditional costumes of villagers in South Serbia. Courtesy of Library of Congress.

The traditional Serbian women's costumes are marked by a remarkable variety of colors, embroideries, and forms, typically geometric and flower motifs. Embroidery is rich and sumptuous, with gold and silver thread adding sheen and contrast. The long, roughly woven one-piece blouse was the customary shirt worn by women, while the *jelek* is a distinctive kind of wool or velvet Serbian waistcoat. Women's jackets were often lined with fur for cold weather, whereas the *nazuvice* (embroidered, knee-length woolen socks) were worn commonly by Serbian women. A *tkanica* is a kind of belt used to contain a variety of skirts, either made of plaited or gathered and embroidered linen. Aprons (*pregace*) were widely worn around the home and usually decorated with floral motifs. The colorful *zubun* is a long hemp waistcoat or dress made of richly decorated red or blue cloth with buttons. Shirts were in the shape of tunics, richly decorated with silver thread, and cords were worn over the shirt. In some areas scarves replaced cords, and caps bordered with cords were worn as headdresses. Girls also wore collars, and clothing was enhanced, especially on special occasions such as weddings, with a string of gold coins hung around the throats of girls, with earrings, bracelets, and caps also decorated with shiny coins or flowers. Girls often wore red caps, while married women covered their heads with folded scarves.

Traditional men's pants in Serbia included both narrow trousers and baggy ones with flared legs (*pelengiri*), one of the oldest and most characteristic forms of clothing in this part of the world. They were typically worn together with straight but overlapping vests (*ječerma*) and short overcoats with sleeves. A leather girder around the belt, known as the *ćemer*, was essential for any self-respecting Serbian or Montenegrin gunslinger and could carry two pistols; gunsmith shops usually made these.

The *šajkača* has been Serbian men's national hat since the eighteenth century and, unlike other traditional dress, is still worn by old people in the countryside. It originally was worn by Serbian sailors from the Danube and Sava rivers fleet in the service of Austro-Hungary. These men were known as the *šajkaši* and bravely conducted raids against the Turks to expedite the escape of Serbian refugees from Turkish territories into the Habsburg Empire. The distinctive hat is easy to recognize. Its top part resembles the curving bottom of a boat's hull when viewed from above, which is how it got its name. The hat became popular as a nationalist symbol from the early twentieth century and was the official hat of the Serbian army in World War I. By contrast, the traditional hat of Vojvodina is thick, and the clothes are marked by black and white tones.

A unique kind of shoe is the *opanak*, a narrow leather shoe with a long, curving hornlike extension on the front. It dates back to the medieval Serb kingdoms and was worn in both Serbia and Montenegro. Montenegrin national dress comes in two main styles: Dinarić (the mountain areas) and the Adriatic, coastal type. The obvious differences relate to cultural influence, temperature, and geography. However, in general, the colors of traditional folk costume in Montenegro are red, blue, and white, like the Serbian flag. The traditional cap used by Montenegrin highlanders (*crnogorska kapa*), a soft, woolen hat with a flat top and embroidery, is very similar to that found in other areas, such as the Republic of Georgia. In Montenegro, this hat typically has the Serbian cross or the initials of turn-of-the-century Montenegrin Prince Nikola embroidered onto a red-colored top. A popular variant replaced this design with the *ocila* symbol conveying the initials for the national motto, "Only unity saves the Serbs" (see chapter 2, "Religion and Thought"). Under Communist rule, the Communist red star replaced these designs, though it was never really accepted. Most recently, a new version depicting the modern coat of arms

Distinctive *opanak* shoes, shown hanging here at a market in the mountain resort of Zlatibor, were the traditional footwear of Serbian and Montenegrin males in olden times. Courtesy of Patrick Horton.

of Montenegro has become increasingly popular, reflecting the latest iteration in a long line of nationalist symbolism.

Modern Fashion

Although the industry is still largely confined to the national and regional level, Serbian designers are starting to make a name for themselves with bold colors and designs. Serbia and Montenegro also boast many fashion models who grace the catwalks of major fashion shows worldwide, blessed by the countries' genes, which make for tall and beautiful people.

Bojana Panić, born in 1985, is one of the top new Serbian models today. She started her international career in Milan and has modeled for important fashion companies in Paris, London, and New York, such as Chanel, Christian Dior, and Yves Saint Laurent. Ana Mihajlović (b. 1986) is another Serbian fashion model who has modeled for Dolce & Gabbana, Givenchy, John Galliano, Prada, Christian Dior, and many others. Mina Cvetković is another young model who was worked with such major companies, as has Vedrana Grbović, a young Belgrade woman named Miss Serbia in 2006. Serbian designers are mainly concentrated in Belgrade and combine chic, minimalist modern styles with expansive cuts and even some counterculture, "rock fashion" patterns. Verica Rakočević is the best known of all. Other famous fashion designers in Serbia include Darko Kostić, Valentina Obradović, and Bojan Božić.

A relatively new forum at home, Belgrade Fashion Week allows Serbian (and international) designers, as well as industry executives and students from Belgrade's Faculty of Applied Arts, to showcase their wares and learn something new about the trends. Belgrade Fashion Week has been held annually since 1996 and operates under the organization of a leading Belgrade designer, Nenad Radujević, and his fashion studio Click, which opened in 1991 as the first private modeling agency in Serbia. Today, this agency works with many of the leading models in the country. The show attracts approximately fifteen thousand guests, though many more watch through various media. It has received plaudits from designers and fashion companies abroad and seems to be going from strength to strength.

NOTES

1. Christopher Deliso, "Bosnian, Serbian Breweries Attract International Investment Interest," February 22, 2004, http://www.balkanalysis.com.

2. For more information, see the festival's official Web site at http://www.belgradebeerfest.com.

3. Indeed, a number of the details of Serbian wines in this chapter come from the Serbian National Tourism Organization's well-illustrated and informative 2007 booklet *Wine Routes of Serbia*.

4. "Slivovitz Becomes Serbia's First Brand," *B92* (Belgrade), September 28, 2007.

6

Literature

ALTHOUGH MOST SERBIAN and Montenegrin writers are not very well known in the West, these countries do have a very rich tradition of literature and poetry. This tradition began with the theological and hagiographical writings of religiously inclined medieval scribes, and it has continued through to nineteenth-century works imbued with the spirit of national awakening, up to the novels and philosophically minded musings of writers in Communist and more recent times. At times, these creators have merged the Serbian and Montenegrin national consciousnesses; at other times, they have taken a highly individual course. Above all, literature in these two culturally (and geographically) close countries has reflected the tactile experience of the human and the natural worlds and the interaction of the nation with a turbulent history of foreign intervention, war, and poverty—and the almost mythic qualities of courage, betrayal, and sanctification born of this experience. In modern times, these characteristics have been tempered somewhat by a wonderful use of comedic devices and juxtapositions meant to poke fun at the behavior of the people, nationalism, religion, or politics.

EARLY SLAVONIC AND CHURCH LITERATURE

Serbian literature is almost as old as the language itself. It is a member of the Slavonic group of languages, which, along with the Romance and Germanic groups, is one of the three largest in the Indo-European family of languages. At the time of the mission of Saints Cyril and Methodius to Moravia, in the middle of the ninth century, the differences among the Slavonic languages were slight, meaning that the heritage of early Slavonic literature is considered a shared one today. By the end of the tenth century, the language created by Cyril and Methodius and their follower, Saint Clement of Ohrid in Macedonia, was known as Old Church Slavonic and had become the liturgical and literary language of Slavs in the Balkans, Central Europe, and Russia.

Serbian ecclesiastical literature was enhanced by contact with the church abroad, especially on Mount Athos in Greece. The "Holy Mountain," as it became known, had been a refuge for ascetics and hermits since the early Byzantine period, becoming more of an organized system of monasteries during the ninth and tenth centuries. The Serbian place in the Orthodox world was amplified considerably by the endowment of a Serbian-populated monastery on Mount Athos, Hilandar, founded by the great King Stefan Dušan. The monasteries here had rich libraries and plenty of interaction with Greek, Russian, Georgian, and other monks, and with the imperial capital of Constantinople, Serbian monks had access to a wide range of texts, including early Church patristics, contemporary commentators, and other theological texts. As a result of their steady translations, they were able to appreciate the content of Byzantine religious and literary thought and its literary style, bringing this understanding back to the monasteries and nobility of Serbia and Montenegro. One of the results of this process was the adaptation of Greek neologisms, many with abstract meanings, into Slavonic, thus enriching the vocabulary of the medieval Serbian tongue.

With Serbian ecclesiastical authors thus developing the skills of expression in the creation of a higher level of language, they expanded the potential to express religious and abstract concepts in their own language, as well as to apply rhetorical figures of speech, following the Byzantine passion for a fairly convoluted literary style. Lingering traces of this influence have survived to the current day in the abstruse and wordy formulations, to Westerners at least, of both ordinary and literary written language.

The oldest surviving example of what can be considered Serbian literature is an illuminated parchment manuscript book known as Miroslav's Gospel (*Miroslavovo Jevandelje*). This 362-leaf manuscript was written between 1180 and 1191. The language used is fairly unique, as it shows signs of linguistic transition between Old Church Slavonic and the first recognizably distinct Serbian language. The manuscript was written by two monastic novices for the brother of King Stefan Nemanja, Miroslav, the Duke of Zahumlje (in modern-day Croatia). Patterned on models of Byzantine didacticism, the manuscript explains the origin of the Cyrillic script and is considered a masterpiece of illustration and calligraphy. Miroslav's Gospel has long resided in Hilandar Monastery on Mount Athos; in 2005, UNESCO added the gospel to the list for its historical and literary significance. The most beautiful surviving Serbian manuscript, however, is the Serbian Psalter of Munich, created in the last quarter of the fourteenth century.

Other medieval Serbian literature included court biographies of rulers and hagiographical texts, or texts about the lives of the saints. Hagiography was by far the most popular style of literature in Byzantium, usually written in very accessible vernacular Greek. The Serbs and other Orthodox peoples picked up this genre, its literary devices, and its themes, from their Byzantine confreres. Hagiographical texts inevitably involve saints providing magical cures, miracles, and other acts of assistance. A permanent suspension of disbelief (i.e., religious faith) is needed to take them at their word; however, historians have found hagiographical texts of great value because they often shed light on social customs, rituals, and even food, drink, and clothing of the common people of the age.

A major Serbian hagiographical writer, Domentian, was a thirteenth-century hieromonk (head monk) in Hilandar Monastery, most famous for writing the *Life of Saint Sava* (1243). Most of what is known about Serbia's patron saint, in fact, derives from Domentian's account. In it, not only Sava but also the whole Nemanja family, and ultimately the Serbian nation, are given divine ancestry. Again under imperial patronage, Domentian also wrote the *Life of Saint Simeon* (1264), influenced by an eleventh-century Ukrainian court eulogy and earlier testimony from Serbian predecessor Stefan Prvovenčani. By the end of the thirteenth century, the hagiography of Saint Sava was rewritten by another monk, Teodosije. While relying on Domentian's account for the facts of his exposition, Teodosije demonstrated a new trend toward realism, attempting to make the saint more human, more palpable, and closer to the reader. He continued this new style of writing in 1310 with *The Life of Petar of Korisa*, a Byzantine hermit. The narrative is even more immediate and offers psychological insights into the mind of the character, thus demonstrating for the first time some characteristics of the modern novel.

FROM FOLK BALLADS AND EPICS TO EIGHTEENTH-CENTURY BAROQUE

Under Ottoman domination, and with an overwhelmingly rural population, medieval Serbia and Montenegro developed a vernacular literature, as did similar European countries; that is, a collection of folk songs and epics passed down orally from generation to generation. The major themes in these epics were historical events, such as the 1389 defeat at the Battle of Kosovo against the Turks. In 1690, the Serbs were forced to leave their lands in Kosovo and Raška with the retreating Austro-Hungarian army. The "Great

Migration," as it would become known, resulted in the transmission of folk literature and poetry into more northern climes, and into a society more influenced by developments in Central Europe. Therefore, while foreign influences began to enter into Serbian literature, an expressive, romanticizing vernacular simultaneously arose, becoming more powerful with the nostalgia-enhancing passage of time.

In Montenegro, the resistance of highland tribes to Ottoman domination meant that a rich and undiluted tradition of folk ballads and legends would remain generally unaffected, protected in the mountain redoubts of shepherds and brigands. However, displaced Serbs adjusting to their new homes in Austrian-held territory soon came under new influences. The academic, well-ordered style of Central European society began to create new generations of Serbian philologists and literary men. And as with art and architecture (see chapter 9), the Ukrainian baroque fashion affected the literature. The direct reason for this influence was a Scholastic gymnasium established in the Serbian city of Sremski Karlovci between 1733 and 1739. Its founders had all previously studied at the Kiev Religious Academy, and from there brought the new baroque literary culture to Serbs' attention. Religious poetry, patriotic verses, and poems written for commemorative events and special occasions began to be penned here, along with two larger verse works: the 1734 baroque drama *Tragedokomedija* (Tragicomedy), by Emanuel Kozačinski, and a collection of poems related to coats of arms and heraldry, *Stematografija* (1741), by Hristifor Zefarović. Another one of the most important Serbian writers of the eighteenth century, and one of the country's first Western-style academics, was Jovan Rajić (1726–1801), a writer of histories, pedagogic texts, and literature.

Another important figure in eighteenth-century literary life was Dositej Obradović (1739–1811), born in a village in the northern region of Banat (today, a part of Romania). Obradović had an extraordinary life, joining the monastic order while young only to become a "fugitive" from his monastery, spending years traveling alone as a wandering monk through southeastern Europe, an experience that deeply affected him and left him very knowledgeable about the various cultures, customs, and peoples to be found in the region. He was especially influenced by the Greeks. However, after striking off for Vienna in 1771, Obradović started to devour Western learning, attending lectures at universities in Paris and London, and he became proficient in both Greek and Latin and all major European languages. No longer a monk, Obradović espoused classic Renaissance learning values and would enthusiastically champion Enlightenment thinking. He urged his countrymen to adopt a new literary vernacular and to eschew the limiting, religion-associated conventions and mind-sets that had always characterized

Serbian thought. Obradović articulated his thought in this regard in texts like his *Letter to Haralampije* (1783) and his autobiographical work *Life and Adventures* (1783–1788). Obradović remains the most important Serbian writer of the eighteenth century and the one who more than anyone else helped introduce the concepts of classical education and secular literature based on Enlightenment thought to his home country.

VUK STEFANOVIĆ KARADŽIĆ (1787–1864)

While not a literary author per se, the nineteenth-century philologist Vuk Stefanović Karadžić is of tremendous importance for the evolution of the Serbian language and the survival of Serbian folk literature. A friend of the German writer Goethe, his work ranged from collecting folk ballads and conducting philological analysis to devising a new system of Cyrillic with "extra" letters for formalized and rational spelling. This was not all, however: leading, and responding to, the growing nationalism of his epoch, Karadžić sought to overthrow the established literary order by replacing the Serbian dialect then prevailing for another. At the time, the so-called Ekavian/Neo-Štokavian dialect, common to Vojvodina and other northeastern regions, was dominant; this owed to more than a century of northerly influence since the Great Migration of 1690 had displaced the Serbs from their ancestral home. However, Karadžić wrote in his own native dialect, Ijekavian, found in Serbian areas of western Serbia, Bosnia, Montenegro, and Croatia. Karadžić's proposals, and the theorizing behind them, appealed greatly to the mass of Serbs who were from these areas and who were then fighting the Ottomans for the full restoration of their lands.

Along with winning the admiration of young Serbian patriots, Karadžić enjoyed respect from scholars abroad. The collections of folk poems he gathered and published fueled a yearning for the "Old Serbia" and enhanced his reputation among nationalists. For scholars today, Karadžić's efforts to commit the oral tradition to pen and paper are an admirable exertion that probably saved poems and stories that would otherwise have been lost. At the same time, his work had obvious political implications. The concept of discovering individual and group identity through language was a new and exciting concept for European thinkers at the time, and in the Serbian case it became the basis for the concept of Yugoslavism, or the inherent similarity of all South Slavs (*yug* means "south"), based on their commonness of language.

In Karadžić's time, concepts of identity in the Balkans were undergoing radical changes because of exposure to trends in the rest of Europe and because of the retraction and replacement of the Ottoman Empire. Under the

Turks, Serbs and other Ottoman subjects had been classified solely according to religion; however, starting in the late eighteenth century, a new focus on ethnic and linguistic identity profoundly altered the course of history and the political aspirations of almost all Ottoman subjects. Critics today sometimes blame Karadžić's linguistic identity logic for the nationalist belief in a "Greater Serbia," in which Croat and Bosnian neighbors are "really" Serbs. Interestingly, however, since the breakdown of Yugoslavia and the establishment of independent republics, the politically encouraged development of distinct Croatian and Bosnian languages, developed with minor alterations of what was essentially a common tongue, seem to show that Vuk Karadžić is back in style.

In his lifetime, Karadžić published ten volumes of Serbian folk poetry he had collected in his travels. Among Karadžić's other major contributions to Serbian linguistics were his lexicographical works: a grammar of vernacular Serbian (1814) and a Serbian dictionary (1818). In 1847, he also translated the New Testament into New Serbian. His successful language reforms included both changing the standard Serbian vernacular and introducing phonetic spellings and new letters to the Cyrillic alphabet. While it certainly seemed unlikely that one man could single-handedly rearrange a whole nation's language, the folk hero prevailed, and by 1868, the Serbian government had removed the last limitations on the use of the revised Cyrillic alphabet.

Petar II Petrović Njegoš (1811–1854)

Deep in the mountains of Montenegro, a literary opus had survived dark centuries of Ottoman domination and, by the early decades of the nineteenth century, was ready to reemerge for the world to see. It was something untouched by foreign influence or studied mannerisms; it was raw, rough, and oddly touching. The *Gorski vijenac* (Mountain Wreath) of the great Montenegrin patriarch-prince Petar II Petrović Njegoš is the culmination of the Serbian folk epic, based on the rhythms of the *gusle* (traditional Montenegrin stringed instrument) that accompanied recitations of the ancient folk songs of this mountain people. The *Gorski vijenac* proved tremendously popular when first published in 1847, and its author remains comparable to Shakespeare or Homer for his stature in the literary history of his language.

The plot of *Gorski vijenac* is set in the context of a contemporary Montenegrin struggle against the Turks. As could be expected, the battle is violent, and this is reflected in the details of the poetry. It is a dramatic poem, in which scenes take the form of dialogues and monologues between the central characters. The major one is a bishop, Danilo, torn between action against the invaders and the desire to preserve his people. This from the start would have struck a chord with the average listener, as this was a choice that many Montenegrins had to make over the years.

In the poem, Bishop Danilo has a vision: he sees the grave threat of Turkish power spreading across Europe, relentless and unstoppable. In his own country, Islamic practices have started to take hold, leaving the bishop to fear the rising power of the infidel amid his own flock. While he and the powerful clan chiefs know that they must wage a war against the Muslims, he fears that the result will be the decimation of the Christian Serbs; thus, Danilo equivocates, like Hamlet, between contemplating action and inaction. By the end of the poem, however, the bishop and his people are cast into the fray, and an epic battle takes place.

The Montenegrin hatred of the Turks, and their constant readiness for battle, shows through clearly. Take the following lines, spoken of an old warlord, Ivan:

In his old hands he held his sword and spear,
and his hands and weapons became bloody.
Counting Turkish corpses with his footsteps,
the old man bounced like a nimble youngster.

The bishop is based on a character from folk tradition; however, Petar II endowed him with some of his own characteristics, making him much more of an intellectual than common folk ballads had him. In addition to his literary work, Petar II is a central figure in the history of the Montenegrin state. Born in 1811 into the ruling family of Vladike (bishop-princes), he studied in monasteries at Cetinje and Kotor at a time when schools did not exist and most of the population was illiterate. After the death of his uncle, Vladika Petar I, he was sent to Moscow at the age of twenty-two to be made bishop, before returning to rule the tiny country. However, before his death in 1851, Petar II had changed history by ending the hereditary theocracy that had ruled Montenegro since the seventeenth century. He was the last Vladika, and after him rule passed to a secular prince. Petar II dreamed of the day when all Serbian territories would be liberated from the Turks, and his literary work reflected this. He idolized Miloš Obrenović, the revolutionary who led the second Serbian uprising in 1815 and established a dynasty that would rule off and on for the next seventy years.

Today, the tomb of Petar II Petrović Njegoš rests more than 5,500 feet above sea level, on the famous Mount Lovcen, where the poet, bishop, and ruler built a chapel for himself. From this peak, one can see all of Montenegro and several other Serbian lands; even in his death, therefore, Petar II was looking toward the lands that had yet to be freed from the Turks. The poet's kaleidoscopic imagination and love of his homeland shine through in evocative lines like these:

> A hundred times I've gazed at floating clouds,
> Sailing as, phantom ships high off the sea,
> And casting anchor on this mountain range!
> Now here, now there I've watched them break away,
> With darts of lightning and with rumblings dread,
> And sudden roar of all the sky's artillery!
> A hundred times have I watched from these heights,
> And quietly basked beneath the genial sun,
> While lightnings flash'd and thunders peal'd below:
> I saw and heard how they did rend the skies;
> Downpours from heaven of most hostile hail
> Robbed Mother Earth of her fertility.[1]

ROMANTICISM AND REALISM

From the mid- to the late nineteenth century, Serbian literature passed through two further influences: romanticism and realism. This was broadly consistent with similar trends then ongoing in the rest of Europe. Considered the founder of Serbian lyrical Romanticism, Branko Radičević (1824–1853) tragically died young, but he left an enduring legacy of poetry. Radičević's work shows an author eager to throw off the creatively restrictive shackles of the baroque style and Enlightenment rationality and to transcend the limits of folk poetry. His sensitive poems show a close appreciation of nature and love, often featuring lyrical stories of young men and women trysting in the great outdoors. Along with these sensual odes to youthful pleasures, however, Radičević also penned more melancholy works such as the harrowing *U licu smrtvi* (In the Face of Death).

Soon after the premature death of Branko Radičević, a new generation of romantic poets appeared in Serbia, establishing the genre as the leading trend in poetry. The first major romanticist after Radičević was the enormously prolific Jovan Jovanović Zmaj (1833–1904). His large body of work consists of poems dedicated to love, the senses, and family. In volumes such as *Dulici* (Roses) and *Dulici uveoci* (Faded Roses), Zmaj expresses a gift for lyricism and heartfelt feeling. His poetry reveals a deep love for his immediate and extended family and a strong affinity for the Serbian nation and humankind in general. Zmaj had an affinity for children, and he also composed children's poetry, creating a marvelous and evocative world of characters and scenes that remains among the best Serbian children's poetry today. Among notable romanticists who wrote more than poetry alone is Đura Jakšić (1832–1878), who also wrote some forty short stories, three full-length dramas, and a novel.

Very different from romanticism was realism, a trend that caught on in the 1870s, at about the same time that realist novels were coming into vogue in America and Western Europe. Realism was in many ways a reaction to romanticism. Rather than sing the lyric praises of nature, beauty, or love, it sought to reveal common life in its simple and unvarnished truth. At the same time, in Serbia, realism meant an almost anthropological examination of local habits and regional singularities. From the archaic to the modern, Serbian realist writers sought to illustrate the customs, characteristics, and dialects of regions within their nation. Along with similar literary production in the West, this impulse also had some overlap with the encyclopedic and journalistic accounts that Western travelers and diplomats were then publishing in the form of books.

By the 1870s, realism had become the leading trend in Serbian literature. This development coincided with the movement of the country's cultural and literary life southward from Novi Sad to Belgrade. As the Serbian state gained more territory and competences in the wake of the Ottoman retraction, there was more of the old "homeland" for curious scholars and writers to explore, and realism lent itself well to the task. In true Serbian style, realism had to proceed according to a theory, and the one that won out was formulated by Svetozar Marković (1846–1875), a socialist and writer. In his articles *Pevanje i mišljenje* (Writing and Thinking) and *Realnost u Poeziji* (Reality in Poetry), Marković emphasized the value of realism in reference to chronicling the stories, historical experience, and folk culture of the peasantry.

The new realist accounts included stories culled from folk life; prominent authors of such included Milovan Glišić (1847–1908), Laza Lazarević (1851–1891), and Janko Veselinović (1862–1905). Other major figures in the nineteenth-century Serbian realist movement were Jakov Ignjatović (1822–1889) and Stefan Mitrov Ljubiša (1824–1878). Again, these writers not only were exploring new territory in the gradually larger and more stable Serbia; many of them were also from these lands. The language reforms of Vuk Karadžić had empowered writers from these previously neglected or underrepresented areas, and the stories they had to tell found an eager readership in the cultivated circles of Belgrade and Novi Sad. As such, writers Glišić, Lazarević, and Veselinović all hailed from western Serbia, while the central region of Šumadija produced two others: Svetolik Ranković (1863–1899), one of the first Serbian novelists and writers emphasizing a psychological reading of characters, and Radoje Domanović (1873–1908), who became known as a satirist.

More major contributions from the "new" Old Serbia included the novelist and playwright Borisav Stanković (1867–1927), known for his most famous play, the 1902 *Koštana* (see chapter 8, "Performing Arts"). Stanković was a realist who has been called the father of the modern Serbian novel. Born in

Vranje in the south of Serbia, an area with strong Turkish and Roma (Gypsy) influences, Stanković had a setting for his work that was exotic in comparison to the Austrianized northern Serbia of Vojvodina, and he told his tales with passion. Along with *Koštana*, he depicted the lives of people in southern Serbia in his novel *Nečista krv* (Impure Blood, or Unclean Blood). This groundbreaking novel was the first Serbian novel to receive favorable reviews when translated into different European languages.

TWENTIETH-CENTURY SERBIAN LITERATURE

In the twentieth century, Serbian literature flourished and myriad young and talented writers appeared. In the second half of the century, under Communism, poetry was considered "safer" than literature, as it was often used to express turgid concepts of Tito's brotherhood and unity and to immortalize the war crimes of non-partisans (i.e., the losing sides) in World War II. However, a rich variety of political and philosophical ideas have exemplified the genre over the past fifty years, and in Danilo Kiš and Milorad Pavić, Serbia has produced two Nobel Prize–nominated authors whose work is regarded very highly abroad.

The most beloved Serbian poet of the twentieth century, Desanka Maksimović (1898–1993) worked as a literature professor and later became a member of the Serbian Academy of Arts and Sciences. Maksimović was expressive and emotional, and her poetry was inspired primarily by scenes of great joy or great tragedy; for example, when the Nazis murdered children in the 1941 Kragujevac massacre, she was moved to write a poem immortalizing the evil in "Krvava bajka" (A Tale of blood). Maksimović had great versatility with the Serbian language and in her poetry was able to evoke deep emotions. Her best poems include "Predosećanje" (Anticipation), "Prolećna Pesma" (Spring Poem), "Opomena" (Warning), and "U Buri" (In the Storm). Another one of her best-loved works is "Strepnja" (Apprehension, or Trembling), a lyrical poem that incidentally won Maksimović her first writing award. The poem is as follows:

> No . . . don't come to me! I want to adore
> and love your two eyes from far, far away.
> For, happiness's beau just while waiting for—
> when only allusion comes out of its way.
>
> No . . . don't come to me! There is more allure
> in waiting with sweet apprehension, fear.
> Just while seeking out everything is pure;
> it's nicer when just foreboding is near.

No...don't come to me! Why that, and what for?
Only from afar all stars spark and glee;
only from afar we admire all.
No...let not your eyes come closer to me.[2]

Another pioneer of women's literature in Serbia was Isidora Sekulić (1877–1958). She is known for creating strong female characters in a time long before feminism, and she had considerable success with her novels, essays, and critical articles. For Sekulić, a major concern were the transformations of modern life as she experienced it, and her stories reflect the issues and problems that came with the Industrial Revolution's transformation of an essentially rural, agriculture-based society into an urban one. Sekulić's most famous work, *Kronika palanačkog groblja* (The Chronicle of a Small-Town Cemetery), is a fascinating collection of tales that Sekulić accumulated following the death of her father, when she began to spend hours by his grave. In the cemetery, she started listening to the gravediggers' stories about the people who were buried there. She assiduously wrote the stories down in a small notebook, publishing the best of them in her novel.

Poet, author, and diplomat, Miloš Crnjanski (1893–1977) started out as a journalist. He went on to become one of the leading figures in Yugoslav literature. As a poet, he was considered a romanticist, but as a novelist he discussed broader themes of history, with emigration and the fate of refugees being recurring themes. Crnjanski's related works, *Lirika Itake* (1919, The Lyrics of Ithaca), *Seobe* (1920, Migrations), and *Druga knjiga seobe* (1962, The Second Book of Migrations), are vividly told historical novels based in the eighteenth century. These highly original accounts examine an unusual event in Serbian history: what became of the Serbs who fled into Hungary and then into Russia, fighting for the czar in epic battles all over Europe. Crnjanski's later book, *Roman o Londonu* (1971, A Novel about London), takes a different angle on the same theme of alienation and emigration, depicting the lives of characters who are diaspora members far away from home in the British capital.

Danilo Kiš (1935–1989)

One of the most important writers in later-twentieth-century Serbian, and indeed European, literature was Danilo Kiš. Born in Vojvodina of a typically ethnically complex family (he was of Hungarian, Jewish, and Serbian background), Kiš was a first-rate, intellectually demanding writer whose modernist list of influences was topped by the Argentinean short-story writer Jorge Luis Borges. Indeed, Kiš once stated that the world of the short story could be divided into two periods: before Borges and after Borges. At the time of his premature death in 1989, Kiš had been expected to receive the Nobel Prize for Literature, and he left tragically unfinished a work that was expected to have been his greatest novel.

The influence of Borges is clear in early works such as *Bašta, pepeo* (1965, Garden, Ashes) and runs up through his masterpiece, a short-story collection titled *The Encyclopedia of the Dead* (1983). Kiš's first two novels, *Mansarda* and *Psalm 44*, were published in 1962. One of his most famous works, *Peščanik* (Hourglass), was published in 1973; it depicts the apparently mundane life of a nameless railway clerk referred to simply as "E. S." However, the story, which is set in 1942, takes on more surreal and horrifying tones as it continues, with the petty family squabbles and bureaucratic concerns that consume the clerk's attention set against the simultaneous mass murders, suicides, and disappearances of local Jews. The overarching literary structure of the book is a series of questions and answers presented to E. S. by an unseen interrogator; at book's end, a final letter discloses that the preceding story was simply a manuscript, the creation of the unnamed clerk, meant to be just "a bourgeois horror story."

Milorad Pavić (b. 1929)

One of Serbia's most inventive and unorthodox writers, Milorad Pavić has been acclaimed far and wide for his innovative work as an author, translator, and literary historian. Each of his five novels has been translated into English, among many other languages. Like Danilo Kiš, Pavić was strongly influenced by eccentric modernist genius Jorge Luis Borges, and in his writing he, like Kiš, plays with form and organization. His stated goal in several of his novels has been to usurp the convention of reading a book from beginning to end.

For example, his novel *The Inner Side of the Wind* (1993) can be read from two different starting points. His 1998 book *Last Love in Constantinople: A Tarot Novel for Divination* comes equipped with tarot cards, for the reader to better understand the book or even to read his or her own fate from it! And Pavić's novel that is most famous abroad, *Dictionary of the Khazars: A Lexicon Novel* (1984), consists of several short stories—he calls them "entries"—and allows the reader to begin anywhere he or she chooses. "I always think of my reader," Pavić has said. "I offer him a choice—millions of possible paths for reading. And, the more the book he has read differs from the one I have written, the better I have dealt with my task."[3]

Such intriguing, demanding, and revolutionary thought has made Milorad Pavić very popular among literature lovers in Serbia and abroad. *Dictionary of the Khazars* is indeed one of the most remarkable novels in world literature today. The subject of the book is, ostensibly, a historical question: the fate of the mysterious Khazar people, a tribal group that inhabited today's southern Russia and Ukraine and converted to Judaism the early ninth century. The Khazars would finally vanish, but Pavić's book does not provide any help in putting the pieces together: rather, he soon departs from his supposedly historical quest, and it becomes clearer and clearer that his characters are primarily fictional.

Although numerous information claiming basis in fact is presented, in the end there is little resemblance between Pavić's depiction of the Khazars and what historians know of them today. Rather, the ostensible topic serves as a device to keep a certain nonlinear narrative line in place: the book takes the form of three cross-referenced mini-encyclopedias, one for each of Christianity, Islam, and Judaism. The novel may thus be read from anywhere, with the connections between individual entries thus becoming subjective and unique. *Dictionary of the Khazars* is thus both a challenge to the reader and to the genre of the novel in general. In the methodical madness of this book, the influence of Borges is quite strong, and one is especially reminded of the Argentine writer's short storys *Tlon, Uqbar, Orbis Tertius*, in which a secret society of intellectuals conspires to create the features, sciences, attributes, politics, and so on of a make-believe planet via their encyclopedia entries.

NOTES

1. The English-language version of *The Mountain Wreath*, in expert translation by Professor Vasa D. Mihajlovič, is available online at the Rastko Project for Serbian Culture Web site, http://www.rastko.org.yu/knjizevnost/umetnicka/njegos/mountain_wreath.html#wreath.

2. This translation is the standard one composed by noted Serbian author and translator Dragana Konstantinović (b. 1961).

3. Ilmars Slapins, "The World from the Viewpoint of Milorad Pavic," http://www.eurozine.com.

7

Media and Cinema

For the greater part of my life I have lived in fiction; in the company of unusual people in even more unusual circumstances.
—Dušan Kovačević, Serbian screenwriter and director[1]

MEDIA IN SERBIA and Montenegro have a very long history. With *Politika*, Belgrade boasts the oldest daily newspaper in the Balkans; even today it is the most respected in the country and is sold in other former Yugoslav republics as well. Serbia and Montenegro have numerous television and radio stations, both public and private, and several of them have influence on forming and directing public opinion on a gamut of issues, from popular music to politics. Recent years, however, have seen numerous difficulties in media development. The problem today is not so much a lack of freedom of speech or state repression (as occurred up through the Milošević regime), but rather economic pressure to conform from new ownership, whether local or foreign. Serbia, with its population of 7.5 million people, remains attractive for foreign investors, as recent acquisitions have shown; nevertheless, the long-awaited improvement of standards resulting from the involvement of major European players in the media industry has failed to materialize. Arguably the biggest lingering problem with media in Serbia and Montenegro is the tendency toward sensationalism, especially in regards to political and security issues, something that can be especially volatile in a region where nationalist emotions typically run high and controversial issues (e.g., Kosovo) remain unresolved.

With cinema, there is a much happier story to tell in regards to Serbia and Montenegro. Although Serbs have been making movies since even before the First World War, their cinema did not become world famous until the breakdown of Yugoslavia in the 1990s, when directors like Emir Kusturica put the country definitively on the map of world cinema. The days of Communism were marked mostly by lighthearted, slapstick comedies accompanied by gratuitous amounts of flesh, as well as the mandatory war movies glorifying the exploits of the Communist Partisans in World War II. Today, a Balkan film genre (which not even its creators agree exists) has arisen in reaction to the convulsions of the 1990s. Employing an often absurd juxtaposition of rational and irrational events and reactions, in seemingly haphazard fashion and with heavy doses of black humor, such films have been used as a means of coming to grips with and describing the chaos and contradictions of the past two decades of war and economic and political turmoil in the Balkans. Although this genre has definitely left its mark, with numerous films gaining international acclaim since the 1990s, there are signs that directors in Serbia (and other former Yugoslav countries) are turning away from this to explore new thematic horizons. Nevertheless, a certain amount of Balkan surrealism and black humor will undoubtedly remain in Serbian cinema of the future.

MEDIA

Throughout all the tumultuous events that have transpired in Serbia and Montenegro since the breakup of Yugoslavia in the early 1990s, the media have followed the stories—but much more than that, they have helped to create them and to create a platform for those with political ambitions. Today, the man who ruled during the entirety of the 1990s, the late Slobodan Milošević, is particularly associated with this phenomenon. In reality, though, media was charitable to all sides at various points. Even today, anyone who has political aspirations in Serbia or Montenegro quickly becomes associated with specific media that support or oppose his or her goals. In Montenegro, this scenario played out between the two largest daily newspapers, *Vijesti* (News) and *Dan* (The Day) during the 1990s and up until the successful independence referendum of 2006. The former newspaper was largely supportive of the government of Milo Đukanović and his close supporters, all of whom came to favor independence. On the other hand, *Dan* was associated with the Serbian party in Montenegro that did not want Montenegro to be independent. Intimidation, accusations, and beatings characterized the relationship between the different camps, and one head of *Dan* was even killed. The struggle has, since the referendum, moved on to the political control of *Vijesti* and the state television station, Radio-Television Montenegro. When, in 2007, the partial owner of

Vijesti, Željko Ivanović, was beaten, critics pointed out that it was "a logical consequence of almost two decades of strife within Montenegrin society in which the media have been mostly seen—and used—as political tools."[2]

Further criticism of the media in general has been registered regarding editorial influence over journalists, professional laziness, and especially the machinations of rival businesspeople, who often have a controlling stake in the media in question. As analyst Dragan Doković put it in a recent study:

The publishers cannot keep their hands off the editorial work; they continue to wage private warfare using their media and give preferential treatment to certain political or business parties. Covert advertising and commissioned or paid articles remain regular practices. Investigative journalism is being neglected, maybe because of the weak interest in finding the truth. There are attempts to promote investigative journalism, but these are somehow limited to enthusiastic ventures, not appealing to professionalism. When some media reveals the truth, it often means that they gain some benefit from doing so, and that they are endangered by an opposing position. But, in Serbia, it seldom happens that editors or owners are ready to pay for an investigation for the sake of truth itself.[3]

In the 1990s, Serbian journalists suffered intimidation and even beatings because of the political clannishness surrounding the Milošević regime. However, the most brazen attack on journalists occurred in April 1999, when the supposed occupants of the moral high ground, NATO's "humanitarian" bombers, targeted the Radio-Television Serbia building in Belgrade, leaving sixteen dead and scores injured, trapped in the rubble for days.[4] Frightened journalists had on the evenings before begged NATO not to kill them on the air; there was an outcry from most international journalist federations afterward, with little contrition expressed on the part of the military alliance. NATO claimed that the broadcasting building was a "legitimate" target because it was airing "propaganda" supporting the Serbian government; of course, no one suggested bombing CNN's Atlanta headquarters, even though it was later proved that a U.S. Army PsyOps (Psychological Operations; i.e., propaganda) team had been "helping" the CNN studio editors in the "production of news" during the Kosovo bombing.[5]

Newspapers

The official Serbian state news agency, essentially a wire service that delivers feeds to the print, broadcast, and online media, is Tanjug. Its Montenegrin equivalent is MINA. Information tends to be simply phrased and sums up accurately official notices from the government, press conference information, briefs of official government activity, and the like. The state agencies in Serbia and Montenegro do not attempt, as does National Public Radio (NPR) in America, to create feature stories, reviews, or other extraneous content. There is no real American equivalent to these state information agencies, which are prevalent in many countries and work in similar ways throughout. Although the Serbian information agency had a bad reputation for disseminating strictly propagandistic information during Tito's Yugoslavia and again under Milošević, this was never actually the case on a comprehensive basis, and it is certainly not the case today. Large Western bodies routinely quote the Serbian and Montenegrin state agencies when they have factual information to share.

Serbia has a number of newspapers, the oldest being *Politika* (Politics). Its very first issue rolled off the presses on January 25, 1904, making it the oldest newspaper in Serbia and indeed in the Balkans. It is considered somewhat akin to the *New York Times* of Serbia, and it can be found on the newsstands of neighboring countries. *Politika*'s slightly retro font and format add to this image. It is considered the best source of "serious" news in the country. The Politika Group consists of three companies: Politika AD, Politika Newspapers & Magazines, and RTV Politika. In 2001, a deal gave German media giant WAZ 50 percent of the company, with 50 percent remaining with the founding Ribnikar family. The complex deal involved numerous leaders and a banker and was led by Zoran Đinđić. Later, WAZ also bought Novi Sad–based *Dnevnik* and the Montenegrin newspaper *Vijesti*, out of Podgorica. The company also bought several papers in neighboring Macedonia, among other places.[6]

At least in circulation, *Večernje Novosti* (Evening News) is probably the most popular in Serbia today, with more than two hundred thousand copies sold a day. It is also a serious newspaper, somewhat less staid than *Politika*, and it has been around for fifty-five years. *Blic*, another daily news provider, sells about 150,000 copies, and its stories are often influential. It was founded in 1996 with German-Serbian capital but in 2001 became wholly owned by a subsidiary of German media giant Bertelsmann. *Glas Javnosti* (Voice of the People) is a more nationalist, right-wing paper that sells eighty thousand copies daily. It was started in 1995 by former *Blic* (Flash) journalists, who originally wanted to call it *Novi* (New) *Blic*, until a judge decided that this would be copyright infringement. *Blic*'s owner, Radislav Rodić, also owns *Kurir* (Courier). He and his media group were targeted by Milošević during the 1990s for opposing his policies.

Other high-circulation dailies are somewhat more lowbrow. *Kurir* is a very popular tabloid, strong on sensationalism, style, and celebrities, but also with some dedicated news coverage and, like the others, with a cut-and-paste synopsis of world news from international sources. It has the highest circulation in Serbia. The newspaper originally emerged after the assassination of Zoran Đinđić, when state regulators attacked *Nacional* (National), the previous Belgrade tabloid, because it had run articles critical of the state's declaration of a state of emergency following the killing. *Svet* (World) and *Skandal* (Scandal) are two other print tabloids, weekly ones that concentrate mostly on sex scandals involving Serbian celebrities and the less intellectual side of Serbian popular culture. *Svet* also has its own local editions in Bosnia's Republika Srpska, in Montenegro, and in Macedonia, meaning that the poor celebrities of those countries are also regularly in for the *Svet* treatment.

Magazines

Serbia's best and oldest existing weekly news and politics magazine is *NIN*, established in 1935. *NIN* regularly offers the best investigative journalism that, though sometimes sensational or nationalistic, is generally more credible than most of the newspapers. Similarly to *NIN*, which was originally launched by the Politika Group but has since largely broken off from it, Serbia's other main weekly magazine, *Dnevnik*, was founded by *Politika* journalists (in 1990). It was funded by the well-known Belgrade lawyer Srđa Popović.

Other magazines include *Danas* (Today) and *Ilustrovana Politika* (Illustrated Politics), the first issue of which came out in 1958. In Serbia, all sorts of magazines exist on many topics, including babies and mothering, autos, computers, and the paranormal. Women's magazines are also popular. *Lepota i Zdravlje* (Beauty and Health) and *Ljubav* (Love), with respective circulations of seventy thousand and forty thousand copies, are two of the most popular. Major Western magazines like *Elle* and *Cosmopolitan* are available in Serbia as well. A problem with such "fluff" magazines in the Balkans, and perhaps further afield, is that they are very prone to borrowing content, both from one another and from outside publications. Usually, this seems to be because there is little fear that the original creators of a magazine or Web site article appearing originally in English-language media will notice—or even look for—translations of the same article in a Serbian- or other Balkan-language magazine. Although statistics are not available regarding this, a quick and careful examination usually reveals a certain amount of recycling. Despite laziness and a lack of original content, this phenomenon also points to occasional allegations that in the region, a number of publications seem to exist largely to assist the money laundering of their owners.

Television and Radio

Whereas print media in Serbia and Montenegro have seen large foreign investment inroads, television and radio largely remain in the hands of powerful local business tycoons. In at least two cases (Pink TV and B92 TV), an original radio format became the launching pad for breaking into the television market. Television remains a very powerful force for shaping ideas, trends and tastes, and even political loyalties.

Of Serbia's many stations, Pink TV has been considered the most popular in recent years. It began life as a radio station specializing in the glitzy Turbo-folk music that became popular in the early 1990s. Owned by businessman Željko Mitrović, who was elected to the Yugoslav Federal Parliament in the 1990s and was very close to the Milošević administration, the station became a potent political force. Critics state that the reason for this influence was its subtlety: its enormous manipulative and political potential is actually based on its (alleged) absolute lack of political interest. This actually runs counter to the Western conventional wisdom regarding Eastern European television and the public, which has tended to argue that state-owned media represents the biggest mouthpiece of any dictatorial administration. However, while Mitrović did get early assistance in starting his company from the head of public television RTS (Radio-Television Serbia) Milord Vučelić, his station turned to be a much more significant lever for controlling public opinion than was RTS.

In 1999, annual revenue stood at US$2–3 million, whereas only four years later total revenues stood at $20 million per annum. Today, Pink is a very large company, one of the largest in Serbia, and has multiple holdings. With its satellite transmission, the station reaches the large Serb diaspora in Europe as well. However, while the company was founded and originally profited from association with the Milošević regime, as soon as that leader's political fortunes changed, the station quickly embraced the new leadership and has since shown other signs of chameleonlike behavior. Most recently, in 2008, it was reportedly approaching an American public relations firm to clean up its image and become a respectable provider of "real" news. This has been reflected by a new policy that has sought to lessen the amount of flesh that female singers can show in the videos and performances aired on the network, thus going against the policy that initially brought Pink so much success.

Another popular network owned by local tycoons is BK TV, founded in 1994. The initials stand for the Braća Karić, or "Brothers Karić." The Karić family is one of the richest and most successful dynasties in Serbia. Their BK television station is just one of around twenty companies in a group that in 2003 enjoyed a profit of more than $200 million. The Karić brothers are also owners of a mobile phone operator and a private university in Belgrade.

Both TV B92 and Radio B92, which started in 1989 as an experimental student-run station, were the darlings of the opposition at the time of Milošević's fall in October 2000. Unsurprisingly, it is 48 percent owned by an American media development fund, which means it has a different variety of political influence. Nevertheless, the B92 broadcast media and Web site remain important and widely viewed news media in Serbia. B92 is one of the few Serbian Web sites with dedicated English-language translation, further increasing its stature as a voice of Serbia in the outside world. It considers itself a voice of democracy and critical viewpoints and has indeed been critical of the various governments from Milošević to today. However, this does not mean that it does not defend the Serbian national interest from time to time, and the station and Web site do also criticize perceived policy mistakes of Western countries as well in relation to treatment of Serbia.

New Media and Internet Usage

The most popular Web sites in Serbia and Montenegro, such as Beograd Cafe (http://www.bgdcafe.com) are, as could be expected, oriented toward popular culture and sports. The major news Web sites are extensions of the biggest print and broadcast outlets in the country; however, most of them do not have dedicated English-language translations (B92 is a notable exception). This indicates that the news in Serbia, even when presented to the world via the Internet, is still largely intended for domestic consumption and domestic interests. However, a number of Serbian and Montenegrin journalists have made names for themselves by writing as local correspondents for English-language Web sites specializing in the Balkans as well as large media outlets such as wire services and newspapers in the United States and Britain. Serbs and Montenegrins have also adapted quite quickly to the YouTube craze and blogging, posting all manner of videos about daily life, sports, national issues, and so on.

Dial-up Internet connections became available in Serbia and Montenegro in 1996 and remain the dominant form of connection today. DSL connections arrived only in 2005. As in other Balkan countries, the monopoly of the fixed operator (in this case, Telekom Srbija) slowed the growth of competitive providers and resulted in high prices compared to other European countries, with customer packages offering meager amounts of bandwidth. Statistics say that Serbia has 1.4 million Internet users, or approximately 14 percent of the population, though this is probably higher in actuality. The same goes for Montenegro's stated number of Internet users, fifty thousand, or 8 percent of the population.[7] Nevertheless, Internet usage is a major fact of life today in Serbia and Montenegro, Internet cafés are widespread, and it is mostly the older generations who have little or no experience of it.

The Internet and computer technology in general are also starting to play a larger part in the new media, advertising, and marketing efforts of companies in these countries. According to a report from the Serbian government in 2007, most private companies now use the Internet in one way or another, with marketing and advertising being the most common use.[8] Some 62 percent of all companies now have a Web site; 82 percent of all large companies do. Between 2005 and 2006, the percentage of companies receiving orders via the Internet doubled (from 8 to 16 percent). However, the surveys indicate that 40 percent of these wired forms are still using dial-up, which slows the pace of business. Nevertheless, as elsewhere in Europe, usage of the Internet for promotion, transactions, networking, and other functions will only continue to grow rapidly in Serbia and Montenegro.

Book Publishing

In Yugoslav days, Belgrade's capital status made it a haven for the literate elite, and it remains a place for book lovers and educated ideas. Serbia and Montenegro have numerous publishers of books, companies that expanded considerably following the end of Communism's stifling hold on publications. They include Mladinska Knjiga-Beograd, a sixty-year-old company with headquarters in Ljubljana, Slovenia, and subsidiaries in several other Balkan countries. Another publisher, Paideia, is relatively new, operating since 1991 and offering a wide range of general-interest titles. The much newer Agora Publishing House was established in 2002 (and originally as merely a bookshop) in Zrenjanin, northeast of Belgrade. This publishing house specializes in contemporary literature, producing works of both local and foreign writers, indicating that Belgrade's old literary culture is not completely dead. Finally, the Academic Thought publishing house is, as the name suggests, a publisher of textbooks and academic studies that number more than 350 at present.

Stubovi Kulture publishing house started in July 6, 1993, primarily as a literary project, but in the following years it grew into a project of general culture and historiography. This approach includes a group of the finest of the Serbian authors and the most prominent ones from the whole world. The Serbian authors of Stubovi Kulture are practically the only Serbian writers whose books are continually being translated in Europe and Northern America.

CINEMA

Cinema in Serbia goes back to the days when Serbia was a kingdom and the Ottoman and Austro-Hungarian empires were still in existence. Owing to its much smaller size and resources, Montenegro has not really been able to make its mark in the world of film. Serbian cinema, however, has achieved worldwide acclaim with the films of directors like Emir Kusturica. Today, Serbian cinema is most often associated worldwide with edgy works of the 1990s and, in more recent years, with large doses of black humor and Balkan absurdity to spice things up, as mastered by Kusturica in award-winning films like *Underground* (1995) and *Black Cat, White Cat* (1998). Movies dealing directly with the recent wars in the former Yugoslavia have also reached an attentive international audience, such as Goran Paskaljević's *Balkan Cabaret* (1998) and Srdan Dragojević's harrowing 1994 take on the Bosnian conflict, *Pretty Village, Pretty Flame.*

Today in Serbia there is a thriving young generation of actors and directors who, bolstered by the success of the previous generation, are working hard to develop and expand the genre beyond its now stereotypical Balkan identity. Despite economic difficulties, Serbian cinema remains capable of turning out up to ten new movies in a down year, many more in a good one.

Cinema in Royalist and Communist Yugoslavia

Serbian cinema dates back almost to the very beginnings of cinema itself, with the first Serbian movie created in 1911. In those days (and after), film-making was considered a new vehicle for spreading patriotic fervor among the nation. A silent film based on the life of Karađorđe Petrović, leader of the first Serbian uprising in 1804, was the inaugural motion picture created in Serbia. The film, *Karađorđe*, was directed by the film pioneer Čiča Ilija Stanojević, who also acted in it. Of the twelve films produced in Serbia before the start of World War II, most had similar nationalist or historical themes, such as Mihail Popović's *The Battle of Kosovo* in 1939, the 550th anniversary of the battle.

During the first half of Tito's Communist reign, some topics became off-limits, or at least not to be contemplated, particularly political ones. Tito's general policy of stifling nationalism in his potentially fractious republics in the name of brotherhood and unity also meant that certain historical epics should take more recent history as their preferred subject matter. In Communist times, the entire Yugoslav cinematic output was approximately eight hundred films; of these, at least five hundred were devoted to events of World War II glorifying the Partisan cause.[9]

Because of his goal of suppressing any possible ethnic nationalism, Tito discouraged cinematic depictions of previous conflicts. Thus, only one film dealing with World War I, for example, was produced, in 1964: *Marš na Drinu* (*The March on the Drina*) by the prolific director Zivorad Mitrovac (1921–2005). This epic film depicts the heroic resistance of the Serbian royalist army at the Battle of Cer in 1914, where the much more powerful Austro-Hungarian forces were beaten back. Since the Communist authorities so disapproved of such nationalist-oriented art, media shunned the film, and the details of its production have remained secret long after the fact.

An example of a World War II epic is the very successful 1969 film *Bitka na Neretvi* (*The Battle of Neretva*), the dramatic account of a key battle in 1943 that pitted the Axis powers against Tito's Partisan rebels on the Neretva River in Bosnia. The film was written by Stevan Bulajić and Veljko Bulajić and directed by the latter. One of the things that makes the film unique is that it featured genuine Western film stars, Yul Brynner and Orson Welles, and the American composer Bernard Herrmann wrote the score for the film's English-language version. Partly because of this star power, the film was nominated for an Oscar in the category Best Foreign Language Film.

Another Serbian filmmaker especially known for his 1960s work was Živojin Pavlović (1933–1998). Obsessed with sweeping aside the curtain of Tito's happy world of brotherhood and unity, Pavlović depicted the world of Yugoslavia's most marginalized and abandoned people. For this, the filmmaker became associated with the so-called black wave realist movement in 1960s film. Among his numerous films was 1967's *Budjenje pacova* (*The Rats Woke Up*). The film revolves around the activities of a downtrodden, depressed man hoping to improve his meager lot in life. In the process he becomes hopelessly deluded when he falls in love with a girl whom he erroneously thinks will elevate his fortunes. Actually, she absconds with his borrowed funds, leaving the man more embittered and miserable than in the beginning. For this film, Pavlović won the Silver Bear at the Berlin Film Festival and the gold at Yugoslavia's main festival, the Pula Film Festival in Croatia, one of several he would receive during his career.

Toward the end of Yugoslavia, filmmakers had success with comedies (indeed, many Yugo-nostalgics today look back on the 1980s as a kind of golden age of social life). *Maratonci trče počasni krug* (*The Marathon Family*) is a dark comedy from Serbian director Slobodan Šijan that has attained cult status in the former Yugoslavia. Today it is widely considered one of the peak moments in all of Eastern European cinema and eerily prescient in light of the subsequent violent breakup of the country. Set in the 1930s, it tells the story of five generations of morticians, the Topalović clan, and the young son, Mirko, who hopes to escape the family business. Times are tough from the economic point of view, and the business becomes even more unsavory when the Topalović's are forced to rely on one Billy Python (played by Zoran Radmilović) and his grave-digging criminal gang to get cheap, recycled coffins. Mirko, however, falls for Kristina, the daughter of this local gang leader. However, when both she and Mirko's best friend betray him, the young man kills her. The film ends with a final, apocalyptic gang war between the Topalović family and Python's criminals. Jelisaveta Sablić, who played the role of Kristina, won the Best Actress award at the 1982 Pula Film Festival in Croatia.

Modern Serbian Cinema

With the decline and dissolution of Yugoslavia, a new genre of filmmaking began to emerge. It was a direct reflection of the experiences of people who, until very recently, had lived in peace and were trying to grapple with the sudden new realities of war, social dislocation, and economic breakdown. While films dealing with such themes can be found the world over, the unique blend of black humor with surreal juxtapositions of sadness and joy, creativity and destruction, logic and irrationality made ex-Yugoslav films stand out.

Dušan Kovačević (b. 1948)

The genius behind much of modern Serbian cinema is a man known more for writing screenplays, often based on his own plays, than for directing. Yet Dušan Kovačević has contributed to most of the important films to be produced in Yugoslavia in the past three decades and composed twenty plays, which have been translated into numerous languages.

Born in 1948 in Mrđenovac in Vojvodina, Kovačević studied in Novi Sad before gaining a bachelor's degree in drama studies from the University of Belgrade in 1973. He worked in television for several years while writing plays. In fact, at the age of twenty-three, he had already composed a play that he would adapt into a screenplay for one of Serbia's greatest films: the 1982 *The Marathon Family* (see above). In 1984, he wrote the screenplay for and co-directed the comedy film *Balkanski špijun* (*Balkan Spy*). A hilarious send-up of the paranoia and irrationality intrinsic to the Communist system, the film centers on the exploits of an ordinary Serb, Ilija, who becomes certain that his neighbor is a dangerous spy and that assassins are out to get him. When the secret police drop in for a "routine" questioning, Ilija starts looking on his neighbor—a man fresh from a business trip to dangerously capitalist Paris—with newfound suspicion and starts his own espionage and surveillance operation against the unwitting man.

A few years later, Kovačević adapted his play *Proleće u januaru* (*Spring in January*) to become the screenplay for Emir Kusturica's award-winning 1995 film *Underground* (see subsequent sections). According to Kovačević, he and Kusturica had to work through sixteen revisions to get the final screenplay down. All in all, this equaled more than two thousand pages of text. "When we agreed to make a film of it, I worked for more than three years. It is a kind of work one could not make any more today. We were a group of workaholics, directed by Kusturica, towards and against all the external pressures," he stated years later.[10]

Along with several other projects, Dušan Kovačević in 2003 wrote and directed *Profesionalac* (*The Professional*), a film that uses the unlikely meeting of two Belgrade men to flash back on a decade of turbulent experience in the Serbian capital. The film concerns the interaction of Teja, the educated director of a publishing house, and Luka, a taxi driver who claims to have been an agent of the state security services. Luka discloses that for a decade he was tasked with keeping Teja under regular surveillance, due to the latter's liberal pretensions and anti-Milošević views. Other unexpected revelations and events happen throughout the film, which has echoes of Kovačević's *Balkan Spy*, made two decades before.

Most recently, he has adapted a play originally written to be the screenplay of *Sveti Georgije ubiva azdahu* (*Saint George Shoots the Dragon*), a film released in late 2008 by acclaimed director Srđan Dragojević. The most expensive Serbian movie ever made, the film is based on a true story that Dušan Kovačević was told long ago by his grandfather, Cvetko Kovačević, who as a boy had been called on to help the war wounded. In 2005, Dušan Kovačević was appointed Serbia's ambassador to Portugal. An ardent nationalist, he also belongs, oddly enough, to the Crown Council of Aleksandar Karađorđević, descendent of the royal line ousted during World War II.

Goran Paskaljević (b. 1947)

Goran Paskaljević is one of Serbia's most respected directors today. His filmmaking career began in 1976, but he really received attention abroad with his 1998 take on the recent Yugoslav wars, *Cabaret Balkan*. The film was actually based on Macedonian playwright Dejan Dukovski's award-winning play *Bure Barut* (*The Powder Keg*; the film is also sometimes referred to by this name). The film takes place in Belgrade, on a cold winter night in which physical and moral darkness has gripped the city. The characters themselves become personified powder kegs, prone to reacting violently to any external threat or challenge. The pressures of war, restrictive politics, and economic privations have left the society on the verge of disintegration.

In the various snapshot vignettes that comprise the film, the lives of twenty people cross and are affected in violent ways; structurally, this device anticipated those of several Hollywood movies made in recent years. The people involved all engage in acts of provocation and retributions, as with the man who destroys an apartment belonging to a man whose son trashed his car. The interactions of estranged lovers, former antagonists, and friends who discover their mutual betrayal are just some of the other stories that play out in the film. All in all, it is a story of a city's misplaced frustration and anger, in which personal suffering is clumsily revisited on innocent victims. Today,

Cabaret Balkan is considered among the top five films to deal with the period of war in Yugoslavia.[11]

Srđan Dragojević (b. 1963)

One of the most successful Serbian directors of the 1990s, Srđan Drago-jević studied directing at the University of Belgrade and soon enjoyed a break-through moment with his first film, the 1992 *Mi nismo anđeli* (*We Are Not Angels*). Along with directing the film, Dragojević also wrote the screenplay. This tragicomic plot revolves around the characters of an Angel (played by Uroš Đurić) and the Devil (Srđan Todorović), comically fighting for the soul of Nikola (Nikola Kojo), a local playboy unaware that he has impregnated a young high school girl named Marina (Milena Pavlović) during a drunken one-night stand. The film was an immediate hit in Serbia and other former Yugoslav countries, with its idiomatic language, frequent pop culture refer-ences, and fresh directing making it an instant classic.

After working in directing television programs for two years, Dragojević returned in 1994 with the much darker *Lepa sela lepo gore* (*Pretty Village, Pretty Flame*) set in wartime Bosnia. The film attracted huge interest, with some eight hundred thousand people flocking to cinemas to see it. Like many war movies, the plot was based on real events taking place on the ground. It tells the story of a detachment of Bosnian Serb soldiers who became trapped inside a tunnel by a Bosnian Muslim detachment, going into the mentality of characters, young soldiers who have different emotions and reactions to the fighting. This dramatic and darkly humorous film sparked controversy in Croatia and Bosnia, as could perhaps be expected. Critics in those coun-tries charged that the movie dramatized wartime atrocities carried out against Serbs, but portrayed those perpetrated by Serbs in an ironic, almost comic light.

Nevertheless, *Lepa sela lepo gore* is considered a modern classic in Serbia. In 1998, Dragojević's following film, *Rane* (*Wounds*), painted a much bleaker and more damning picture of wartime Serbia, perhaps partially a reaction to comments made about his previous film. A film critical of Serbia under the Milošević regime, *Rane* depicts the violent lives of two Belgrade boys trying to become gangsters. The contextual backdrop of the film is war in Yugoslavia and especially the growing level of hatred between Orthodox Serbs and Catholic Croats. When asked about the film's violence and depressing nature while promoting this film in America in 1999, the director made a memorable response: "I can't escape the subject; this is my life. If I were a Swiss director, I'd probably be making films about garden roses."[12] Critics have praised Dragojević as being "one of very few people who manage to show how things look from the point of view of Serbs."[13]

After these two films raised interest in Dragojević internationally, he got a deal with American film giant Miramax. However, despite spending two years in America and coming close to working with major American actors on multiple occasions, the opportunities all fell through in the end and the Serbian director ended up returning home in 2003. Since then, Dragojević has continued making films, his most recent being *Sveti Georgije ubiva azdahu* (*Saint George Shoots the Dragon*), released in late 2008, a World War I drama that will be the most expensive film in Serbian history (excluding Yugoslavera war epics) at 5 million euros.[14] A significant amount of the funding has come from the governments of Serbia and Bosnia's Republika Srpska, owing to its national significance.

The film covers the period from 1912, when Serbia was at war with the Turks, through the ensuing Great War. It tells a fascinating story of the jealous rivalry between one village's able-bodied young men packed off to fight and its substantial population of invalid veterans from previous wars. When the former are sent to the front lines, rumors begin to circulate that the latter are wooing their womenfolk left behind in the village. To prevent a mutiny, the army chiefs are forced to recruit the invalids, too. The leading role in the film (that of the village policeman, Đorđe) is played by Lazar Ristovski, famous for his role in Kusturica's *Underground*, among many others. In the film, Đorđe becomes suspicious that his wife will be seduced by her former lover, Gavrilo, who lost his arm in previous battles.

Interestingly, the idea for the film comes from a true story that Dušan Kovačević, the film's screenwriter, was once told by his grandfather, Cvetko Kovačević. In 1914, Cvetko had been a young boy ordered to help the war effort by transporting the dead and wounded via oxcart to a field hospital during an important battle, the Battle of Cer in Vojvodina, in which the Serbs beat back the mighty Austro-Hungarian army. It is fascinating to note the symmetry between this film and the only non–World War II military history drama to be made during Communist times, the 1964 *Marš na Drinu* (*The March on the Drina*). Both films focus on aspects of the same epic battle, though telling the story was an infinitely riskier venture during Communism, when Tito sought to suppress any iterations of ethnic nationalism, including *The March on the Drina*. To Serbs, therefore, it is a bit of poetic justice that the story can finally be told and supported as they believe it deserves.

Emir Kusturica (b. 1954)

Arguably the best and certainly the most celebrated film director in Serbia today is Emir Kusturica, the only director other than Francis Ford Coppola to have won the Cannes Palme d'Or twice. Born into a secular Muslim family (his father described himself as an "atheist," Kusturica later recalled),

Kusturica moved to Serbia and has spent most of his life there since. Bosnian Muslims have expressed anger at the director for allegedly "turning his back" on his native country by moving to Serbia. However, Kusturica himself grew embittered when, during the war, Muslim paramilitaries ransacked his family's uninhabited apartment in Sarajevo. His shocked father died three weeks later of a heart attack; Kusturica said "this war killed him too."[15] Devout Muslims were even more irritated when Kusturica converted to Christianity and built an Orthodox shrine atop the traditional village he built in western Serbia's Mokra Gora mountains, Drvengrad (Wooden Town) or Kustendorf, as it is now officially called.[16] The impulsive director recalled the moment when the idea first dawned on him, revelation-like, to create the town: "one day when I was shooting I noticed a shaft of light hit the hillside. 'There I will build a village,' I thought."[17]

Kusturica has always been a controversial figure, but one whose larger-than-life behavior and blunt honesty have also won him many admirers. Although he has plenty to say and even plays guitar in a side band (the internationally known No Smoking Orchestra), Emir Kusturica primarily lets his films do the talking. He first sparked attention in the late 1970s, when winning awards while still a film student. His career began with television shorts in Yugoslavia, but he was quickly catapulted to fame when his first full-length film, *Do You Remember Dolly Bell?* (1981), took the Golden Lion at the Venice Film Festival. The setting for the film was 1960s Sarajevo, where a young Bosnian man, Dino, enjoys himself with an escapist world of cinema, rock music, and hypnosis. However, when he falls in love with a cabaret girl who is actually a prostitute, things take a wild turn. The uproarious film piqued the interest of Western film lovers eager to see what was going on in the still exotic Eastern European world of cinema.

Kusturica's second feature film, *Otac Na službenom putu* (*When Father Was Away on Business*), was also critically acclaimed, winning the prestigious Palme d'Or at the world's premier cinematic event, the Cannes Film Festival, in 1985. The film also won five first-place awards at Yugoslav film festivals and was nominated for an Oscar in the Best Foreign Film category. Set in 1950 in Bosnia, the film unfolds from the point of view of a Bosnian youth who believes that his father has gone away on a business trip when, in fact, he has been sent to a labor camp after authorities suspect him of working for the Soviet Cominform. Numerous bizarre things happen throughout the film, such as when the boy finds out about his father's affair with a female pilot, who later tries to commit suicide with a toilet's flush cord.

In 1988, Emir Kusturica moved to telling the unsung tales of Yugoslavia's most marginalized people, its large Roma (Gypsy) population. His fantastical *Dom Za Vešanje* (*Time of the Gypsies*) explores their unique, transient, and somewhat chaotic culture. The complex film tells the story of a Roma teen named Perhan and his tumultuous relationships with his family and girlfriend. Perhan aspires to marry a local girl but is prevented from doing so by her mother. Ahmed, a Roma man of ill-gotten wealth, comes to town, and Perhan leaves his caring grandmother Khaditza, ostensibly to put his lame sister Danira in a Slovenian hospital. However, Ahmed deceives him and recruits him into his criminal ring in Milan. After becoming rich, Perhan returns to his village to find that his love, Azra, is pregnant, he angrily suspects, by another man. However, they marry in spite of his concerns, until Azra dies after giving birth to the baby. Among other odd twists, Kusturica's unusual hero Perhan is blessed with telekinetic powers (which, incidentally, led to a minor craze among Yugoslavs attempting to move things with their minds), and in the end he uses them to kill enemies Ahmed and his brother communicate telekinetically with a fork. However, Perhan is then killed by Ahmed's bride, and in the end, at Perhan's funeral, the coins ceremonially placed over his eyes are stolen by his son.

The bizarre film received both plaudits and criticism, primarily from Roma community leaders in the Balkans, who claimed that Kusturica had just shown the worst elements of their culture with his film. However, it became another favorite (young audiences were especially excited when Azra, played by Macedonian actress Sinolicka Trpkova, bared her breasts in one romantic scene). The Roma element nevertheless continued, in the form of a soundtrack consisting mostly of traditional Gypsy brass band music, in Kusturica's next film, *Podzemlje* (*Underground*), which features a screenplay by the eminent Dušan Kovačević. Released in 1995, *Underground* became Kusturica's biggest hit to date, winning him another Palm d'Or for Best Feature Film at the Cannes Film Festival that year. The pulsating soundtrack, heavy on infectious, chaotic brass band music, was created by Serbian composer and musician Goran Bregović and featured the famous Serbian Roma trumpet player Boban Marković (see chapter 8, "Performing Arts").

The complex storyline of the film takes place between the years 1941 and 1961, a period running from the war to Communist Yugoslavia. Although therefore a period piece, *Underground* had clear modern implications for the conflict in Yugoslavia, which was winding down when the film was released. The overarching plot is of the deception of one man, Blacky (played by famous Serbian actor Lazar Ristovski) by his best friend, Marko. After being accused of being Communists in German-occupied Yugoslavia, the two go underground in Marko's grandfather's cellar, along with Marko's brother and Blacky's pregnant wife, to escape arrest. After an intolerably long time underground, Blacky resolves to return to the world and kidnap his actress lover, Natalie, who has gone with a German officer. However, she turns him down, and Blacky is arrested. His friend Marko comes to save him, but a grenade accident results in a severe injury to Blacky, and he is forced to recuperate underground. As time wears on, he is led to believe by Marko that danger remains and dutifully remains underground, preparing munitions for a war long over. By the end of the film, Marko has married his friend's former lover and is enjoying the prestige of a high-ranking Communist post in Tito's new Yugoslavia. The slogan of the film—"Once upon a time, there was a country"—indicates its symbolic value, pointing out the tragically fratricidal nature of the breakup of Yugoslavia.

On the heels of this success, Emir Kusturica went on to win the Venice Film Festival's Silver Lion for yet another Gypsy film, the 1998 *Crna mačka, beli mačor* (*Black Cat, White Cat*), set in a Roma settlement on the Danube in eastern Serbia. This film was so over the top that some Roma voiced their indignation with the director's portrayal of a wild, violent, drug-taking society of wheeler-dealers with little regard for conventional principles of morality. However, the film simply reflected some of the characteristics of Roma life as the director had experienced them and featured excellent examples of traditional Roma music.

In *Black Cat, White Cat* there is a bewilderingly large cast of characters, most of them members of two local families. The head of the first, Matko Destanov, seeks to pay off a large debt by marrying his seventeen-year-old son Zare to the undersized sister of a wealthy local gangster, Dadan. However, Zare is in love with someone else, and the sister, Afrodita, is waiting for the man of her dreams. While everything ends happily ever after, at least for some, it is a wild ride along the way, the surreal gags involving imploding outhouses, dead men on ice who reawaken, accordions stuffed with money, and, of course, a black and white cat, the only witnesses to Zare's ultimate marriage to his love, Ida. Although some critics found *Black Cat, White Cat* too preposterous for its own good, others recognized that it was just a madcap director having a bit of well-deserved fun and that, as in all fiction, there was a little bit of truth to it.

Emir Kusturica's most recent major success was the 2004 *Life Is a Miracle*. Much more relaxed and contemplative than his previous films, it nevertheless does take place in a wartime setting, in 1992 Bosnia. The film is based on the true story of a Bosnian Serb engineer, Luka, who refuses to believe that war will soon break out. His son, Miloš, is drafted into the Bosnian Serb army but captured by the Muslims. When Luka is offered Sabaha, a Bosnian Muslim woman, as a hostage to exchange for his son, he experiences tormented loyalties because he and Sabaha, confused by the irrational chaos gripping their land, end up falling in love. Unlike many other war movies, *Life Is a Miracle* is balanced in that there are both good guys and bad guys to be found among both the Bosnian Serb and Bosnian Muslim warring sides.

As a director, Emir Kusturica is known for his demanding, and sometimes seemingly irrational, perfectionism. In *Life Is a Miracle*, he shot the same scenes for twelve full nights—and in the end, never used a second of the footage.[18] In recent years, Kusturica has been increasingly outspoken in his criticism of Western consumerism and Hollywood's "factory-produced movies," which he argues are debasing the art of filmmaking. Posing the rhetorical question of where the Frank Capras of the world have gone, Kusturica argues: "What you have now is a Hollywood that is pure poison. . . . Hollywood was a central place in the history of art in the 20th century: it was human idealism preserved. And then, like any great place, it collapsed, and it collapsed into the most awful machinery in the world."[19]

In fact, Emir Kusturica has only directed one Hollywood film, the offbeat *Arizona Dream* (1992), which starred Johnny Depp and Jerry Lewis. Although the film was not a huge commercial success, it did win critical acclaim with a Silver Bear at the Berlin Film Festival in 1993. While Hollywood has knocked several times on his door, Emir Kusturica has shown little interest in compromising his ideals for the sake of American exposure and lucre. He also has strong political views, openly opposing globalism and the American wars in Kosovo and Iraq, for example. In 2008, he made a splash at the Cannes Film Festival, though he did not enter his film in any competition, with his biographical documentary of Argentinean soccer legend Diego Maradona. Some loved it, while others were less impressed, with one British reviewer pronouncing that in the film, "Kusturica's egotism has met its match in Maradona's."[20]

Regardless of what some of his critics think of him, Emir Kusturica shows no signs of slowing down, and his legions of fans eagerly await his next films. His success has put Serbia definitively on "the map" of European cinema, and has served as an example for young Serbian filmmakers and actors of the generations to come.

NOTES

1. Quoted in Jasmina Lekić, "Dušan Kovačević: u potrazi za proćedranim vremenom," *Novine* (Toronto), http://www.novine.ca/intervju/intervju-1088-kovacevic.html.

2. Dragoljub Duško Vuković, "Beating Lifts Veil on Dirty War for Montenegro's Media," Balkan Investigative Reporting Network (BIRN), September 12, 2007.

3. Dragan Dokovic, "Media Ownership and Its Impact on Media Independence and Pluralism: Serbia." Ljubljana, Slovenia: Peace Institute.

4. Richard Norton-Taylor, "Serb TV Station Was Legitimate Target, Says Blair," *The Guardian*, April 24, 1999.

5. See Christopher Deliso, "The CNN Factor and Kosovo," May 11, 2005, http://www.balkanalysis.com.

6. See Christopher Deliso, "Analysis: Print Media Moves on S.E. Europe," United Press International, July 28, 2003.

7. Information according to the CIA World Factbook on Serbia, https://www.cia.gov/library/publications/the-world-factbook/.

8. Dragan Vukmirovic, Kristina Pavlovic, and Vladimir Sutic, *Usage of Information and Communications Technologies in the Republic of Serbia.* Statistical Office of the Republic of Serbia, 2007.

9. These estimates were made by Dušan Kovačević; see Lekić, "Dušan Kovačević."

10. Dušan Kovačević's comments are recorded on Emir Kusturica's official Web site, http://www.kustu.com.

11. John Anderson, "A Serbian Director's Eye Remains Fixed on Uncomfortable Truths," *New York Times*, January 9, 2008.

12. Nancy Ramsey, "Film: Growing Up in Belgrade with Suitably Black Humor," *New York Times*, August 22, 1999.

13. Ibid.

14. At time of writing, the movie had not yet been released. See its official Web site for any updates or changes: http://www.azdaha.com.

15. Dan Halpern, "The (Mis)Directions of Emir Kusturica," *New York Times*, May 8, 2005.

16. Information about this unusual project, and all of Kusturica's work, is available on his official Web site at http://www.kustu.com/.

17. Fiachra Gibbons, "I Will Not Cut My Film," *The Guardian*, March 4, 2005.

18. Ibid.

19. Halpern, "(Mis)Directions."

20. Andrew Pulver, "Diego Maradona and Emir Kusturica: A Meeting of Egos," *The Guardian*, May 20, 2008.

8

Performing Arts

In a house where the *gusle* is not heard, both the house and the people there are dead.
　　　　—Petar II Petrović Njegoš, nineteenth-century Montenegrin poet, in
　　　　　　　　　　　　　　　　　　　　　　　　　The Mountain Wreath

Britney Spears and Madonna could never be a success here like I am.
　　　　　　—Svetlana "Ceca" Ražnatović, Serbian Turbo-folk singer[1]

MUSIC, DANCE, AND theater have been at the heart of life in Serbia and Montenegro for centuries, and these countries have given the world many acclaimed and imaginative creative works. Over time, they have both reflected and responded to larger socioeconomic and political developments, but at all times they have proved a critical release for the Serbian people.

THEATER

Serbia's tradition of large-scale, organized theater dates to 1861, when the Serbian National Theater was first established in Novi Sad. It was the oldest professional theater in the South Slavic lands. Seven years later, founder Jovan Đorđević answered a request from Prince Mihailo Obrenović and opened a national theater in Belgrade as well.[2] Opera performances started from the end of the nineteenth century, with a permanent national opera (which in turn established a national ballet) not being established until 1947.

During the second half of the nineteenth century, when resurgent nationalism was gripping Serbia and the Balkans, this was also reflected in the productions of the Serbian National Theater. Along with the "compulsory" classics and modern masters (e.g., Sophocles, Shakespeare, Molière, Ibsen, Chekhov), numerous theatrical performances, grand and heroic spectacles inspired by Serbian medieval and more recent history, were on the bill. One of the first plays to break this trend in the early twentieth century was the *Koštana* of Borisav Stanković (1902), a recognized classic today. The action takes place in Stanković's native town of Vranje in southern Serbia and incorporates several of the playwright's favorite themes, such as longing for lost youth, love of women, and local patriotism. The play includes references to Serbian folklore and village customs of the time, which are part of its enduring attraction.

The Belgrade Drama Theater, or Beogradsko Dramsko Pozorište (BDP), is the city's official urban theater and has been active since 1947, when it excited audiences particularly with performances of contemporary American playwrights. The memorable productions of the 1950s and 1960s included the Serbian adaptations of *Death of a Salesman*, *The Glass Menagerie*, and *A View from the Bridge*. Today, the BDP works with a repertory artistic company and performs both classic and avant-garde plays. A reconstruction of the theater building in 2003 has brought the BDP to a high European theater standard. The long-running but recently restored Pozorište na Terazijama (Theater on Terazije), named for the area of Belgrade where it stands, is a Broadway-style theater and the only one to perform musicals exclusively. Serbia is also an important destination for theater lovers in Europe. The Belgrade International Theater Festival (BITEF), founded in 1967, is one of the world's oldest theater festivals. Today it is considered one of the top five European theater festivals.

Founded in 1953, the Montenegrin National Theater (Crnogorsko Narodno Pozorište) is located in the capital, Podgorica, and is the little country's only professional theater, working closely with the University of Montenegro's Faculty of Drama in Cetinje. However, Montenegro's seasonal theater offerings increase dramatically with the influx of tourists to the coast in summer. In July and August, the action shifts to the Adriatic town of Budva, where regular theatrical performances featuring productions and actors from the Balkans and outside world are held.

OPERA

The Serbian National Opera developed within the Serbian National Theater, and after some interruptions held its first performance on February 11, 1919. Conductor Stanislav Binički led the performers through Giacomo Puccini's opera *Madame Butterfly*, to generally favorable acclaim. The operas that followed this were also mostly from Italian composers such as Verdi and

Rossini, and they were also received very favorably. Serbian composers of the day who had their operas performed here include Stevan Hristić, with his *The Sunset*, and Petar Konjović, with his *Prince of Zeta* (see the section "Classical Music" herein). Konjović also wrote an opera based on the beloved 1902 play *Koštana* by playwright Borisav Stanković.

Aside from the National Opera, an intimate private opera house, the Madlenianum Opera and Theatre has been working since 1998 in Zemun, a northeastern suburb of Belgrade. The founder and main benefactor of the opera house, Madlena Zepter, made with Madlenianum the largest such investments in opera in Europe. Although it does not have a permanent ensemble, the opera has continuous organization and administration, and in 2005 it was completely refurbished and reconstructed. This opera is the major cultural and artistic center in this populous area of Belgrade.

The standout Serbian opera singer of the twentieth century was Bosnia-born Miroslav Čangalović (1921–1999). A powerful bass, he is considered today among the top operatic voices in Serbian and Yugoslav history and in his long career starred in more than ninety roles. He debuted in 1946 in Belgrade National Theater's opera house, playing the role of the jailer in Puccini's *Tosca*. Critics consider his superlative role, however, that of Boris Godunov from the eponymous Modest Mussorgsky opera. All in all, his concert repertoire consisted of 520 pieces, including solos, song cycles, cantatas, and oratorios. In his career, Čangalović received numerous international operatic awards, including the French government's chevalier de L'ordre des Arts et des Lettres, given for Čangalović's contribution to promoting French culture.

Today, Serbian opera continues to flourish, with many world-known opera singers. One of the most renowned living opera singers is soprano Jadranka Jovanović. Her first role, after she earned two degrees in the theory of music and solo singing in Belgrade, was at the National Theater in Belgrade, where she played the character of Rosina in Rossini's famous *The Barber of Seville*. Soon after, Jovanović began a career internationally in Milan, appearing in *Carmen*, and continued to sing primarily in Italy but also in opera houses, festivals, and theaters the world over. Slavko Nikolić, currently first tenor at the Belgrade Opera, has had a similarly distinguished career. He is noted for his expressive voice and great range, and has appeared in starring roles in all of the classic operas by composers such as Verdi, Rossini, Tchaikovsky, and more in opera houses around the world.

Two other contemporary Serbian female singers, sopranos Jasmina Jasna Šajnović, Biserka Cvejić, and Suzana Suvaković-Savić, are also considered among the best that Serbian opera has to offer. Both are principal singers at the Serbian National Opera in Belgrade. The former became a star when just sixteen years old while dazzling the judges at an English choir competition with an interpretation of an aria from Mozart's *The Marriage of Figaro*. The latter launched her solo career after winning five international competitions in the mid-1980s. Since 2002, she has appeared at all of the major Italian opera houses.

MUSIC

Music in Serbia and Montenegro has always been close to the heart of the people and throughout history has both accompanied mysterious rituals associated with religion and has been associated with things like politicians and big businesspeople—not mysterious at all, except as to their sources of funding. Music today continues to play a powerful role in society in general. Serbs and Montenegrins, with many festivals and celebrations on their annual calendars, keep especially close to their roots with folk music and dancing at weddings and other events. In some parts, especially the eastern edges of Serbia, wailing funeral laments of long tradition are also kept up. Raucous and fast-paced brass band music, as seen in summer festivals and films from the region, is especially characteristic of the Serbs and their minority Roma (Gypsy) population.

Early and Traditional Music

Traditional music among the Serbs and Montenegrins goes back to the rituals of their Slavic tribal forebears in the pagan, and subsequently Christian contexts. One ritual with undoubtedly pagan roots involved the flower-bedecked "rainmaker" girls of the village, who would organize to dance about their villages to coax the skies to open with rain. Processional songs accompanied by cross and icons characterize rural life after Christianization, and the synthesis between the two civilizations can be found in the songs performed on traditional instruments in adopted Christian winter carnivals and ceremonies for saint's days and the like. It is known from the records of Byzantine historians and foreign travelers that the Slavs were using stringed instruments (at least) as early as the Middle Ages.

Serbian medieval music would develop under Byzantine influences, especially after the twelfth century. Certainly the strongest and most enduring such influence was religious—the tradition of Byzantine chant. Technically, the style employed in Serbian churches developed under Byzantine influence, and especially from practices on Mount Athos in Greece, where the Serb-endowed Hilandar monastery allowed Serbian monks access to a steady stream of Byzantine cultural practices. Any visitor to an Orthodox Church or monastery in Serbia and Montenegro today can enjoy this form of vocal music and appreciate that it has remained relatively unchanged for many centuries.

The academic Miloš Velimirović (1922–2008), who studied in Belgrade but afterward went on to study and teach for most of his life in America, was a pioneering researcher on the subject of Byzantine chant and its adoption in the early Slavic and Serbian worlds.

Forms of culturally unique popular music started to take shape during, and essentially in reaction to, the Turkish occupation of the late fourteenth to nineteenth centuries. During this time, "official" music of the state died out along with it, and it was left to the rural populations, with their simple instruments and folk ballads, to preserve the musical heritage of the Serb people. Only in Austrian-controlled Vojvodina was the situation somewhat different. Here, musical (as other) styles were more integrated with Central European culture, and here as well the development of Serbian classical music occurred first, in the eighteenth century.

The content of Serbian and Montenegrin folk music is fairly predictable: epic ballads of bravery commemorating the struggle against the Turks, often based on historical events, and more uplifting tunes meant to accompany rural seasonal celebrations, especially weddings. Serbian folk music, as elsewhere in the Balkans, can be tricky for Westerners to tap along with, since many songs use unusual time signatures that are less simple than the steady 4/4 of pop-rock tunes. This adds to the hypnotic, slightly Eastern feel of much Balkan folk music, characterized by long, tonally static tones enhanced by repeated trills as a kind of lead. Brass band music, on the other hand, often features rapid changes of tone and time signature and complex, multiple riffing in bands that may often have more than fourteen members.

The provenance of traditional instruments used in Serbian and other Balkan music is a never-ending question of influence in which most countries claim that the (fairly identical) instruments they use were either invented by themselves or else are to at least be especially associated with their nation. Leaving this vexed question aside, we can say that Balkan music and its instruments are a result of a unique synthesis of indigenous sounds and instruments and the Eastern ones brought by the Ottomans, with some areas, however, having very specific and unique characteristics. In the case of Montenegro, the national instrument is the *gusle*, a maple-wood, long-necked instrument quite similar to the *rebab* used among Arabian Bedouin tribes. The fact that the *gusle* has but one string and that Montenegrin folk songs are fairly monotone in nature have only added to the traditional jokes about their stereotypical laziness.

Gusle players, known as *guslari*, play a double role: they are also minstrels, able to memorize and sing or recite back the long narrative poetic epics that refer to the country's dark but glorious past. The *guslari* also often improvise their own additional lyrics, all of which follow a decasyllabic (ten-syllable) count, unlike Byzantine folk poetry in Greek, which followed a fifteen-syllable pattern. *Gusle* players played a crucial part in ensuring that Serbian epic poetry survived through the centuries, passing on these epics in the oral tradition before the days of sound recording could save them for posterity. The great nineteenth-century philologist Vuk Stefanović Karadžić collected many of these epics in his research.

One of the best-known Serbian traditional instruments is the *frula*, basically a small wooden flute with six holes. As elsewhere in the Balkans, the *frula* was traditionally played by shepherds to help pass the time while tending their flocks up in the hills. A very famous Balkan instrument is the *gajde*, a single-chamber bagpipe that possibly originated in the plains of Anatolia and was brought by the Turks. It is usually made from sheepskin or goatskin, and playing it correctly requires tremendous lung power. The *gajde* features prominently in many folk songs, not only in Serbia and Montenegro but also around the region. Other popular instruments include the accordion, especially associated with the northern Banat region and elsewhere in Vojvodina, where Central European and Romanian influences predominated. The violin (*violina*) is a widely used instrument, both in traditional and classical music. It is used mainly in ensembles.

Brass Band Music

The form of traditional music closest to the Serbian soul, however, is the music of the brass band. It has its historical roots in the revolutionary, military spirit of the early-nineteenth-century uprisings of Karađorđe and Miloš Obrenović, when the trumpet was first brought to Serbia from the West, where it had already been established in martial music. Official brass bands, with European melodies and grand presentation, came into being. Alongside the disciplinary and ceremonial nature of this music, in its official use by the military, the trumpet began to be used not long after its introductions for entertainment purposes. With it, Serbs even began to transpose their folk songs into a new medium. However, Serbian brass as we know it today would attain its ultimate form, combining musical complexity with passion, only when it was adopted by the Roma (Gypsy) populations living in Serbia and the Balkans in general. Gifted with innate musical ability and bringing their full, complex variety of rhythm and melodies into play, the Roma created a popularized, danceable, and somewhat exotic genre that we know today as "Gypsy brass."

The most famous masters of this genre tend to lead orchestras, many of eight or more members. Internationally, the best-known Serbian representative of Gypsy brass is the Bosnian-born composer Goran Bregović (b. 1951). Originally emerging as a guitarist in the early 1970s Yugoslav rock

Roma (Gypsy) children playing for passersby. Serbia is renowned for its Gypsy brass bands, and brass music is an important part of traditional customs and ceremonies such as weddings, funerals, and feasts. Each summer, a raucous three-day celebration and musical competition, the Guča Trumpet Festival, is held in the small village of Guča. Photograph by Rafael Estefania.

scene, he became known for brass music when he ventured into writing film scores. Bregović's breakthrough project was when he wrote the score for Emir Kusturica's *Time of the Gypsies* (1989), the beginning of a fruitful partnership with the legendary director (see chapter 7, "Media and Cinema"). He then composed the music (which was actually performed by rock star Iggy Pop) for Kusturica's next film, *Arizona Dream* (1993), which Johnny Depp starred in. Bregović became associated permanently with Gypsy brass, however, when he composed the film score for Kusturica's cult classic, *Underground* (1995). Bregović's music here is an exciting fusion of traditional Serbian brass music, Balkan polyphonic music, pop themes, and even Latin tango. The composer's rock origins are in evidence in the *Underground* soundtrack as well, and the driving intensity of much of the music made it very danceable and an instant hit. Today, many favorites from that album, such as the vibrant "Kalashnikov," are still played widely on television and at bars and events. Since *Underground*, Bregović has been much in demand, writing several other film scores and touring with his infectious Orchestra for Weddings and Funerals.

   While Bregović is the best-known composer of brass music worldwide, the most acclaimed performers of the music include Fejat Sejdić, Bakija Bakić, and Boban Marković. The last of these is especially well known and was the only trumpeter to win perfect scores from every judge at the annual Guča Trumpet Festival (see chapter 4, "Holidays, Customs, and Leisure Activities"). The Boban Marković Orchestra has been the leading brass band in Serbia for almost twenty years and has won numerous awards. Many trumpeters, such as Fejat Sejdić, are self-taught. This often owes to the poverty of life in Roma communities and the lack of formal schools or academies for such music, which is passed on from generation to generation. For example, Marko Marković, the son of Boban Marković, joined his father's orchestra after having practiced ten hours a day by himself to earn his place. Sejdić himself has been a leading figure in Serbian music for four decades, playing in front of the highest Yugoslav leaders, such as Josip Broz Tito and Slobodan Milošević. The best Serbian brass bands have expanded their audiences significantly over the past decade or so and are to be found in festivals, documentaries, and concerts the world over with their highly distinctive sound.

Classical Music

Classical music in Serbia and Montenegro sprang up somewhat later than in the rest of Europe because of the political instability and economic deprivations that accompanied the transformation of an Ottoman possession into an independent state. Theater music was performed in Kragujevac in central Serbia as early as the period of Miloš Obrenović (leader of the second Serbian uprising in 1815), and later in the National Theater in Novi Sad (founded in 1861). Orchestra concerts began in 1842 in Belgrade and received a major boost not long after eminent composer Johann Strauss appeared for a guest performance with his orchestra. His musical selection included original compositions inspired by Serbian folk melodies. After Strauss, other foreign composers and performers began to appear in Serbia as well. Gradually, Serbia began to produce its own stream of composers, musicians, and singers, some of whom by the end of the nineteenth century had achieved success performing in Germany, Hungary, and France.

Stevan Stojanović Mokranjac (1856–1914) was one of the pioneers of classical music in Serbia, and he remains the most accomplished Serbian composer and music teacher of the nineteenth century. With Mokranjac, a strong sense of folk and ecclesiastical music was fused with the classical style to create unique compositions; his most famous such compositions were the fifteen "Rukoveti" (literally, works by hand, or handmade), an assortment of classicized folk songs from across Serbia and former Serbian lands. He also wrote choral arrangements for church services based on traditional Serbian melodies, which are still sung today.

The next major classical composer after Mokranjac was Stevan Hristić (1885–1958), who played a dominant role on the classical orchestra and opera scene in the first half of the twentieth century and founded the Belgrade Philharmonic Orchestra. His two major works were the *Symphonic Fantasy for Violin and Orchestra* and *Rhapsody for Violin and Piano*. His other works drew inspiration from Serbian tradition and history, such as the *Opelo in B minor* (a Serbian Orthodox requiem), and the ballet *Ohridska legenda* (The Legend of Ohrid, after the fortified Macedonian town held by the Serbs in the Middle Ages), his most famous work. His composition *Resurrection* was the first Serbian oratorio (1912). Petar Konjović (1883–1970) was another significant Serbian composer of the Yugoslav periods, whose expressive works often evoked nationalist and folk themes. Many were for opera scores, at a time when that genre was just getting off the ground in Serbia. His most famous works are the operas *Vilin veo* (A Fairy's Veil), *Knez od Zete* (The Prince of Zeta), *Seljaci* (Peasants), and *Otadžbina* (Homeland). His *Koštana* was an adaptation of the very popular play of the same name by Vranje-born playwright Borisav Stanković.

Classical music in Serbia has survived the various wars and political uncertainties that have plagued the country over the past two decades. Among noteworthy modern-day performers is the young violin maestro Stefan Milenković (b. 1977), who began playing under his father's tutelage at the age of three. Today a concert violinist and teacher at the Juilliard School and the University of Illinois, Milenković's illustrious career has included performances before then–U.S. President Ronald Reagan in 1987 and subsequently Mikhail Gorbachev and the late Pope John Paul II. At the age of twenty-six, he was named a faculty member at Juilliard, where he also became a teaching assistant of the famous Itzhak Perlman, an Israeli-American violinist, conductor, and pedagogue, one of the most distinguished violinists of the late twentieth century. Milenković has already won numerous prizes and competitions for his skill and released several albums.

Rock and Controversy

Rock-and-roll music has a long history in Serbia, and indeed in the former Yugoslavia, whereas in other Eastern European countries it manifested as both innocuous pop and on occasion pointed political or social critique that brought performers into a collision with the Communist (and post-Communist) authorities. However, compared to Soviet states, Tito's Yugoslavia was a fairly liberal place, so much so that it appealed to American hippies and liberal theorists in the 1960s and 1970s. Rock first came to the country early on, influenced by American and British acts from Elvis to the

Beatles and the Rolling Stones. From the late 1960s, a number of homegrown rock groups became popular in Yugoslavia, like the YU grupa, a pioneer in using Serbian folk music elements in rock music, and Smak, which combined its rock approach with jazz and blues influences. As in many other things, Belgrade became Yugoslavia's capital of rock, with the biggest concerts and some of the best bands being from there.

The 1980s represents what many look back on as the golden age of Yugoslav rock. With Tito's death and the future of the country more uncertain than ever, rock music provided an outlet both for public doubts and unrest and for simple, straight, to-hell-with-the-future exuberance. During this decade, the Belgrade scene gave birth to various new wave bands, such as Električni Orgazam, Ekatarina Velika, Oktobar 1864, and Partibrejkers.

Riblja Čorba

Among the groups to emerge from the Belgrade scene in the 1970s was Riblja Čorba (literally, fish stew, though also a slang term for menstruation). When the group began in 1978, it combined a 1970s-style hard-rock sound with blues riffs and satirical lyrics. The band's leader, Bora Đorđević, has often caused controversy with his (usually) socially critical lyrics. This biting sarcasm was evident in the band's very first single, "Lutka sa naslovne strane" (Doll on the Front Page), a hard-rock ballad about a fame-hungry model that quickly became a hit on the radio. Riblja Čorba's debut album, *Kost u Grlu* (Bone in the Throat), was released the following year and spawned several more hits, selling a then-notable 120,000 copies.

The band's zenith as social critics occurred a few years later, when the Communists went after them for songs that could be read as dismissive of Tito's revolution. Actually, one did not have to dig deep into lyrical analysis to get the point behind "Za ideale ginu budale" (Fools Get Killed for Their Ideals) and "Kreteni dižu bune i ginu" (Jerks Rise Up and Get Killed). Before a concert in Sarajevo, lead singer and songwriter Đorđević had to write an "explanation" for the offending lyrics. Then, in 1983, Yugoslav state censors decreed that two songs—"Mangupi vam kvare dete" (Those Rascals Are Ruining Your Kids) and "Besni psi" (Wild Dogs)—were "ethically unacceptable." The embarrassed authorities were reacting to the indignation of Arab, African, and Greek diplomats at the lyrics to the second song: *Grčki šverceri, arapski studenti, negativni elementi, maloletni delikventi i besni psi* ("Greek smugglers, Arab students, negative elements, juvenile hooligans, and mad dogs"). Several embassies lodged official protests, and the Yugoslav Ministry of Culture ordered an "analysis" of the song by a panel of "experts." For the average Serb, however, the song, drawing on common stereotypes, was just amusing.

However, Đorđević's later involvement in more serious political causes damaged the band's popularity among fans in Croatia and Bosnia, when he came out in favor of the Bosnian Serb fighters and the Serb rebels in the Krajina region of Croatia, based around the city of Knin. Together with a Knin band of the time, Minđušari, he recorded a controversial song titled "E moj druže Zagrebački" (Oh, My Zagreb Comrade). It was a reaction to an anti-Serbian song by Croatian singer Jura Stubljić, "E moj druže Beogradski" (Oh, My Belgrade Comrade).

However, Đorđević and Riblja Čorba were not unthinking nationalists, as their enormously popular satirical song "Baba Jula" would prove. The song alludes, critically, to Mirjana Marković, the corrupt wife of Slobodan Milošević, who had recently started her own political party, JUL–Jugoslavenska Levica (Yugoslav Left). The band thus became associated with the anti-Milošević, pro-Western protest bloc. However, after the toppling of the dictator in 2000, Riblja Čorba never really regained its former popularity in Serbia; more than simply having gotten old, Đorđević alienated some with his support for Vojislav Koštunica's Democratic Party of Serbia. However, the band still continues to release new material.

Other Rock Groups

When English rock icons the Rolling Stones played Belgrade in 2007, the opening act was a similarly long-lived Serbian band, Električni Orgazam (Electric Orgasm). The band began on Belgrade's punk and new wave scene in 1980 and became a mainstream rock band, led by Srđan "Gile" Bojković. They were an important band on the Yugoslav new wave scene. Električni Orgazam has eight albums and is still a popular live act in Serbia and around the former Yugoslavia; like many Serbian rock groups, it appeals to those feeling "Yugo-nostalgia" for the good old days.

Another pioneer on the Yugoslav scene, Ekatarina Velika (Catherine the Great, also known simply as EKV) formed in 1982 and disbanded twelve years later following the tragic death of lead singer Milan Mladenović. In that time, the new wave and rock-influenced band had built up a loyal following that actually grew after the band itself was no more. Ekatarina Velika's ten albums included three live ones. Critics and fans consider its best to be *Ljubav* (Love), released in 1987. Two years later, the band released the much darker *Samo par godina za nas* (Just a Few Years for Us), which seemed to predict the civil war and social upheaval that was to grip Yugoslavia beginning in the following years. Leader Mladenović later considered one hit from that album, "Srce" (Heart), to be EKV's best song.

The Partibrejkers (Party Breakers) is another important Serbian rock group to have emerged from the former Yugoslav rock scene. The band's eclectic influences include the Rolling Stones, the New York Dolls, the Stooges, rhythm and blues, and American rockabilly music. Major hits include "Kreni prema meni" (Come to Me), "Ona Zna" (She Knows), and "Mesečeva kći" (The Moon's Daughter).

Today the rock group Van Gogh remains one of Serbia's most popular rock bands, with a following in other ex–Yugoslav republics as well, despite the fact that most of their success came in the 1990s. MTV Europe named Van Gogh the Best Adriatic Act at the MTV Europe Music Awards in 2007.

A popular group that combines rock with arty and electronic tones is Darkwood Dub, which is still among the headliners on large regional music festivals like the EXIT Festival in Novi Sad (see chapter 4, "Holidays, Customs, and Leisure Activities"). Formed in 1988, the group pioneered musical trends in Serbia then beginning in Western Europe, such as electronic percussion, ambient bass, and sampling, combining these with more traditional rock elements. Aside from appearing at festivals and releasing six original albums, the band has also contributed to several film scores and has been associated with pro-democracy projects and initiatives in Serbia.

Rambo Amadeus

One of Serbia's most over-the-top musicians, and an outstanding if irreverent performer, is Rambo Amadeus (real name, Antonije Pušić). This self-titled musician, poet, and media manipulator, sometimes compared to American rocker Frank Zappa, has recorded fifteen albums since emerging on the Yugoslav scene in 1988. He has had a major impact on the development of music here, not only for his own songs but also for his categorization of styles; indeed, it was Rambo Amadeus's lighthearted comment that his music could be called "Turbo-folk" that created a name later applied to a much different genre of popular music (see the section herein on Turbo-folk).

Following in the tradition of earlier Serbian performers, Amadeus's songs often satirize social trends and politics. His concerts have always been marked by improvisation, unexpected (and usually comic) events, and intense performances. From the beginning, Amadeus perceived the value of spectacle and illusion: as an "unknown commodity" at the time of his arrival on the scene, he was able to develop a reputation as a trickster by introducing himself as Nagib Fazlić Nagon—allegedly, a poor mine-shaft operator who had been saving up enough money to record an album. His first album, *O, tugo jesenja* (O, My Autumn Sadness) was a hit, coarsely combining Serbian folk riffs with rap, opera, rock guitar, and irreverent lyrics. Oddly enough, before becoming a singer, Amadeus had actually enjoyed a successful career in sailboat regattas off the Montenegrin coast.

Zdravko Čolić

Serbia and Montenegro have their share of crooners (both male and female) who turn up on the concert stage and at television galas to sing soaring pop ballads and folk numbers. Among them, arguably the most beloved is the Bosnian-born Zdravko Čolić (b. 1951). The fifty-seven-year-old singer, who started out as a balladeer in the early 1970s, could perhaps best be described as Serbia's version of Tom Jones. A charismatic performer, Čolić retains a youthful charm (and, in his videos, youthful women). He was already acknowledged as one of Yugoslavia's greatest pop stars by the time the country fell apart in the early 1990s. Blessed with a melodic and powerful voice, and great personal charisma, Zdravko Čolić is one of the few pop singers to appeal to both the older and the younger generations in the former Yugoslavia.

Čolić began his career in 1968, making hits with romantic numbers like "Sinoć nisi bila tu" (Last Night You Were Not Here) and "Gori vatra" (The Fire Is Burning). Some of the best-known songs from the singer's long career also include "Zvao sam je Emili" (I Called Her Emily), "Mađarica" (The Hungarian Woman), "Zločin i kazna" (The Crime and the Punishment), and "Moja draga" (My Darling). The last, from the melodic, rock-influenced 2004 album *Čarolija*, is a plaintive, beautiful ballad about love lost, while the album's lead track, the joyous "Biti il ne biti" (To Be or Not to Be) restores festive spirits. Today, Čolić still performs regularly in the major cities of the former Yugoslavia, and he attracts big audiences for New Year's Eve and other special concerts.

Turbo-folk

The one style of Serbian popular music that has caused just as much wincing as cheering is the ubiquitous Turbo-folk, a genre that seems just as much a social order as a form of music. Perhaps because its main stars have been so closely affiliated with controversial politicians and salacious lifestyles, Turbo-folk has acquired a checkered reputation over the years. But what exactly is it?

The moment the term itself actually came into being can be defined fairly precisely. In 1988, Serbian rocker Rambo Amadeus used it, jokingly, to describe his own eclectic sound, which included smatterings of percussive pop, Balkan traditional, and exotic Turkish music, combining various styles and influences. A few years later, in 1991, the bland Novi Beograd (New Belgrade) neighborhood, which consists of identical concrete apartment blocks hosting a large percentage of the city's population, hosted several illegal radio stations. One DJ in Novi Beograd, W-ICE, started mixing Serbian folk with electronic dance beats, and a specific form was set. The commercialization of the new music developed quickly, with producers starting to put busty, scantily clad female singers and tough-guy, mafia look-alikes behind the microphone and in the salacious background choreography. Economic difficulty and the ensuing mass depression caused by the suffering of Serbs in neighboring Bosnia and Croatia during the wars, and most acutely United Nations trade embargoes on Serbia, helped nationalist subtexts in the lyrics find a large audience. An early example was the song "Ne može nam niko ništa" (No One Can Touch Us) by the singer Mitar Mirić. Although the overt meaning of the song was the drama of a young couple trying to keep their love against all odds, the implicit reference was a defiant statement of Serbian national unity at a time when it seemed to Serbs that the whole world was against them.

Turbo-folk clearly had appeal, therefore, as a form of escapism, and it proved a lucrative industry for the singers, managers, and production companies involved. But more than this, it also developed into a cultural index when its stars began to cultivate various unsavory associations. The most famous was the 1995 marriage of Arkan, the notorious paramilitary leader in the Bosnian war, to a young Turbo-folk singer named Svetlana ("Ceca" for short). The popularity of both, and what this said about the ideals of men and women in contemporary Serbia, horrified many observers both at home and abroad. Turbo-folk became a more omnipresent factor in televised media as well, in both music videos and "live" performances (usually lip-synched) on talk shows and music galas. Serbian television is still full of such events today, though trends toward reining in some of the lewder bits seem to have begun on the programs of the genre's standard-bearers, like Pink TV (see chapter 7, "Media and Cinema").

By the early 1990s, a distinct style would be known by the name of *Turbo-folk*. Short-skirted, leggy girls such as Lepa Brena, Ceca, Dragana Mirković, and Snežana Babić embraced the new, more uninhibited style, becoming overnight stars. The largely generic nature of the lyrics, music, and looks also meant that producers could manufacture public tastes by taking any attractive young woman (and sometimes man) with a decent voice and dressing (or undressing) him or her in the right way. Television programming filled with scantily clad young women dancing salaciously and singing vapid lyrics had a pleasantly numbing effect on the public, provoked copycat behavior and values in "real life," and—most important—brought in significant advertising dollars that helped advance the media moguls' business and political ambitions. The performances of the stars, and their lifestyles as constantly investigated by the tabloids, introduced a range of unhealthy examples for young women and men in society, with a noticeable increase in plastic surgery and various surgical enhancements being among the most worrying.

The matriarch of Turbo-folk is Lepa Brena, the best-selling singer of any Balkan pop performer. A star since the early 1980s, Brena was the inspiration for the Turbo-folk genre of the 1990s, combining the silliness of Yugoslav candy pop with Serbian folk melodies. Her music was meant to be danced to, and for the first time, the traditional two-step group circle dance (the *kolo*) was applied to pop. With a backing band called Slatki Greh (Sweet Sin), Brena reeled off a string of hits starting with 1982's "Mile voli disko" (Mile Likes Disco). The song went like this:

Mile likes disco,
But I like Shumadija's kolo,
To be closer with each other,
The accordion is playing disco.[3]

Despite, or perhaps because of, the inherent silliness of the lyrics, such songs went on to become classics of late Yugoslavia. Controversially, Lepa Brena herself was an outspoken supporter of Yugoslavism, even singing her popular hit "Živela Jugoslavija" (Long Live Yugoslavia) at the opening ceremony of the 1984 Winter Olympic Games in Sarajevo. Brena recorded many other albums over the years, and she continues to be popular in concert and on the Belgrade talk shows. Her newest album was for release in 2008.

Turbo-folk's biggest star of the modern era, however, is the busty, raven-haired Ceca. Ironically, she got her showbiz start at the age of seventeen, when cast in the role of the decent country maiden Koštana from the beloved 1902 play of the same name. Her phenomenal popularity in recent years was attested by a June 2002 stadium concert in Belgrade in which she performed in front of an estimated one hundred thousand fans. In January 2007, she was part of a multigroup Orthodox New Year's concert, also in Belgrade, that drew 350,000 people. Since 1988, Ceca has recorded thirteen albums, all of which have generated numerous hits and sold more than 10 million copies in all. In recent years, she has increasingly started putting out polished dance tracks, with more pure pop than folk to them, in line with the prevailing trends. However, Ceca's musical legacy will forever be associated with one album, *Maskarada* (Masquerade, released in 1997), and its hit single, "Nevaljala" (Naughty Girl). The album sold almost four hundred thousand copies in the first two weeks of its release, and "Nevaljala" became the only song in Serbian pop history to top the charts for seventeen consecutive weeks. Its racy lyrics reflect a favorite theme of the Turbo-folk genre, that of the love triangle. The most famous lines from it go like this:

All month long I've been sleeping alone
What you would do in my place?
Why should it be something sacred to me,
That it's good for you to be with her?
The blue nights in satin,

The coconut milk—
It would be better for you to be with me,
But oh you have no taste!

You love her, I love you,
Oh, does she know? So what if she knows—
She should give you to me,
Because tonight I'm a naughty girl.[4]

Ceca's career has also had its share of controversy, beginning with the 1995 marriage to the paramilitary leader Arkan. In March 2003, she was arrested and detained for four months after the assassination of Serbian Prime Minister Zoran Đinđić. She was accused of helping his killers, the mafia group Zemun Clan, but was subsequently cleared of all charges. However, in 2008, Ceca was accused of being involved with illegal financial transactions with FK Obelić, a soccer club owned by her. Ceca has also started and is president of a humanitarian fund that donates money to families with three children or more—which oddly enough brings the queen of lascivious living into perfect harmony with the stated goals of the somewhat more staid Serbian Orthodox Church.

NOTES

1. Matt Prodger, "Serbs Rally to Turbofolk Music," BBC.
2. The official Web site of the Serbian National Theater is http://www.narodnopozoriste.co.yu/cms/.
3. Translated by the author.
4. Translated by the author.

9

Art and Architecture

The development of shipping in Boka Kotorska in the past, and the consequent relative prosperity of this region of our country, unique for its natural beauty, was particularly reflected in the rational architecture of the captains' houses built during the eighteenth and at the beginning of nineteenth century. ... The size and equipment of the house expressed, in the manner typical of pioneers, the achieved earnings, the thought-out savings, and the personal vanity.

—Milan Zloković, Serbian modernist architect[1]

The iconographers of Serbia were great masters, so much so that those who have some conception of the art of fresco painting are astonished. They surpassed many of the Italians who, more than others, worked at frescoes.

—Photios Kontoglou, art historian[2]

Belgrade does not have to seek a remedy for the heterogeneity and colorlessness of its architecture in the national style based on our old sacred architecture. ... It has its own life, its own needs and habits. Its financial means, climate, work conditions, etc., will dictate the special and characteristic style of Belgrade Modernist Architecture.

—Branislav Kojić, Serbian modernist architect[3]

SERBIA AND MONTENEGRO have a long and vivid history of art and architecture, based on the ancient and medieval examples of the Roman, Byzantine, and medieval Serbian kingdoms, with other influences right up through the Ottoman and national revival periods, and finally a brief modernism period truncated by Tito's Communist regime. Since the fall of Communist

Yugoslavia, architecture has not been distinguished by anything special—just more "modern" constructions as elsewhere in Europe. In art, however, Serbian painters both continue to push new ground in abstract works and to invoke the past with the time-honored creation of Byzantine-style religious icons, perhaps the country's greatest gift to the world in terms of historical art.

CHURCHES, MONASTERIES, FRESCOES, AND ICONS

There is no part of the artistic and architectural heritage of Serbia and Montenegro to match the Byzantine and medieval Orthodox churches of these lands and Kosovo, which is why Serbs have been so devastated by the loss of that southwestern province to Albanians; since 1999, when the United Nations and NATO took over control of the province, more than 150 churches and monasteries have been damaged or destroyed, a catastrophe for Serbian and world cultural heritage and a crime for which none of the perpetrators has ever been found or held accountable.[4] Since 2004, UNESCO has listed the Visoki Dečani Monastery in western Kosovo as a World Heritage site; although this book does not include this or other great Kosovo churches, such as the Gračanica Monastery, the reader should understand that for Serbs, these are considered very much part of the national architectural treasure.

Early Byzantine Architectural Influences

Serbian and Montenegrin church architecture derives originally from Byzantine influences, though in coastal Montenegro and Vojvodina in northern Serbia there are Catholic influences from the Venetians and Austro-Hungarians, respectively. Since stonemasons and builders at different times also came from the Montenegrin coast, and in turn had influence from European sea trade and commerce, this proved another way for Western styles to creep into Serbia and Montenegrin church architecture. In general, churches in the Byzantine style are distinguished by their plaster-and-brick outer walls, vivid frescoes, grand inner arches, and side chambers, and most of all by the plethora of curving outer domes that seem to emerge one from the other magically. One feature of a Serbian Orthodox church that distinguishes it from the original Byzantine style is the frequent addition of a tall clock tower adjacent to the main church building.

Early Byzantine architecture simply continued existing Roman architectural innovations, such as the famous Roman arch, but it increased the geometric complexity of structures. It also began to use more bricks and plaster than simple stone, and it added complex dome structures set on massive piers. Finally, the heavily frescoed walls were enhanced by a constantly changing interplay of light and shadow, when thin beams of sunlight passed through specially designed narrow windows and portals by day, or with the flickering of candlelight at night. From an architectural point of view, however, what fundamentally separated the Byzantine from the Roman style was the technical breakthrough made by architects of Emperor Justinian the Great. In the middle of the sixth century, the Byzantines figured out how to take a square church design and convert it into a circular dome design by using squinches and pendentives (ceiling corner constructs to help support the weight of a dome). The classic examples of this early Byzantine architecture include Justinian's grand cathedrals in Ravenna, Italy, and of course the Hagia Sofia in Constantinople—to this day, one of the world's architectural masterpieces.

When Serbia converted to Christianity from the seventh to ninth centuries, it developed a hybrid style of church architecture, combining the early Byzantine three-nave (single-vault) basilica with Romanesque styling. By the end of the eighth century, cruciform churches with pillared cupolas started to appear. Saint Tryphon's (originally built in 809 and rebuilt in 1166), a Catholic cathedral in Kotor, Montenegro, is especially representative of Romanesque architecture, characterized by round arches and thick vaults. This influence arrived "by sea" (i.e., through maritime contact with Italy). After the cathedral was damaged by an earthquake in 1667, it was refurbished only in stages because of irregular financing, a fact that accounts for its oddly asymmetrical towers. The cathedral remains the major attraction in Kotor, and it is one of the most impressive such structures on the whole Adriatic coast.

The Raška School (c. 1150–1370)

The first notably Serbian style of church architecture is the one associated with the Nemanjići—the so-called Raška school," named for the location of the Serbian dynasty of the twelfth to fourteenth centuries. Early versions of this style, influenced heavily by middle Byzantine architecture, appear with the church of Saint Nicholas in Kuršumlija (built in the 1160s), a structure built with a single nave and cupola resting above a central square bay, and the similar church of Đurđevi Stupovi at Novi Pazar (1171). However, what is considered the first great example of Serbian Raška school architecture is the superlative Studenica Monastery, 39 kilometers southwest of Kraljevo in central Serbia.

Begun by Nemanjić dynasty founder Stefan Nemanja from 1183 to 1196, Studenica remains one of Serbia's largest monasteries. Its founder made it a heavily fortified monastery, with thick surrounding walls, and wanted it to serve as his future mausoleum. The monastery features two churches: the Church of the Virgin and the Church of the King. While the ravages of time, natural disasters, and foreign invaders have destroyed much of the original structures, Studenica has been reconstructed in elaborate fashion. King Stefan's unique goal was to create a monastery that resembled the theological conception of the ideal, heavenly city. The result was a symmetrical structure, with circular outer walls surrounding the complex, and the inner center falling exactly beneath the cupola of the larger, central church. Ten towers and two reinforced entrances appeared along the outer walls.

Studenica provided the model for several other Nemanjić churches, including Mileševa (built in the 1220s) and Morača (1252). Another major example of the Raška school of architecture is the church at Sopoćani (1265), which combines Byzantine and Romanesque styles. Its three-nave basilica structure reflected Romanesque architecture of the time, while the monumental interior is typical of middle Byzantine architecture. (Sopoćani was later deserted for two centuries and left exposed to the elements, but when reconstructed its frescoes were almost like new, something Serbs attribute to the work of divine Providence). The church at Gradac, built a few years later, also employs Western themes, being Gothic in its structure and shape; this reflects the style of southern Italy, from where, it is believed, some of the artisans involved came.

The Morava School (1377–1459)

The second identifiable trend in Serbian church architecture is known as the Morava school, beginning in the late fourteenth century, when the Serbian state was forced to relocate northward to the Morava River basin to escape the advancing Turks, and continuing to the mid-fifteenth century. The Serbian prince Stefan Lazarević is especially associated with the Morava school because of his endowments of the great churches of Ravanica (1377–1381) and Lazarica in Kruševac (1377–1380). What distinguishes Moravian architecture from its predecessor is the geometric juxtaposition of cupolas and arches, with alternating stone and brick layers, and especially the highly ornate stone decorative sculpturing around the windows, arches, door frames, and columns. These sculpted forms were most often geometric or floral in nature; only in late Moravian churches do we find human and animal figures as found in Roman and early Byzantine stonework (as well as in medieval Georgian and Armenian churches). Most unusually, the Morava school sculptures were usually painted in vivid colors. It is believed that Serbian architects in this period were influenced by monastic builders on Mount Athos in Greece.

The second characteristic of Moravian churches was their increasingly fortified nature—testament to the growing threat from Ottoman forces. During sieges or attacks on outlying villages, monasteries became safe havens for the citizens and therefore had to be equipped defensively, as well as with everyday provisions and water. The Manasija Monastery (built from 1407–1418, also known as the Church of Resava) in Despotovac exemplifies this trend, with its imposing structure, five cupolas, and massive outer walls dotted by ten towers. This church was also endowed by Prince Stefan Lazarević, and after he died it became his mausoleum. Until the Serbian Moravian principality fell to the Ottomans in 1459, Manasija was the center of Serbian culture and art. For art historians and ethnologists, the wall paintings of this church are notable because they show people wearing feudal Serbian costumes.

Modern Church Architecture

The construction of Serbian churches, embracing both traditional and more modern forms, coincided with the beginning of an independent Serbian state after the uprisings of 1804 and 1815. These churches therefore tend to be associated with specific dynastic families and to be located in more northerly areas that had not previously been major centers for Serbs, most notably the new capital of Belgrade.

These include Belgrade's Saborna Crkva Svetog Arhangela Mihaila (Cathedral Church of St. Michael the Archangel) and the Church of Saint Sava (1929). The cathedral was built in the style of classicism with late baroque elements; architects building the Church of Saint Sava were inspired by modernist architecture.

Another very important religious structure in Belgrade is Saint Marko's Church. In the very center of the capital, it houses the sacred remains of the fourteenth-century emperor Stefan Dušan. The architecture was largely inspired by that of Gračanica Monastery in Kosovo. The church of Sveta Ružica, located within the sprawling Kalemegdan Fortress above the Danube, is considered especially holy because for several years after the Ottoman invasion, it housed the body of Saint Petka, a female saint who is one of the most revered by the Orthodox people (in Greek she is known as Saint Paraskevi).

One of the most awe-inspiring sights in Serbia is the magisterial Church of Saint George at Oplenac in the western Šumadija region, site of the first rebellions against Turkish rule. It was built by the Karađorđević dynasty as its family mausoleum in 1912. This imposing, five-domed church built with gleaming white marble is most remarkable for its fifteen-thousand-piece mosaic, which depicts biblical scenes from assorted frescoes from more than seventy Serbian monasteries.

HISTORIC DEFENSIVE ARCHITECTURE

Nonreligious historical architecture in Serbia and Montenegro consists mostly of castles and other fortified structures, the oldest ones dating from

Roman times—a testament to the country's unfortunate placement in the middle of a perennial conflict zone. These structures, spread out over a large and diverse geographical area, display much variety—a result of their different outside influences and specific purposes. Fortifications were almost always built of stone and in strategic places that could be easily defended, such as hilltops, ravine entrances, or overlooking important river or seaports. Fortresses served to protect governing authorities and families, monasteries and monks, economic centers, and, of course, the soldiers required to defend the realm.

The oldest fortress in Belgrade, and today one of its most popular places for relaxing or taking a stroll, dates from the days when the city was known as Singidunum. Built by the Romans in A.D. 86, the Kalemegdan Fortress was built along a high, curving bluff overlooking the confluence of the Sava and Danube rivers. This militarily and economically strategic placement allowed the Romans to monitor ships coming and going and to defend the city in case of attack. As with other elevated fortresses, Kalemegdan could also be used as a safe haven for the citizens in the case of an enemy siege. This massive complex today includes parks, museums, and tennis and basketball courts.

Byzantine texts from the middle of the tenth century attest to the first Serbian defensive architecture. One such site, now mostly ruined, is near the small Montenegrin town of Spuž. Surviving remains, including a great tower, indicate that the structure was originally a palace complex in the principality of Zeta/Duklja in the tenth century. More intriguing ruins lie in the medieval Serbian mining center and town of Novo Brdo, where a partial citadel stands over foundations set in an irregular pattern that fanned out to include six thick towers connected by bulwarks. Another low bulwark created a protected pathway along the outer walls, reminiscent of Byzantine fortifications, such as the great Theodosian Walls of Constantinople. A good example of riverside defensive architecture is the medieval settlement of Golubac, on a hill guarding the Đerdap Gorge on the Danube. Although most of the settlement has not survived, the remaining ring of towers, starting from the waterfront and rising up in a circular pattern to the ridgeline, indicates the builders' strategic goals. Also set near a river (the Morava) is the former capital of Prince Lazar at Kruševac. Along with the famous Lazarica Church, visitors today can see the remains of the structure's towers and palace.

Perhaps the most famous example of medieval Serbian defensive architecture is the well-preserved Smederevo Fortress, built from 1428–1430 along the Danube by the despot Đurađ Branković. The extensive walls and towers of the lengthy fortress survive, though little of the original inner structures do. Smederevo is considered the pinnacle of Serbian medieval defensive architecture, after which Turkish occupation prevented the construction of similar large-scale fortresses. Smederevo was built under Byzantine supervision, along a long, flat area above the Danube. A high and enclosed tower stands guard at the tip of the triangular fortress closest to the river. Towers with defensive parapets run along the walls, which were built with stone and bricks glued together with lime mortar. It should be noted that the major reason the Turks took Serbian (and other Byzantine) fortresses owed less to the skill of the invaders than to the progress of military technology, in the form of gunpowder and the first cannon. Repeated and heavy cannon fire was needed to breach the walls of well-fortified cities like Constantinople and even smaller ones, such as Novo Brdo, as archeological evidence has attested.

Montenegro is especially rich in grand defensive architecture from medieval times. Here, however, the architects were mostly Westerners—the Venetians, who controlled much of the Adriatic coast to further the commercial interests of their maritime empire, which stretched from Italy to the Near East and the Black Sea. Stara Budva (Old Budva) consists of narrow stone streets culminating in a citadel over the protected bay: today this warren of chic shops is a favorite place for tourists to stroll, but it was once the key defensive point for

The little town of Perast is situated at the convergence of the bays of Risan and Kotor in the Boka Kotorska, Montenegro's most beautiful waterway, lined with mountains and fjords. It was the earliest inhabited part of the area, with civilization dating back to Neolithic times. Perast reached its architectural and political peak during the rule of the Venetian Empire (fifteenth–eighteenth centuries). Photograph by Rafael Estefania.

On the far northwestern edge of Montenegro, the evocative town of Kotor stretches along its eponymous bay, the Boka Kotorska. Its outstanding architecture, a legacy of three centuries of Venetian rule, has led it to be protected by UNESCO as a site of world heritage. Courtesy of Patrick Horton.

the Venetian-held town. The foundations of Stara Budva include remnants of walls dating back to Hellenistic times. A slightly different site is Stari Bar (Old Bar), further down the coast but a few kilometers inland. In medieval times a significant center of economic, cultural, and ecclesiastical life, Stari Bar was constructed on raised rocky terrain for strategic purposes. The surviving ramparts date from Venetian times, though these were built over early medieval structures.

The most impressive fortified site in Montenegro, however, is Kotor, one of the most defensively strategic coastal sites in Europe. Built at the back of a long, meandering bay framed by limestone cliffs, Kotor has always been coveted property. Now a UNESCO World Heritage site, Kotor is backed by an impregnable mountain and surrounded by city walls built by the Nemanjići dynasty. From 1420 to 1797, it was controlled by Venice, which expanded the city walls. When that republic fell soon afterward, it passed into the hands of Napoleon, who subsequently turned Cattari (as it was then known) over to the Austro-Hungarian Empire. Getting Kotor back became an obsession for

Montenegrin princes, right through World War I, after which they finally succeeded.

TRADITIONAL VILLAGE ARCHITECTURE AND URBAN DESIGNS

There is considerable charm to be found in the traditional architecture of the Serb and Montenegrin peasantry, which you can still see today in rural areas. The distinct styles of these structures vary according to geographical necessity (i.e., lowlands and mountain areas) and, according to cultural influence, most markedly between the formerly Austro-Hungarian northern province of Vojvodina, the center of the national revival, Šumadija, and southern areas more affected by the Ottoman influence.

Village houses, wherever the location, were built with functionality in mind. Their builders assessed climatic conditions and relied on readily available local materials. In mountainous Montenegro, therefore, stone houses with stone-shingled roofs predominated, while in forested Šumadija, Zlatibor, and Fruška Gora, log cabins with high, wood-shingled roofs were most frequently built. Finally, in less forested southern, central, and eastern Serbia, houses of mixed construction were made. These involved timber frames, the walls created of stone, mud, and wattle. The roofs of such houses were often thatched or partially thatched. This style, known as the Morava style, is the closest to houses in the north, on the Pannonian Plain of Vojvodina, where houses were constructed of tightly packed clay, mud, and straw, as well as unbaked bricks. Of course, for wealthy and important families, houses were often much more ornate and built of finer materials.

While many traditional houses in Serbia and Montenegro are now dilapidated and in a state of disrepair, some are being renovated into smart bed-and-breakfasts for foreign tourists. The most remarkable use of traditional styles, however, has been the Drvengrad (literally, "Wooden City") project, also known as Kustendorf, by filmmaker Emir Kusturica (see chapter 7, "Media and Cinema"). This specially built town in the Mokra Gora area between Mount Zlatibor and Mount Tara consists of traditional, western Serbian, arched wood houses. It won the European design award from the Philippe Rotthier European Foundation for Architecture.

FROM THE BAROQUE TO MODERNISM

The baroque style of architecture in Europe was originally conceived as part of the Catholic Counter-Reformation reaction against the rationalism and idealized symmetry represented by Renaissance painters and the Protestant

Reformation thinkers. It came to Serbia in large part with the Catholic Austro-Hungarian Empire, whose long rule in the north left Vojvodina and Belgrade with the greatest number of baroque structures. In Belgrade the period of so-called urban renewal lasted from 1718 to 1739, and it was in that period that the Austrians built Knez Mihajlova (Prince Michael) Boulevard as part of a baroque-inspired urban plan. Even today, Knez Mihajlova remains Belgrade's main pedestrian street, where residents and visitors go to enjoy a long, relaxed stroll, shop, or sip coffee along the small squares that abut it.

Baroque architecture during the eighteenth century in Serbia also began to appear as a trend in church and monastery construction. By 1726, high, baroque-style bell towers were being added to existing monasteries, while new churches were built in a higher and wider style; here, the Counter-Reformation thinkers' goal to create awe and grandeur befitting the Divine coincided quite nicely with free Serbians' desire to finally enjoy more expansive and grand structures, since the Turks had prevented Christians from building any church larger than a mosque in areas under their control. The best example of ecclesiastical baroque architecture in Serbia remains the Cathedral of Saint Nicholas in Karlovac (built 1758–1762). The church is characterized by an enormous facade and two massive flanking towers—thus achieving the appropriate goal of an awe-inspiring architectural display. This was followed by further baroque-style churches built throughout the eighteenth century, notable for their ornate pilasters and lizenes and featuring few pillars, unlike earlier Morava school churches.

The near contemporary cathedral in Belgrade (1841) and Church of Saint Mark (1836) were massive expressions of the vitality of the new Serbian state. Grand, classicist facades and baroque touches (like the bell tower) characterized these churches, which featured intricate painted art as well. Such churches were designed to leave visitors in awe, as was the case when Stefan Nemanja and his descendents built the first great Serbian churches in the thirteenth century. The new Belgrade churches became models for church architecture elsewhere in Serbia.

In the nineteenth and early twentieth centuries, as Serbia and Montenegro gradually recovered more and more territory from the Ottomans, they also moved firmly within the European aesthetic orbit. Informed and enthusiastic Serbs and Montenegrins helped to popularize Western political, philosophical, artistic, and architectural theories back home. A prime example of the spirit of Serbian architecture in this period is found in the national theater in Belgrade (built in 1868), designed by Aleksandar Bugarski.

During this period, Serbian architects also began to study in European universities, with assistance from the Serbian government's Ministry of Construction, which then used the returning students' expertise for creating urban structures. The ferment of ideas that characterized the nineteenth century is evidenced in the eclectic combination of styles ranging from Renaissance to academic and secessionist forms employed by nineteenth-century Serbian architects. In 1897, Belgrade's Technical Faculty opened a department of architecture, allowing knowledge acquired abroad to be transmitted to younger generations of students. Serbian and Montenegrin architects were recruited to design not only public and corporate buildings but also the mansions of the rich and famous throughout the country.

One of the most beloved buildings in Belgrade and an emblem of the city is the Hotel Moskva (Hotel Moscow), which stands at a central point near the top of the major pedestrian street, Knez Mihajlova Boulevard. Built in 1907, the Moskva is an imposing, rectangular structure with a narrow facade and numerous windows. Its interior features stained-glass windows.

The Hotel Moskva, which has hosted countless luminaries since opening in 1908, preserves Belgrade's turn-of-the-century ethos. It is one of the city's major landmarks, its big-window café being much frequented even by locals. Photo by the author.

It was designed by Serbian architect Jovan Ilkić. Similarly monumental and ornate structures built in Belgrade at around the same time as the Moskva include the Belgrade Cooperative Building (1905), designed by Andra Stevanović and Nikola Nestorović, and the Telephone Exchange Building (1908), designed by Branko Tanazović, who also designed the Ministry of Education building four years later. Although it was designed slightly later, in 1930, the magnificent Post Office and Telegraph Administration Building, designed by architect Momir Korunović, is a similar grand, multiwindow structure.

The modernist period of architecture in Serbia (1919–1941) is now being critically appraised, gaining new admiration from critics abroad. Architects of this period were also practicing intellectuals, heavily influenced by artistic and philosophical developments then taking place in Western Europe. What really propelled the movement, however, were the exigencies of the times; a war-shattered Serbia had to be rebuilt, and villagers migrating to the capital had to be housed and served. Answering the call was an eclectic group of four young architects who, in November 1928, formed a society with the grandiose name Group of Architects of the Modern Movement in Belgrade. Although it was not a secret society planning to overthrow a government or assassinate someone, it was typically Balkan in that it had its own bylaws and customs and met in a café—the celebrated Ruski Tsar, to this day a fashionable spot for coffee and cakes in the heart of Belgrade.

The group's founding members were Czech architect Jan Dubovy (1892–1969), Bosnia-born Dušan Babić (1896–1948), Milan Zloković (1898–1965), a Serb from Trieste in Italy, and Branislav Kojić (1899–1987), the only native of Serbia. All of these architects would have long and eminent careers in subsequent years. Their group's prestige was enhanced significantly in 1930 when the established architect Dragiša Brašovan joined. The group had an effect by spreading new ideas to students, awarding prizes at special design shows, and generally sparking a new creative energy into the growing capital city. According to a Serbian architect and historian of architecture, Liljana Blagojević, these newcomers on the scene "were adamant about establishing a contemporary identity for Serbian architecture." Their group "seemed to be the way ahead in their struggle against the hostile traditionalist environment."[5]

Some of the buildings Brašovan designed included Novi Sad's Provincial Administration building, the Cable Industry in Jagodina, and the State Printing House in Belgrade, considered a prime example of Belgrade modernism. Zloković, also considered a father of Serbian modernism, designed many distincitve buildings, such as the Belgrade Children's Hospital (1940).

Serbia's second city, Novi Sad, is the capital of the northern province of Vojvodina. Its architecture is strongly influenced by its previous history of Austro-Hungarian rule. The city also hosts the famous EXIT Festival each summer, bringing partygoers from all over Europe to hear some of the most-best known local and international musicians. Courtesy of Patrick Horton.

Communist-Era Architecture

Although most people wince when they see it now, architecture in Tito's Yugoslavia was considered cutting edge at the time, and perhaps future generations will someday find something to be fascinated by in these concrete monstrosities, bulky and cut by sharp angles and awkward forms, reflecting the esoteric and abstract nature of Communist ideology being propounded at the time. Yugoslav architects were frequently recruited to design buildings in foreign countries (often in the Middle East), and their contemporaries from foreign lands were sometimes called in to design Yugoslav buildings, as when Japanese architect Kenzo Tenge designed the new post office in then-Yugoslav Skopje, Macedonia, a lingering eyesore that resembles an enormous concrete pineapple.

Postwar architects in Serbia were allowed to use their creativity, but it was also constrained to some extent by the limits of the form and content that Tito the Communist preferred. A parallel example from a different artistic genre was the case of wood-carvers: then, rather than produce hand-sculpted wooden blocks decorated with religious motifs, they were to illustrate their carvings with forms that could not be mistaken for anything other than secular. In architecture, things were similar: the underlying Serbian penchant for monumental grandeur—as witnessed since the first great churches of the Nemanjić kings—remained dominant, it was just applied to a different style.

This is the case with Belgrade's Western Gate Towers (1950), designed by Mihajlo Mitrović: two massive skyscrapers joined together at the top by a funnel-shaped central tower. The multiterraced Military-Medical Academy in Belgrade (1973), curving symmetrically in a double ellipse, is an impressive example of Communist architecture, as is the city's Museum of Modern Art (1965), the work of Ivan Antić and Ivanka Raspopović.

FRESCOES AND ICONS

Without doubt, the historically most significant form of visual art produced in Serbia and Montenegro, in the opinion of most locals and foreigners alike, comes in the form of the Byzantine-influenced painted icons and frescoes for which Serbia is long renowned. Byzantine icons are sacred paintings that depict Jesus and Mary, as well as the angels and saints of the Orthodox Christian Church, which sometimes include earthly rulers who are considered important by the church and in some cases have been sanctified, such as King Stefan Nemanja. The artistic style of iconography is quite remarkable; unlike most other forms of painting, they are not three-dimensional, but show figures and objects marked by elongated or disproportional arms, legs, and eyes. The "missing" dimension symbolizes the unknowable spiritual existence of God. Everything shown in an icon indeed has a symbolic meaning, and pondering this requires deep concentration, something ameliorated by the vivid colors and striking figures of the icon, which is not uncommonly flanked by gold backgrounds or preserved in an ornate silver outer case.

Most practically, an icon is meant to be a window or portal into the spiritual world, through which one can communicate his or her deepest prayers to the personage depicted in the picture. A very potent feature of icons, therefore, is the reputation that some have acquired for being miraculous; stories of people being cured from diseases, freed of some psychological or emotional burden, cured of infertility, and so on, were widely attested to in medieval times and apparently continue to occur today for the faithful. Some icons have also acquired magical reputations for withstanding fires, appearing miraculously out of nowhere, and protecting Christian cities in times of war. It is thus little wonder that people who paint icons are considered not only artists but also theologians of a sort. People who paint icons for a living are usually very religious, frequently praying and following the Orthodox calendar in periodically fasting and participating in other rituals.

Although all iconography derives from a similar model, the march of time and geographical differences (i.e., the styles of different nations) influenced the development of the genre. Serbian icon and fresco painting passed through numerous subtle stages, beginning with the simplest of early Byzantine styles to Russian- and Ukrainian-influenced romanticized paintings of the eighteenth and nineteenth centuries. Especially to be noted is the style of icon painting that developed in Serbia during the thirteenth- and fourteenth-century Nemanjić dynasty, the so-called Morava school, the same name given to the architectural style of churches constructed then. As with church architecture, this visual art was strongly influenced by Byzantine mores. The cultural transmission occurred both from the interaction and cooperation of Serbian monks in Constantinople and especially the Serb-endowed Monastery of Hilandar on Mount Athos in Greece. Works of art, architecture, literature, and philosophy developed in Byzantium during this time are known as Palaeologan, named for the Palaeologos dynasty that ruled from 1261, when Constantinople was recaptured from Latin knights following their fifty-seven-year occupation, to 1453, when the city fell to the Ottomans. The direct influence of Byzantine artists and artisans in Serbia itself grew after 1204, when many were forced to flee from Constantinople following the (mostly Christian!) sack of the city by the knights of the Fourth Crusade in 1204. This Greek influence can be seen today in the wall frescoes of the Church of the Ascension at Mileševa, as well as at the Sopoćani Monastery.

Some further interesting details are provided by Serbian-Canadian professional icon painter Svetlana Novko:

Art historians can tell the Serbian, or Moravian school of iconography by its darker, earthier undertones of skin and garments (in comparison to, say, Russian bright pinks, blues and greens and almost blond holy personages, including Christ representations) and by oftentimes distinctly "Serbian" features of the holy personages. The Mileseva *Resurrection* fresco (dubbed "White Angel") is an example of an icon that looks quite "Serbian." A number of extant Moravian School frescoes and icons offer a glimpse into the daily life of Serbs then, such as the Hilandar icon of the Entry of the Mother of God into the Temple (*Vavedenje*) from around 1320. In the background of the main event, the icon depicts a scene from Serbian patriarchal family life in the zadruga communal system, including such details as the hair styles, features, clothing and hair covers etc., of the peasant women and girls.[6]

While a number of medieval icon painters (most of them monks) are known by name, most are unknown because they rarely signed their names,

thinking it vain and unfitting the holiness of their work. Production of religious art was affected by the Ottoman conquest of Serbian lands, because it
displaced or destroyed the nobility and church and the sources of wealth that
had allowed them to patronize the arts. This meant a relatively lower production of icons during the fifteenth and sixteenth centuries. However, efforts
resumed with the restoration of the Serbian patriarchate in Peć (Kosovo) in
1557. A renaissance of Serbian icon and fresco painting occurred during the
seventeenth and eighteenth centuries, when a number of regional schools of
icon painting sprang up. One of the most interesting cross-cultural developments was the influence, in the early part of this period, by the so-called
Cretan school of icon painting. The name refers to iconographers from the
Greek island of Crete, which from 1204 to 1669 was under the control of
the Venetian Republic. Here, a unique Italo-Greek style sprang up, creating a
fusion in art and literature between the Byzantine East and the Italian West.
The icons of this school are characterized by a more full-bodied, expressive,
and "softer" Italian Renaissance look. Such icons were usually commissioned
by wealthy patrons, decorated with gold trim, and lavishly ornamented.

After the Great Migration northward into Austro-Hungarian territory in
1690, Serbian religious art began to incorporate Western European influences.
However, traditionalism remained strong, with many leading icon painters
clinging to the simpler High Byzantine style of the eleventh to fourteenth
centuries. Nevertheless, developing trends in eighteenth-century Serbian art
reflected the new social and political realities of the "New Serbia" and settlements along the Danube, especially Sremski Karlovci (also referred to as
Karlowitz). Here, the influential patriarch Arsenije IV championed the
adoption of the more realistic, baroque-style Ukrainian iconography. Thus,
Arsenije's court painters began to follow this style in their work. The following
two centuries of artistic development would be characterized by the tension
between, and synthesis of, Byzantine traditionalist and modern Western and
Ukrainian baroque aesthetics.

The Serb Đorđe Mitrofanović is considered the leading painter of the early
seventeenth century; his work on the church at the Morača Monastery is considered among the best of the period. Other important Serbian iconographers
of the period include Dimitrije Daskal, the head of the Rafailović-Dimitrijević
family known for producing several iconographic masters, all inspired by traditionalism. Daskal's work in 1689 at the Church of Saint Luke in Kotor,
Montenegro, is considered exemplary, though his most important work was
done in 1717–1718 in the Church of Pelinovo; here he created an elaborate series of icons depicting the life of Saint Nicholas, the Virgin Mary, and
the entire menology. Daskal's descendents were active throughout the eighteenth and early nineteenth centuries, when they became known as the Boka

Kotorska school of icon painting. Similarly conservative art was championed by Father Simeon Lazović, who, like his son Aleksije, followed Byzantine models in his paintings.

The "modern" school of painting, influenced by South Russian and Ukrainian baroque in the eighteenth century, had its own masters, among whom are found some of Serbia's first great modern painters. Hristifor Zefarović, painter of the Monastery of Bodjani in Bačka (1737), was the first to truly embrace the liberating use of form and color embodied in Ukrainian baroque. His work demonstrates an expressive and imaginative rereading of sacred art, and many art historians believe that with Zefarović, modern Serbian art was born. The wall paintings created at the Monastery of Krusedol (1750–1756) also represent the new baroque trends, of further interest by the presence there of an actual Ukrainian—the artist Jov Vasilijević—who had become a court painter for Patriarch Arsenije IV. Among other aesthetic exemplars, Vasilijević took his inspiration from illustrated baroque bibles from Germany and Holland.

Other iconographers influenced by the Ukrainian baroque style include the prolific Nikola Nešković (1740–1789)—author of more than a thousand icons, frescos, and other paintings—Dimitrije Bačević, Dimitrije and Jovan Popović, Jovan Popović, Vasa Ostojić, and Ambrosije Janković, all active in churches in the Sremski Karlovci diocese between the 1750s and 1780s, when new Western influences began to gain influence. However, the acknowledged master of the baroque period, considered the first great modern Serbian painter, was Teodor Kračun.

Kračun's dated works begin with the frescoes of the Church of Saint George in Sombor (1772) and continue through 1780, when he painted more outstanding icons in the patriarchal church at Sremski Karlovci. In an exciting departure from the past, Kračun also employed rococo themes in this work. Kračun's work embodies the synthesis of older Byzantine traditionalism—characterized by strictness of form, meant to imply the spiritual dimension—and the more explicit spirituality and emotiveness of the new baroque style. His contemporaries and successors in the 1780s and thereafter, such as Jakov Orfelin and Teodor Ilić Češljar, would be influenced by Kračun's vision, though they would not equal his genius. With the prolific, Vienna-trained Češljar, who painted the iconostases in Mokrina, Stara Kanjiža, Kikinda, and Bačko Petrovo Selo, a turn away from the baroque and toward the rococo palette and more subdued, lyrical form then gaining prominence in the West is witnessed. The work of Češljar marks the beginning of a new, more austere style of Serbian ecclesiastical art, heavily influenced by the Viennese art academies, where many Serbian painters would be trained during the nineteenth century. Major painters of this style, known as the Serbian Biedermeier school, include Arsa Teodorović, Pavel Đurković, Nikola Aleksić, and especially Konstantin Danil, the greatest representative of the genre. This period also marks the emergence of formal (and secular) oil portrait painting.

MODERN PAINTING

Modern painting of a nonecclesiastical nature combined a range of Western influences, especially German, Austrian, and French, reflecting the most common destinations for Serb and Montenegrin art students abroad. Throughout the nineteenth century, their artwork would increasingly be marked by a mixture of styles forced to conform with the wishes of their patrons—increasingly, a wealthy and nationalist-minded aristocratic class seeking to have the best (and worst) moments of Serbian history immortalized on canvas, often in bombastic fashion. This need, and the Serbian upper crust's vain desire for European-style portraits of themselves, did not always prove greatly inspiring for the artists, but a commission was a commission, and so it went.

In the 1840s, Serbian painting gradually departed from its classicist Biedermeier severity in favor of romanticism, which was marked by three distinct qualities. The first was a gripping emotiveness that embellished the nationalistic and patriotic content of these paintings (much to the satisfaction of their patrons). The second was a new conceptualization of landscape. Whereas landscape had previously played a subordinate, background role in Serbian paintings, works of nineteenth-century masters like Novak Radonić and Steva Todorović elevated it, for the first time, to the central theme. The third aspect of Serbian romanticism was embodied especially by Đura Jakšić, who studied in Vienna and was deeply influenced by Rembrandt. In his paintings, he imitated the Dutch master's use of light and shadow and exploration of color. With Jakšić, Serbian romanticism reached its peak between 1850 and 1870.

After 1870, a number of Munich-trained painters brought a new German style of realism into vogue in Serbia. This genre is characterized by dark, rich colors; the subject matter continued to include landscapes and, especially, still-life and peasant village scenes. Proponents of this school included Miloš Tenković, Đorđe Krstić, and Đorđe Milovanović. Uroš Predić (1857–1953) and Pavle Jovanović (1859–1957) were two of the greatest painters of the late-nineteenth-century Munich style. The former created a harrowing series of evocative nationalist-themed painting such as the dark *Turkish Burning of the Relics of Saint Sava* and the *Kosovo Maiden*, spurred by the folk legends of a Serbian girl giving water to wounded soldiers on the battlefield at the 1389 Battle of Kosovo. Jovanović created arguably the most famous Serbian painting of all time in 1896 with *The Great Migration under Arsenije III Čarnojević in 1690.* This grandiose, nationalist-minded work is undoubtedly moving, with its depiction of the patriarch leading his devastated flock out of Kosovo together with the Austrian army retreating from battle with the Turks. This painting was commissioned at a time of high nationalism and nostalgia, following the Russo-Turkish War of 1877 that reshaped the Balkans, and it was finished just seven years after the five-hundredth anniversary of the great Battle of Kosovo, which signaled the end of the medieval Serbian empire. In this fin-de-siècle period, a number of other patriotic-minded works focusing on Serbia's medieval greats were also commissioned.

THE TWENTIETH CENTURY

The turn of the century in Serbia marked a breath of fresh air for artists, as contemporary trends elsewhere in Europe began to be adopted, such as fauvism, cubism, and avant-garde. The country's first school of art was opened in 1895 by Kirilo Kutlik, whose students also studied in France and Germany, where they (and other Serbian artists) came into contact with such styles of art. After the First World War, another important sign of progress occurred when the Belgrade School of Painting was opened. In 1904, the National Museum in Belgrade opened the Yugoslav Gallery, to be devoted to twentieth-century paintings; today, it preserves some three thousand paintings and watercolors created between 1889 and 1999.

One of the first important twentieth-century painters in Serbia was Milan Konjović (1898–1993), a native of Sombor in Vojvodina. He studied abroad and lived for eight years in Paris, where he had numerous successful exhibitions. In his lifetime, Konjović had 297 one-man and 700 group exhibitions, both at home and in many foreign countries. His work, which defies easy description, falls into six periods, divided by art historians into color phases. In his lifetime, the prolific Konjović created some six thousand oil paintings, pastels, watercolors, temperas, drawings, tapestries, stained-glass windows, mosaics, and other forms of graphic art. A contemporary, Marko Čelebonović (1902–1986), is regarded as one of Serbia's finest modern painters. Čelebonović pioneered a style called intimism, defined by its use of colors. The painter had a colorful life as well, living in various European countries and volunteering in the French Resistance in World War II. Čelebonović's notable French colleagues included Antoine Villard, Paul Signac, Albert Marquet, and Andre de Segonzac, and from them he adopted some of the contemporary ideas of the French tradition, and his work indeed is paralleled by the tradition of French artists of the 1930s. However, what makes

Čelebonović's work original is his juxtaposition of this French flavor with eastern, Balkan tones. As his life wore on, Čelebonović considered himself more and more to be a Yugoslav painter, with his roots ultimately in Serbia and the Balkans with all of their Byzantine and Turkish heritage.

A close colleague and contemporary of Marko Čelebonović was the Montenegrin Petar Lubarda (1907–1974), whose influence was especially pronounced after World War II. While Yugoslav Communist ruler Josip Broz Tito preferred "socrealism," or social realism, Serbian artists, led by painters like Petar Lubarda, started to liberate themselves from Communist kitsch in the 1960s. Lubarda, who spent World War II in German concentration camps, was inspired by Montenegrin history and landscape in his paintings. Lubarda was the winner of many international awards, and he traveled widely through his career. The same affection for his homeland reflected in his works was also evident in Lubarda's efforts to establish the first art academy of Montenegro. A second distinguished Montenegrin painter was Milo Milunović (1897–1967), known for his works in both impressionist and cubist styles. He was educated in Florence, Italy, and later in Paris, where he fell under the influence of the great impressionist Paul Cézanne. Milunović's most successful works were created between 1926 and 1932 and combined impressionism with a more abstract, rationalistic approach.

Among several other notable twentieth-century painters is the internationally acclaimed Vladimir Veličković (b. 1935). In the 1970s, he became one of the major promoters of surrealist figurative painting. From 1983 to 2000, he was a professor at the École Nationale Superièure des Beaux-Arts in Paris and is especially popular in France.

NOTES

1. Liljana Blagojević, *Modernism in Serbia: The Elusive Margins of Belgrade Architecture, 1919–1941* (Cambridge, MA: MIT Press, 2003), 191.

2. Photios Kontoglou and Constantine Cavarnos, *Byzantine Sacred Art: Selected Writings of the Contemporary Greek Icon Painter Fotis Kontoglous on the Sacred Arts According to the Tradition of Eastern Orthodox Christianity* (Belmont, MA: Institute for Byzantine and Modern Greek Studies, 1992), 71.

3. Liljana Blagojević, *Modernism in Serbia*, 61.

4. For a graphic and detailed assessment of the scale of this destruction on a case-by-case basis, see the Serbian Orthodox Diocese of Raska-Prizren, *Crucified Kosovo*, book available online at http://www.rastko.org.yu/kosovo/crucified/default.htm.

5. Liljana Blagojević, *Modernism in Serbia*, 57.

6. Quote taken from the author's interview with icon painter Svetlana Novko.

Selected Bibliography

Bieber, Florian, ed. *Montenegro in Transition: Problems of Identity and Statehood.* Baden-Baden, Germany: Nomos, 2003.

Blagojević, Liljana. *Modernism in Serbia: The Elusive Margins of Belgrade Architecture, 1919–1941.* Cambridge, MA: MIT Press, 2003.

Boehm, Christopher. *Blood Revenge: The Enactment and Management of Conflict in Montenegro and Other Tribal Societies.* Philadelphia: University of Pennsylvania Press, 1984.

Collin, Matthew. *Guerrilla Radio: Rock 'n' Roll Radio and Serbia's Underground Resistance.* New York: Nation Books, 2002.

Cormack, Robin. *Byzantine Art.* Oxford: Oxford University Press, 2000.

Denton, W. *Montenegro: Its People and Their History.* London: Daldy, Isbister, 1877. Reprint, Whitefish, Montana: Kessinger Publishing, 2007.

Efthymaides, Stephanos. *Byzantine Hagiography: A Handbook.* Aldershot, U.K.: Ashgate, 2008.

Evans, Helen C., ed. *Byzantium: Faith and Power (1261–1557).* New Haven, CT: Yale University Press, 2004.

Goulding, Daniel J. *Liberated Cinema: The Yugoslav Experience, 1945–2001.* Bloomington: Indiana University Press, 2002.

Goy, E. D. *Excursions: Essays on Russian and Serbian Literature.* Nottingham, U.K.: Astra Press, 1996.

Gruenwald, Oskar. *The Yugoslav Search for Man: Marxist Humanism in Contemporary Yugoslavia.* South Hadley, MA: J. F. Bergin Publishers, 1983.

Hall, Richard C. *The Balkan Wars, 1912–1913: Prelude to the First World War.* London: Routledge, 2000.

Hammond, Lila. *Serbian: An Essential Grammar.* London: Routledge, 2005.

Hoddinott, R. F. *Early Byzantine Churches in Macedonia and Southern Serbia: A Study of the Origins and the Initial Development of East Christian Art*. New York: St. Martin's Press, 1963.

Holy Resurrection Serbian Orthodox Cathedral. *The Serbian Family Table*. Carlsbad, CA: Seraphim Press, 2006.

Iordanova, Dina. *Cinema of Flames: Balkan Film, Culture and the Media*. London: British Film Institute, 2008.

———. *Emir Kusturica*. London: British Film Institute, 2008.

Karanovich, Milenko. *The Development of Education in Serbia and the Emergence of Its Intelligentsia*. Boulder, CO: East European Monographs, 1995.

Kijuk, Predrag Dragic. *Mediaeval and renaissance Serbian poetry*. Belgrade: Serbian Literary Quarterly, 1987.

Laughland, John. *Travesty: The Trial of Slobodan Milošević and the Corruption of International Justice*. London: Pluto Press, 2007.

Marković, Mihailo. *From Affluence to Praxis*. Ann Arbor: University of Michigan Press, 1974.

Marković, Mihailo, and Robert S. Cohen, *Yugoslavia: The Rise and Fall of Socialist Humanism: A History of the Praxis Group*. Nottingham, U.K.: Spokesman Books, 1975.

Marković, Mihailo, and Gajo Petrovic. *Praxis: Yugoslav Essays in the Philosophy and Methodology of the Social Sciences*. New York: Springer, 1979.

Mihajlovic, Jasmina. "Milorad Pavic and Hyperfiction." *Review of Contemporary Fiction*, June 22, 1998. Available at http://www.khazars.com/en/pavic-and-hyperfiction/.

Miloš, Velimirović. *Byzantine Elements in Early Slavic Chant: The Hirmologion*. Copenhagen: E. Munksgaard, 1960.

Mirodan, Vladimir. *The Balkan Cookbook*. Gretna, LA: Pelican Publishing, 1989.

Norris, John. *Collision Course: NATO, Russia and Kosovo*. Westport, CT: Praeger, 2005.

Pavkovic, Aleksandar. *The Fragmentation of Yugoslavia: Nationalism in a Multinational State*. New York: St. Martin's Press, 1997.

Peic, Sava. *Medieval Serbian Culture*. New York: Alpine Fine Arts Collection, 1993.

Popović, Ljubiša et al. *Art Heritage of Serbia*. Belgrade: Nation Museum, 1984.

Project Rastko. *The History of Serbian Culture*. Edgware, U.K.: Porthill Publishers, 1995.

Roberts, Elizabeth. *Realm of the Black Mountain: A History of Montenegro*. Ithaca, NY: Cornell University Press, 2007.

Ruiz, Diego. *Vlade Divac*. Whittier, CA: Los Andes Publishing, 1995.

Sher, Gerson S. *Praxis: Marxist Criticism and Dissent in Socialist Yugoslavia*. Bloomington: Indiana University Press, 1977.

Stana, Aurici-Klajn. *A Survey of Serbian Music through the Ages*. Belgrade: Association of Composers of Serbia, 1972.

Stephenson, Paul. *Byzantium's Balkan Frontier: A Political Study of the Northern Balkans, 900–1204*. Cambridge: Cambridge University Press, 2000.

Stulhofer, Aleksandar. *Sexuality and Gender in Postcommunist Eastern Europe and Russia*. New York: Routledge, 2004.

Temperley, Harold William Vazeille. *History of Serbia*. New York: AMS Press, 1970.

Tradigo, Alfredo. *Icons and Saints of the Eastern Orthodox Church*. Guide to Imagery Series. Los Angeles: Getty Publications, 2006.

Treadway, John D. *The Falcon and the Eagle: Montenegro and Austria-Hungary, 1908–1914*. West Lafayette, IN: Purdue University Press, 1983.

Velimirovich, Nicholai. *The Life of Saint Sava*. Eastchester, NY: St. Vladimir's Seminary Press, 1989.

Ware, Timothy. *The Orthodox Church: New Edition*. London: Penguin, 1993.

West, Rebecca. *Black Lamb and Grey Falcon: The Record of a Journey through Yugoslavia in 1937*, 2 vols. London: Macmillan, 1941.

Wilson, Duncan. *The Life and Times of Vuk Stefanović Karadzić, 1787–1864; Literacy, Literature and National Independence in Serbia*. Ann Arbor: University of Michigan Press, 1986.

Zdenko, Zlatar. *Njegos's Montenegro: Epic Poetry, Blood Feud, and Warfare in a Tribal Zone*. New York: East European Monographs, 2005.

Index

Abortion, 46, 51–52
Adrianople, 12
Albanians, 4, 7–8, 12–14, 23–24,
    33–34, 39, 79, 152
Amadeus, Rambo, 146
Austro-Hungarian, 8, 15, 17–18, 53,
    84, 87, 89, 91–92, 103, 122–23, 128,
    152, 158–60, 163, 166
Austro-Turkish War, 14

Baljak, Aleksandar, 29, 39–40
Balkan Wars (1912–1913), 16–18
Battle of Kosovo, 12–13, 36, 67, 103,
    123, 168–69
Battle of Pločnik, 12
Battle of Srem, 21
Bayezid, Ottoman Sultan, 13
Belgrade Aphoristic Circle, 37–38
Belgrade University, 43
Bijelo Polje, 6
BK Television, 54, 120
Bobotov Kuk, 7
Boka Kotorska, 6, 151, 157–58,
    166

Bologna Process in European education,
    56
Bosniaks, 7–8, 34
Branković, Vuk, 13
Brasovan, Dragiša, 163
Bregović, Goran, 69, 130, 140–141
Broz, Josip Tito, 20–21, 40, 142, 170
Bulajić, Stevan and Veljko, 124
Bulgarians, 8, 11, 16–18
Byzantine Empire, 10, 12

Čangalović, Miroslav, 137
Čarnojević, Arsenije, 14
Catholic Church, 20–21, 34
Cetinje, 6, 52, 55, 107, 136
Christianity, 9–10, 29–32, 113, 129,
    153, 170
Clinton, President William, 24
Čolić, Zdravko, 147
Communism, 8, 21–22, 34, 37, 41,
    45–46, 52, 60, 110, 116, 122, 128
Constantine the Great, Byzantine
    Emperor, 30
Cotrić, Aleksandar, 39

Corfu, 18
Croats, 8, 17–20, 23–24, 34, 74, 127
Cyril and Methodius, 3, 31, 101–2

Dacians, 10
Damnjanović, Milan, 42
Danube River, 4–5, 10, 62, 92, 97, 131
Dayton Accords, 24
Dečani Monastery, 33, 152
Dimitrijević, Branislav, 47
Dinaric Alps, 5
Divac, Vlade, 75
Doković, Dragan, 117
Dragojević, Srđan, 123, 126–28
Drina River, 5, 123, 128
Drvengrad, 129
Duklja, Kingdom of, 11, 156
Durmitor Mt., 7
Dušan, Stefan, 11–12, 32
Dušanov Zakonik, 12
Đerdap, 5
Đinđic, Zoran, 25, 118–19, 124, 150
Đurđevi Stupovi Monastery, 32
Đurić, Mihajlo, 43
Đoković, Novak, 78, 80, 82

Ekatarina Velika, 145
European Credit Transfer System, 57
EXIT Festival, 68, 146

Ferdinand, Franz, 17, 68
Folk Literature, 104–5
Fruška Gora Mt., 5

Glagolitic alphabet, 3
Glišić, Milovan, 109
Gospels, 52, 102
Gorski vijenac (The Mountain Wreath), 106
Great Powers of Europe, 16
Great Serbian Migration (1690), 14, 103–5, 166–68

Guča Trumpet Festival, 61, 68–69, 142
Gypsies (Roma), 3, 5, 8, 10, 11, 13, 19, 21, 46, 69–70, 110, 129–32, 138, 140–142

Hagiography, 103
Hague Tribunal, 25–26, 39
Herceg-Novi, 6
Hilandar Monastery, 11, 32, 93, 102–3, 138, 165
Hitler, 19–20, 24
Holocaust, 20
Holy League, 14
Homosexuality, 57–58
Hungarians, 8, 20, 34, 159

Inat, concept of, 48–50
Islam, 13–14, 33, 36, 113
Italians, 8, 20, 151
Ivanović, Ana, 61, 79–80
Izetbegović, Alija, 22

Jaksić, Đura, 108
Janissaries, 14
Janković, Jelena, 79–80
Jarić, Marko, 76
Jews, 13, 20, 34, 112
Jovanović, Jovan Zmaj, 108
Jovanović, Pavle, 168

Kalemegdan Fortress, 62, 91, 155–56
Kangrga, Milan, 40
Karić Brothers, 54–55, 120
King Aleksandar I Karađoređvić, 19, 21
King Milutin, 11
King Peter II, 19–20
Kingdom of Serbs, Croats and Slovenes, 18
Kingdom of Srem, 11
Kiš, Danilo, 110–112
Kojić, Branislav, 151, 162
Konjović, Milan, 169
Konjović, Petar, 137, 143
Kopaonik Mt., 5

Kosovo Liberation Army, 24
Kosovo Polje, 12
Koštunica, Vojislav, 25, 61, 145
Kotor, 6–7, 16, 55, 107, 151, 153, 157–58, 166
Kovačević, Dusan, 115, 125–26
Kracun, Teodor, 167
Kragujevac, 20, 27, 54, 94, 110, 142
Kumanovo Agreement, 24
Kusturica, Emir, 29, 116, 122, 125, 128–33, 141, 159

Lake Plav, 7
Lake Skadar, 6–7
Lazarević, Stefan, 13
Lepa Brena, 78, 148–49
Lovćen Mt., 7, 43, 107
Lubarda, Petar, 170

Macedonians, 8, 10, 23
Makarije, Patriarch, 32
Maksimović, Desanka, 110
Marić, Božo, 39
Marković, Boban, 69, 130, 142
Marković, Mihailo, 40–42, 45
Marković, Svetozar, 109
Megatrend University, 55
Mihailović, Draža, 20–21
Mihajlović, Momčilo, 39
Milanović, Igor, 77
Milenković, Stefan, 143
Milošević, Slobodan, 23, 25, 42, 91, 116
Miroslav's Gospel, 102
Mitić, Boris, 38
Mokranjac, Stevan Stojanović, 142–43
Morava River, 5, 154
Morava School, 154, 160, 165
Murat I, Ottoman Sultan, 13–14
Museum of Contemporary Art, 47

NATO, 12, 22–24, 27, 30, 39, 50–51, 54, 56, 59, 117, 152
Nemanja, Stefan, 11, 31, 32, 153, 160, 164

Nešković, Nikola, 167
Nikčević, Vojislav, 3
Nikola I of Montenegro, 16
Nikolić, Aleksandar, 74
Nikšić, 55, 83, 91, 93
Novi Pazar, 7, 54, 55, 153

Obilić, Milos, 12
Obradović, Dositej, 104
Obrenović, Milos, 15, 69, 93, 107, 140, 142
Old Church Slavonic, 31, 102
Orfelin, Zaharije, 93
Ottoman Empire, 2, 14, 32, 35, 84, 105

Paganism, 30
Pannonian Plain, 5, 159
Partisans, 19–21, 110, 116
Pašić, Nikola, 19, 21
Paskaljević, Goran, 126
Patriarch Arsenije II, 32
Pavić, Milorad, 110–113
Pavlović, Živojin, 124
Peć Patriarchate, 32–33, 52, 166
Petrović, Gajo, 40
Petrović, Karađorđe, 15, 123
Petrović, Petar II Njegoš, 16, 43, 106–7, 135
Phanariots, 32
Pink Television, 47
Pliny, 9
Praxis School, 40, 41, 43–44
Predić, Uroš, 168
Prince Lazar, 13, 156
Princip, Gavrilo, 17
Prvovenčani, Stefan, 32, 103
Punisa Radić, 19

Radić, Stjepan, 19
Radičević, Branko, 108
Radmanovic, Vladimir, 76
Rajić, Jovan, 104
Rakočević, Verica, 99
Rankić, Zoran, 39

Rasević, Mirjana, 52
Raška, 31
Ražnatović, Svetlana (Ceca), 46–47, 90, 135, 148–50
Ražnatović, Željko (Arkan), 46–47, 148, 150
Red Army, 21
Republika Srpska, 24, 119, 128
Riblja Čorba, 144–45
Roman Catholic Church, 30
Romanians, 8, 10
Russia, 8–10, 15–16, 25–27, 31–32, 46, 63, 81, 102, 111, 113
Ruthians, 8

Saint Clement of Ohrid, 3, 102
Saint Sava, 14, 36, 67, 103, 155, 168
Šapić, Aleksandar, 77
Savičević, Dejan, 76
Šekarić, Jelena, 81
Sekulić, Isidora, 111
Seleš, Monica, 78–79
Serbian nationalism, 23, 46, 47
Serbo-Croatian language, 2
Simić, Slobodan, 39
Smederevo, 13, 93, 156–57
Socialist Party, 29, 42
Sokolović, Mehmed Pasa, 32
Sombor, 52, 167, 169
Sopočani Monastery, 52, 154, 165
South Slavic linguistic group, 2
Soviet Union, 19, 40
Sremski Karlovci, 92, 104, 166, 167
Stanković, Borisav, 109–10
Stara Planina Mt., 5, 92
Stefanović Karadžić, Vuk, 105, 140
Stojaković, Predrag, 75
Stojković, Dragan "Pixie," 76
Studenica Monastery, 32

Tacitus, 9
Teodosije (hagiographer), 103

Tesla, Nikola, 46
Thracians, 10, 16
Topić, Dragutin, 81
Turbo-folk, 45–47, 90, 120, 135, 146–49
Turks, 12–18, 29–30, 32, 48, 67, 97, 103, 106–7, 128, 139–40, 154, 157, 160, 169

Ulcinj, 6, 26
Ulemeg, Milorad (Legija), 25
United Nations, 23, 25, 39, 148, 152
University of Belgrade, 42, 52, 60
University of Montenegro, 55
University of Pristina, 54
Ustaša, 19–21, 33

Van Gogh (Serbian rock group), 146
Vardar River, 5
Veličković, Vladimir, 170
Vendetta in Montenegrin society, 48–49
Vlachs, 10
Vladika system of governance, 16, 48, 107

World War I, 17–18, 97, 123, 128, 159
World War II, 19, 21, 33, 37, 41–42, 51, 110, 116, 123–28, 170

Volga River, 9

Zagreb, 2, 40, 145
Zakić, Rastko, 38
Zemun Clan, 25, 150
Zeta, 6, 11, 13, 137, 156
Zeta Plain, 6
Živojinović, Slobodan, 78
Zlatibor Mt., 5, 159
Zloković, Milan, 151, 162
Zrenjanin, 50, 91, 122

About the Author

CHRISTOPHER DELISO is an American journalist, travel writer, and author specializing in the Balkans. He holds an MPhil with distinction in Byzantine Studies from Oxford University.

**Recent Titles in
Culture and Customs of Europe**

Culture and Customs of Spain
Edward F. Stanton

Culture and Customs of Germany
Eckhard Bernstein

Culture and Customs of Italy
Charles Killinger

Culture and Customs of the Baltic States
Kevin O'Connor

Culture and Customs of Ireland
Margaret Scanlan

Culture and Customs of the Czech Republic and Slovakia
Craig Cravens

Culture and Customs of Ireland
W. Scott Haine

Culture and Customs of Europe
Adriana Helbig, Oksana Buranbaeva, and Vanja Mladineo

Culture and Customs of the Caucasus
Peter L. Roudik